Routledge Revivals

Rethinking Labour-Management Relations

First published in 1991, *Rethinking Labour-Management Relations* explores how the contemporary system of industrial relations developed and outlines proposals for a better alternative.

The book examines the positives and negatives of three systems of industrial relations: a freely operating market for labour where workers bargain individually with employers; a strike-based system of collective bargaining; and, a compulsory arbitration system. It discusses how the strike replaced individual bargaining, highlighting the deficiencies in these respective systems and presenting arbitration as the more efficient and effective way of settling disputes. In doing so, the book emphasises the role of the parties involved in finding solutions and considers how government intervention could be kept to a minimum.

Exploring a wealth of literature relating to compulsory arbitration systems around the world and formulating a set of criteria for establishing the best possible form of arbitration, *Rethinking Labour-Management Relations* will appeal to those with an interest in the history of trade union theory, public policy, and labour law.

Rethinking Labour-Management Relations

The Case for Arbitration

By Christopher J. Bruce and Jo Carby-Hall

First published in 1991
by Routledge

This edition first published in 2020 by Routledge
2 Park Square, Milton Park, Abingdon, Oxon, OX14 4RN
and by Routledge
605 Third Avenue, New York, NY 10017

Routledge is an imprint of the Taylor & Francis Group, an informa business

© 1991 C. J. Bruce and J. R. Carby-Hall

All rights reserved. No part of this book may be reprinted or reproduced or utilised in any form or by any electronic, mechanical, or other means, now known or hereafter invented, including photocopying and recording, or in any information storage or retrieval system, without permission in writing from the publishers.

Publisher's Note
The publisher has gone to great lengths to ensure the quality of this reprint but points out that some imperfections in the original copies may be apparent.

Disclaimer
The publisher has made every effort to trace copyright holders and welcomes correspondence from those they have been unable to contact.

A Library of Congress record exists under LCCN: 90026703

ISBN 13: 978-0-367-68621-5 (hbk)
ISBN 13: 978-1-003-13857-0 (ebk)

Rethinking labour–management relations

The case for arbitration

Christopher J. Bruce
and Jo Carby-Hall

London and New York

First published 1991
by Routledge
11 New Fetter Lane, London EC4P 4EE

Simultaneously published in the USA and Canada
by Routledge
a division of Routledge, Chapman and Hall, Inc.
29 West 35th Street, New York, NY 10001

© 1991   C.J. Bruce and J.R. Carby-Hall

Typeset in Baskerville from the author's wordprocessing
disks by NWL Editorial Services, Langport, Somerset

All rights reserved. No part of this book may be reprinted
or reproduced or utilised in any form or by any electronic,
mechanical, or other means, now known or hereafter
invented, including photocopying and recording, or in
any information storage or retrieval system, without
permission in writing from the publishers.

British Library Cataloguing in Publication Data
Bruce, Christopher   *1933–*
  Rethinking labour-management relations: the case for
  arbitration.
  1. Collective bargaining. Arbitration
  I. Title   II. Carby-Hall, Joseph R. *1948–*
  331.89143
  ISBN 0–415–02213–4

Library of Congress Cataloging in Publication Data
Bruce, Christopher John.
  Rethinking labour-management relations: the case for
  arbitration/Christopher J. Bruce and Jo Carby-Hall.
      p.   cm.
  Includes bibliographical references and index.
  ISBN 0–415–02213–4
  1. Arbitration, Industrial.   2. Collective bargaining.
  3. Strikes and lockouts.
  I. Carby-Hall, J.R. (Joseph R.)   II. Title
  HD5481.C35   1991   90–26703
  331.89'143 – dc20   CIP

Contents

Preface	vii
Acknowledgements	x

1 The origins of the strike-based system — 1

Introduction	1
Collective bargaining and the industrial revolution	2
Experiments in collective bargaining	3
The evolution of the strike-based system	8
Conclusion	10

2 'Perfect' collective bargaining — 12

Introduction	12
Collective voice	14
Efficiency	20
Equity	28
Legal structuring	37
Conclusions	38

3 The strike-based system — 41

The characteristics of a strike-based system	41
Union voice	50
Efficiency	52
Equity	56
Legal structuring	62
The right to strike	63
Summary	65

4 Possible modifications to the strike-based system — 67

Replacement workers	67
Secondary industrial action	69
Union democracy	71
Statutory strikes	73
Conclusion	74

vi   Contents

5   Arbitration systems: a taxonomy   75
Type of dispute   75
The legal structure   76
Arbitrators   78
Role of mediation   80
Information   81
Selection procedure   84
The settlement   88
Conclusion   89

6   The role of arbitration   90
The nature of the bargaining process in compulsory arbitration   90
Collective voice   92
Efficiency   93
Equity   97
Legal structuring   102
Operational difficulties   102
Conclusion   107

7   The market for arbitration   109
Voluntary versus compulsory arbitration   110
Types of arbitration procedures – private versus public law   112
Selection of arbitration procedures   131
Payment of the arbitration fee   133
Publication of awards   135
Penalties   139
Summary   140

8   Wages councils   141
The wages council system   142
Wages councils as a system of collective bargaining   146
Summary   152

9   The arbitration of industrial disputes: a proposal   153
The goals of industrial relations systems   153
Arbitration practices in Britain   156
Compulsory arbitration   161
Arbitration as an industrial relations system   167
Conclusion   168

Notes   169
List of cases and statutes   197
List of arbitration awards   198
Index   199

Preface

In both the United Kingdom and North America, the primary source of trade union power is the threat of the strike. Public discussion in these jurisdictions generally takes as a given factor that this threat is fundamental to the operation of the collective bargaining system. It is rare for analysts to consider the possibility that union–management disputes might be resolved through some means other than the use of force.[1] Rather, the implicit assumption which is normally made is that society is faced with only two choices: either making minor revisions to the strike-based system – for example, by altering laws concerning picketing or secondary boycotts[2] – or abandoning collective bargaining altogether.[3]

We believe that this approach restricts public discussion unnecessarily. Before it can be concluded either that the strike-based system is the best form of collective bargaining available to us or that society would be better off with no form of collective bargaining at all, a thorough review of all possible forms of collective bargaining must be undertaken. The purpose of this book is to contribute to this review, primarily by contrasting the strike-based system of collective bargaining with an arbitration-based system, but also by introducing an analysis of an institution-free idealisation which we call 'perfect' collective bargaining.

Chapter 1 opens the book with a brief review of the development of collective bargaining. What this review suggests is that during the eighteenth century experimentation was conducted with respect to numerous models of employer–employee relations in both Britain and the United States. Out of these competing models, only one major approach

viii Preface

survived – that in which (i) workers were organised according to either industry or craft, (ii) unions agreed (perhaps reluctantly) to operate within the capitalist mode of production, and (iii) unions used the threat of the strike to force employers to the bargaining table. What we ask in Chapter 1 is whether we can interpret the success of this approach to be an indication that society considers it to be the most desirable method of organising employer–employee relations; or whether there are historical reasons why various superior approaches failed or were not tried.

As it is our conclusion in Chapter 1 that the dominance of the strike threat system does not necessarily reveal its superiority over other systems, in Chapter 2 we begin our analysis of the advantages and disadvantages of alternative collective bargaining systems. This we do by developing and analysing an idealised form of industrial relations which we call 'perfect' collective bargaining. Our purpose in developing this model is to avoid what we perceive to be a major drawback to most discussions of collective bargaining: namely, that the advantages and disadvantages of collective bargaining (relative to no collective bargaining, or to purely individualised bargaining) are normally discussed with reference to the particular form of collective bargaining which happens to be in force at the time. But until it has been determined that the existing form of collective bargaining is the most desirable form, this approach biases the findings against collective bargaining. To avoid this problem, we initiate our analysis by reviewing the characteristics of an ideal form of collective bargaining, our assumption being that it is only if this form can be shown to be preferable to individualised bargaining that it becomes worthwhile to attempt to determine whether a 'real world' system of collective bargaining can be developed which achieves the ends of the ideal system.

We argue in Chapter 2 that our idealised form of collective bargaining offers sufficient advantages relative to individualised bargaining to justify the search for a 'real world' equivalent. We begin this search in Chapter 3 by reviewing the advantages and disadvantages of the strike-based system as it is currently practised in Britain and North America; while in Chapter 4 we consider a number of modifications to that system which have been suggested, such as the introduction of 'statutory strikes' and the alteration of laws concerning secondary boycotts and picketing.

Since it will be suggested in Chapter 4 that one alternative to the strike-based system which deserves closer attention is arbitration, an analysis of this technique is considered in Chapters 5 and 6. Chapter 5 is strictly tautological, in the sense that its sole purpose is to categorise the different types of arbitration systems which have been tried or suggested in various jurisdictions. In Chapter 6 the question is asked as to whether arbitration, in general, can serve as a viable alternative either to other collective bargaining systems or to the free market system.

As it will be shown in Chapter 6 that arbitration does offer potential as an alternative to the strike-based system, Chapters 7, 8, and 9 are devoted to analyses of the manner in which arbitration systems might be introduced into the private sectors of Britain, Canada, and the United States. We begin this discussion in Chapter 7 with a review of the arguments for and against government intervention in the arbitration process. One possible model for private sector arbitration is provided by the British Wages Council system, and a brief description of this system is given in Chapter 8. Finally, Chapter 9 summarises the arguments made in this book and we outline an industrial relations system which we believe combines the best elements of the free market, the strike-based system, and arbitration.

Acknowledgements

The authors wish to express their gratitude to HMSO for giving their permission to reproduce certain materials to be found in this book, and in particular the table of incidence rates from work stoppages to be found on page 54.

Both the Advisory, Conciliation, and Arbitration Service and the Central Arbitration Committee have been most helpful in answering the authors' questions in connection with various matters relating to arbitration, mediation, and conciliation. Our special thanks go to Mr Campbell of ACAS for the detailed and helpful answers given to questions raised by the authors. We would also like to acknowledge the advice and encouragement given at various stages in the writing of this book by James Pemberton, Arthur Seldon, Richard Posner, and Robert Cooter.

We wish to thank our various publishers for allowing us to use in this book materials previously published elsewhere. Particular thanks go to Charles Knight & Co.; Barcelona University Press; the *Solicitor's Journal*; and the *International Review of Law and Economics*.

Finally, our deep thanks are due to Messrs Routledge for their patience and understanding during the various stages of production of this book and for putting up with last minute changes necessitated by recent legislative developments. In particular, our thanks go to Peter Sowden and Alison Walters for acting so efficiently and speedily during the production process, thus making our task that much easier.

Chapter 1

The origins of the strike-based system

INTRODUCTION

A recurring theme in the literature of law and economics is that democratic societies possess a tendency to generate laws and legal structures which are efficient.[1] According to this hypothesis, which we shall call the theory of *legal evolution*, either by design or through the relative atrophy of those aspects of the law which prove unsatisfactory, society gradually develops the legal system which best suits the needs and desires of the age. Concomitant with this evolutionary view of the process is the assumption that the prevailing system is, if not superior to, then at least the equal of, any alternative system which might be proposed; for, in the evolutionary battle, it is the existing system which has won through. If the theory of legal evolution is accepted, it becomes incumbent on those who wish to recommend that a new legal structure be substituted for the existing one to show not only that the proposed structure is the theoretically superior one, but also to explain why the existing system was able to dominate its rivals in spite of its supposed inferiority. In particular, if an argument is to be made for the replacement of the strike-based system, it must first be shown that that system has superseded all alternatives, not because it is necessarily the best system of industrial relations for our current age, but because the circumstances of the age in which it arose gave it advantages which no longer apply. That is the purpose of this chapter. Accordingly, we begin by reviewing, briefly, the origins of the trade union movement in Britain and North America and by identifying the reasons why it was the strike-based model of collective bargaining which proved to be successful.

COLLECTIVE BARGAINING AND THE INDUSTRIAL REVOLUTION

According to the Webbs,[2] the origins of trade unionism can be traced to the early stages of the industrial revolution. Three elements of this revolution were of particular importance to the development of employer–employee relations: (i) the creation of large, depersonalised workplaces; (ii) the attenuation of the guild system; and (iii) the automation of many processes which had previously employed skilled tradespeople.

The development of the factory system and of large-scale mining operations was crucial to the evolution of a *collective* form of bargaining. First, individuals who had previously enjoyed an element of self-autonomy in cottage industries, small craft shops, and agricultural villages found that the demands of the new technologies required the transference of control to their masters. At the same time, bargaining power in the labour market shifted away from workers towards employers. In the small workshops of the pre-industrial era, the revenue earned by the employment of one worker may have produced a significant portion of the employer's profits, thereby providing each employee with some power for bargaining with his employer. In the larger factories and mines of the nineteenth century, however, no individual employee performed a crucial role within the company, thereby increasing the credibility of employers' threats to lay off workers who refused to accept the conditions of employment offered to them. The contract of employment became a *contract of adhesion* – the employee could accept or reject the terms of employment, but had no direct input into their determination. Thus, at the same time that employees had begun to feel an increased desire to regain control of their worklives, their power, as individuals, to obtain this control had decreased.

Industrialisation increased the probability that workers would react to this feeling of powerlessness by turning to collective action. First, the contract of adhesion, by its very nature, applied equally to all workers within the establishment. Accordingly, all workers felt a common interest in the terms of employment of each of their fellow employees. Second, whereas the primitive means of transport and communication of the eighteenth and nineteenth centuries had made it difficult to coordinate the efforts of workers spread throughout the land in small workshops and villages, industrialisation brought workers into close proximity in factories and mines. Thus industrialisation had provided manual workers not only with the desire but also the ability to act collectively.

The second major effect of the industrial revolution was to reduce the importance of the guild system. Whereas under that system, apprentices and journeymen could aspire to become masters, under the factory system the number of workers per master was so increased and the amount of money required to become a master so great that these aspirations could seldom be realised. As a result, the commonality of purpose between the employers and employees was severed and a class of skilled wage workers was created – workers who no longer expected to become profit- earners and who, therefore, no longer could be persuaded that wage reductions were in their long-term interests.

Finally, the introduction of mass production techniques, primarily in the second half of the nineteenth century, reduced the demand for, and therefore the wages of, many skilled trades-people, such as cutlers, hatmakers, tailors, and glovemakers. Seeking strength in numbers, these workers attempted to defend their positions through the use of collective action.

In every instance, the industrial revolution increased the likelihood that workers would turn to collective action in their dealings with their employers. Industrialisation removed workers' control over their places of employment, reduced their ability to apply personal skill and initiative, and weakened their bargaining power with their employers. At the same time, it standardised workpractices such that more workers shared common complaints and aspirations and it brought workers into closer proximity to one another, where they could more easily organise collectively. The result was that from the end of the eighteenth century in Britain and from the middle of the nineteenth century in North America, workers began to experiment with numerous forms of collective action. So why did the strike-based system succeed where these other experiments failed?

EXPERIMENTS IN COLLECTIVE BARGAINING

In the late twentieth century we have become so accustomed to the idea that collective bargaining will be conducted by craft or industrial unions bargaining in the shadow of the strike threat

4 Rethinking labour–management relations

that we tend to forget that experiments with many other forms of labour–management relations were conducted in the eighteenth and nineteenth centuries. Before asking, in the following section, why the strike threat system became predominant, it will be useful to review briefly the factors which led to the demise of a number of alternative forms of employer–employee relations. Five of these will be discussed in this section.

Statutes

Until late in the eighteenth century, the primary means through which skilled workers could obtain control over their working conditions took the form of petitions to the legislatures and courts. In Britain, under the celebrated Statute of Apprentices, for example, the justices of each locality were empowered to set wages and apprenticeship regulations, after hearing representations from citizens of the district.[3] Furthermore, it was not uncommon for associations of operatives to appeal directly to Parliament for regulation of wages or of certain workpractices – such as the introduction of new, labour-saving technology. However, two events placed severe restrictions on this practice by the early stages of the nineteenth century. First, in the mid-1700s, the pace of technological change began to increase substantially. As a result, whereas entreaties to restrict the introduction of labour-saving techniques had previously been relatively rare events, which could be acceded to without having an apparent effect on GNP, those entreaties became much more common. Gradually, an implicit understanding seems to have grown up among parliamentarians that if agreement was given to all of the petitions which were being received, the economy would stagnate – particularly relative to Britain's continental competitors. Second, it was at this time that Adam Smith published his famous treatise on *The Wealth of Nations* (1776), in which he argued that social output would be maximised if competition among producers was encouraged. Parliament, which had been groping towards this conclusion on its own, quickly adopted Smith's *laissez-faire* doctrine wholeheartedly and used it to reject all restraints on trade, including those resulting from combinations among workers. In this atmosphere, worker petitions for regulation of wages and apprenticeship requirements fell upon deaf ears. The practice of government regulation of working conditions was not resurrected until the early twentieth century, with the development of Wages Councils,[4] well after the modern structure of trade unions had been established.

Coercion

With the adoption of a *laissez-faire* approach towards the economy, governments in both Britain and North America became hostile to collective bargaining. In Britain, for example, the Combination Acts of 1799 and 1800 were passed, making it illegal for workers to combine to fix wages. The effect of these Acts and other anti-labour policies of the government was to drive worker associations underground. From that vantage, the primary methods available to workers to 'bargain' with employers were those which derived from violence. Hence, much of the early history of trade unionism was marked by what Hobsbawm[5] called 'collective bargaining by riot' and occasionally by overtly criminal acts, such as the murder in America of foremen by the 'Molly Maguires' of the Pennsylvania coalfields.[6] Whether or not these activities met their short-term goals, however, it is clear that they could not form a long-term model for industrial relations in a civilised society and they soon gave way to alternative forms of collective bargaining.

Socialist/Utopian

One of these alternatives was what might be called the socialist, or utopian, general unions. In Britain, these included the Owenite[7] Grand National Consolidated Trades Union and National Union of the Working Classes; while the most prominent example in America was the Knights of Labor, and in Canada, the One Big Union. In each case, an attempt was made to bring together workers of all kinds under one umbrella organisation which was to represent, not the narrow interests of individual trades, but the broad interests of the 'working classes'. Thus, for example, the Knights of Labor included among their ranks farmers, members of the cooperative movement, and unorganised workers as well as members of identifiable unions.

None of these organisations was able to maintain cohesion for more than a few years. In part, their failure arose from the

6 Rethinking labour–management relations

strength of employer opposition to their socialistic goals and from a lack of leadership among men whose utopian idealism far exceeded their practical abilities. In the main, however, it appears that the collapse of such organisations derived from internal stress. Whereas self-interest often provided sufficient motivation to induce workers to support strikers in their own or related trades, the desire to maintain 'worker solidarity' proved inadequate to induce skilled workers to support unskilled, native workers to support foreign-born, or farmers to support professionals. The struggle to establish the legitimacy of the trade union movement required such intense dedication, in the face of concerted opposition from employers, that only the strongest of incentives were capable of persuading workers to commit themselves to its support.

Radical unions

Workers responded in two ways to the failure of the utopian unions. Some concluded that the general unions should be disbanded, to be replaced by inward-looking, trade-based unions which would be connected to one another only loosely. Others, however, concluded that the problem with the utopian unions had not been their attachment to the cause of worker solidarity, but their *lack* of attachment. They argued that the utopian unions had failed because they had treated labour–management contracts on a case-by-case basis, rather that seeing each contract as being part of the larger conflict between the capitalist and working classes. These *radical* unionists, who were best exemplified by the leaders of the North American union, the Industrial Workers of the World (the 'wobblies'), preached that the explicit goal of the union movement should be the overthrow of the capitalist system.

These organisations failed for a number of reasons. One of these was that their revolutionary rhetoric attracted individuals who were willing to use violence in the pursuit of their goals, a willingness which was not always shared by the average worker of the time. Indeed, in many jurisdictions, radical unions found themselves opposed directly by the members of skilled trades, whose (relatively) high incomes had made them supporters of the capitalist system. Second, like the utopian unions, the radicals spread their attacks too broadly, attempting to resolve so many issues simultaneously that the money and the patience of their supporters began to run dry. Finally, employers were so violently opposed to socialism that they used every means at their disposal to squash the radical unions. The combination of these factors has, to this day, left radical unions in the definite minority.

Arbitration

At a number of times in the history of the trade union movement it has been suggested that the parties use arbitration, instead of the strike threat, as the means of inducing them to reach agreement. Why has this technique been so unsuccessful? First, as we have seen, in the nineteenth century governments, as well as employers, stood in opposition to the trade union movement at almost every turn. Hence, the method chosen for bringing employers to the bargaining table had to be implementable without the support of the law. But arbitration could not fulfil this role. In the absence of a legal requirement, employers could only be induced to enter arbitration if workers first developed an extra-legal threat, such as the strike. But once this threat had been developed, it became difficult to supplant it with arbitration. The reason for this was that in those sectors in which it gave employers more bargaining power than they would have enjoyed under arbitration, employers preferred the strike threat; and in those sectors in which it was the unions who obtained more power from the strike than from arbitration, it was the unions who preferred the strike. Only in the unlikely event that arbitration maintained the same balance of power which was provided by the strike would the two sides agree voluntarily to submit to binding arbitration. But even under that circumstance, arbitration suffered relative to the strike threat during the nineteenth century because it was difficult to identify a group of educated individuals which was perceived to be sufficiently unbiased that its members would have been acceptable to both sides as arbitrators.[8] Furthermore, once the struggle to entrench the strike-based system had been won, unionists became very wary of government- and employer-led moves to substitute any alternative industrial relations system, including arbitration.

THE EVOLUTION OF THE STRIKE-BASED SYSTEM

We have argued in this chapter (pp. 2–3) that the industrial revolution created the conditions for the development of a system of collective bargaining between employers and their employees. It created the demand for collective action by reducing the control which individuals had over their worklives and by placing workers in a situation in which many individuals shared a common work experience; and it simplified the mounting of collective action by bringing workers together in large factories and mines and by introducing speedier, more reliable means of communication. At the same time, however, the industrial revolution acted to increase the relative bargaining power of employers and it created the conditions in which *laissez-faire* became the dominant economic philosophy of the ruling classes. Thus, while worker demand for collective action was rising, employer readiness and ability to oppose collective bargaining was also rising. This set the stage for a lengthy, acrimonious, often violent struggle. At the beginning of the nineteenth century it was far from clear how this struggle would be resolved and many models of collective action were tried and discarded before one came to dominate the rest.

With hindsight, it appears that a successful industrial relations system would have to embody the following characteristics: first, it would have to provide workers with some form of collective voice, in order to satisfy the demand identified above. Second, it would have to be implementable in the face of concerted opposition from employers and governments. And, third, it would have to take a form which could rally a wide cross-section of the labouring class.

All of the models discussed in the previous section (pp. 3–7), above, met the first of these criteria – providing support for the thesis that workers in the nineteenth century felt a strong need to act collectively. However, only one of the models could meet the second criterion. Appeal to the courts and legislatures, which had been successful in the Middle Ages, could not survive the *laissez-faire* philosophy of the nineteenth century; arbitration would not be introduced voluntarily by employers who were under no external compulsion to bargain with their employees; and the coercive and radical models simply raised such strong opposition from employers that they proved untenable. Only the socialist/utopian model was able to surmount these two hurdles. It

The origins of the strike-based system 9

provided a collective voice, and it offered a sufficiently 'reasonable' face to capitalists that it might have been able to survive had it been able to present a cohesive front. It failed in this last test, however, because it overestimated the selflessness and homogeneity of the 'working classes'. In the initial euphoria of organisation, workers had been willing to provide their financial support to strikes and a variety of other industrial actions. But soon those workers who did not benefit directly became disillusioned and the utopian unions all failed within short periods of time.

These failures opened the way for an industrial relations system which was based upon the following principles:

1 Workers combined to present a common front to their employers – in order to meet the demand for *collective action* which had arisen from the changes brought about by the industrial revolution.
2 Employers were brought to the bargaining table by the *threat of a strike*. Employer and governmental opposition to trade unions had forced workers to rely upon extra-legal means of obtaining employer compliance. This ruled out both petitions to the government and arbitration; and violence could not provide a long-term solution to the need for cooperation between management and labour. Workers had found that the only means by which they could obtain a significant amount of bargaining power without either the cooperation or the total opposition of the government was the use of the collective withdrawal of labour.
3 Unions were to be composed of workers who shared a *common experience* and among whom the gains obtained by one group could be expected to redound to the benefit of the remaining groups. The experience of the socialist/utopian and radical unions suggested that the closer the struggle of their fellow workers to their own cause, the easier it would be to convince workers to assist one another. Workers would be more willing to assist others within their own trade than within other trades and within their own industries than within other industries, in part because they shared a common outlook with their fellow workers and in part because they could see that it would be easier to obtain gains for themselves, the greater were the gains of similarly situated workers.

10 Rethinking labour–management relations

4 Unions were to work within the *capitalist system*, rather than attempt to bring it down. This policy arose for two reasons. First, opposition from employers to socialist policies was so strong that overtly socialist/radical unions found themselves locked in a constant struggle, a struggle which they lacked the forces to win. Second, employer opposition to even the most conservative of unions was sufficient that only workers of great political skill, backed by large financial resources, could hope to prevail. In general, this implied that early union organisation occurred only among craft workers, who were relatively well educated and well paid. Because these 'aristocrats' of the working class had succeeded within the capitalist system, they had less incentive to attack that system than had many of their fellow workers.

Accordingly, closely following upon the failure of the socialist/utopian unions, craft-based unions arose in both the United States and Britain. The first of these were the 'New Model Unions' which developed in Britain in the middle of the nineteenth century, based upon the example of the Amalgamated Society of Engineers (1851). In the United States, with the collapse of the Knights of Labor during the 1880s, Samuel Gompers of the American Federation of Labor (AFL) developed what became known as 'business unionism'. In both cases, the new unions rejected socialist ideals, refused assistance and recognition to industrially based unions, and pursued narrowly selfish goals – in Gompers' famous words, all that the AFL-led unions wanted was 'More'.

CONCLUSION

In this chapter we have argued that the collective bargaining system which dominated labour–management relations in both Britain and North America in the last decade of the twentieth century was shaped largely by the socio-economic circumstances of the nineteenth century. But these circumstances have changed dramatically, suggesting that the strike-based system of 'business unionism' which we inherited from that past age may no longer be the one best suited to modern realities. Certainly, there has been sufficient change that a review of the various advantages and disadvantages of alternative systems is, at the very least, a useful exercise. In particular, the public and the government are no longer so strongly opposed to collective bargaining that unions are necessarily forced to rely upon extra-legal means to obtain their objectives. For example, that governments in North America have proven themselves willing to use minimum wage laws to intercede on behalf of low-wage workers, and that the British government has supported (at least until recently) the wages council system, suggests that some form of government-organised system for settling wages and working conditions may no longer be out of the question. The fact that governments have provided arbitration procedures to resolve labour–management disputes in both Britain and North America suggests that the advantage which the strike held over arbitration in the nineteenth century may not be as strong in the twentieth and twenty-first centuries.

For these reasons we believe that a thorough review of present labour relations systems is in order. This review should not restrict itself to an analysis of changes to the existing system, but should begin from an examination of the fundamental arguments for and against collective bargaining itself. Only in this way can it be ensured that all possible alternatives are given complete, unbiased consideration. We initiate this review in the following chapter, in which we analyse the advantages and disadvantages of an idealised form of collective bargaining, which we call 'perfect' collective bargaining.

Chapter 2

'Perfect' collective bargaining

INTRODUCTION

Most analyses of collective bargaining begin with a description of the existing industrial relations system. The advantages and disadvantages of this system are then contrasted to those of one or two alternative systems and a conclusion is reached as to whether the current system ought to be maintained – perhaps in a slightly revised form – or replaced with one of the alternatives.

For two reasons, we find this approach to be inappropriate. First, literally hundreds of alternative industrial relations systems have either been put into practice or have been suggested by theoreticians. The fewer the number of these analysed in any discussion, the greater the probability that an important alternative will have been excluded and, therefore, that the conclusions which are drawn will not be generally applicable. It may well be true, for example, that the system of collective bargaining in some jurisdictions is so flawed that workers would be better off if they were to bargain individually with their employers. But this does not 'prove' that individual bargaining is superior to all possible forms of collective bargaining, nor to some other system of industrial relations. Second, in an analysis which is restricted to the discussion of specific examples, it is difficult to uncover principles which will be of general applicability to all systems of employer–employee relations. An analysis of the role of British shop stewards in the bargaining process is unlikely to be of significance to the understanding of collective negotiations in Australia, with its system of arbitration before labour courts, for example.

In an effort to minimise these problems, we have chosen to

begin our investigation with an analysis of an idealised system of collective bargaining which we call 'perfect' collective bargaining. By this we mean a hypothetical situation in which: (i) all employed workers are equally free, without constraint, to combine together to bargain collectively for the wages and conditions of employment with their respective employers; and (ii) a costless method exists for ensuring that the agreements reached between each firm and the group of employees with which it bargains maximise the joint utilities of the employees and that firm.[1] That is, a situation in which perfect collective bargaining exists is one in which all of the purported advantages of collective bargaining prevail without the disadvantages which arise from inequalities in bargaining power, costliness of the bargaining process (for example, arising from the use of the strike), or lack of uniformity of coverage.

The use of the perfect collective bargaining paradigm allows a clear distinction to be made between the advantages and disadvantages of collective bargaining *in general* and those of the particular bargaining system which happens to be in place in the 'real world'. As we argued above, this distinction is important because the prevailing practice among critics of the institution of collective bargaining has been to assume, implicitly, that a finding that the *existing* system of collective bargaining is inferior to a free market in labour is synonymous with a finding that the free market is superior to *all* systems of collective bargaining; and also because the corresponding practice among defendants of collective bargaining has been to assume, again implicitly, that it is the existing system of bargaining, and not bargaining in general, which must be shown to be superior to the free market. In our view, both approaches lead to an underinvestment in the search for the general, desirable principles of a collective bargain. In turn, in the absence of a foundation of such principles, the search for new systems of bargaining has been forced to proceed on an *ad hoc* basis. Development of a paradigm such as perfect collective bargaining will help to direct attention away from the institutionally bound approach towards one which is more conducive to the development of alternative systems of bargaining.

It will also be suggested that the model of the perfect collective bargain parallels that of the perfectly competitive market, from

14 Rethinking labour–management relations

microeconomic theory, in the sense that both models are able to act as standards against which the effectivenesss of 'real world' institutions can be measured. That is, although we cannot expect the assumptions of the perfect collective bargain to be realised, their statement can serve to remind us of the goals which we are seeking to attain when investigating the characteristics of actual institutions.

In this chapter we will contrast the advantages and disadvantages of perfect collective bargaining with those of the freely operating (i.e. 'competitive') labour market. We begin in this way because it is our view that the search for a system of collective bargaining cannot be justified if even an ideal form, such as perfect collective bargaining, is found to be inferior to the free market. Thus, in the remaining sections of this chapter, we identify four major factors which are held to be of importance when measuring the advantages and disadvantages of collective bargaining. We outline the impact which perfect collective bargaining can be expected to have upon each category and review the available empirical evidence. In a summary section we will ask whether it can be concluded that perfect collective bargaining is superior to a free market in labour.

COLLECTIVE VOICE

Human beings are social animals. When placed in adversarial positions, we find safety and security in banding together to act in concert. This primal instinct may be one of the most important factors motivating workers to form associations which can speak for them in a *collective voice*.[2] Regardless of whether or not they expect to increase their power, workers may derive some comfort from a collective expression of their views to their employers. As Ulman and Sorensen have argued recently,

> the most serious case for collective bargaining as a social institution has not rested on the grounds that it pays for itself – or that it is innocuous – but rather that it has generated non-economic gains for democratic society, flowing from the replacement of a regime of paternalism in the workplace with 'industrial democracy' and 'industrial jurisprudence'. [3]

Alienation

One of the most important outcomes of the industrial revolution was the development of the large-scale workplace. Whereas workers had previously retained some personal control over their day-to-day worklives – because they were independent craftspeople, because they were home workers, or because they worked in relatively unstructured environments, such as on farms – once they entered the factories and mines of the late nineteenth century every aspect of their work activities became closely directed by their employers. With this loss of control also came a loss of a feeling of responsibility for, and pride in, the product of their labour. Workers came to feel that they were mere 'factors of production' rather than human beings. They responded by seeking some way to reassert their sense of human dignity.

The strength and pervasiveness of this desire is reflected in the observation that it has been commented on by researchers working within virtually every discipline in the social sciences. Sociologists speak of the worker's 'alienation' from his work and of workers' desire for 'industrial democracy'.[4] Psychologists argue that workers' mental health can be improved through the use of 'job enrichment'.[5] Economists have written about the effects which improvements in the 'quality of working life' can have on labour productivity.[6] Furthermore business academics have developed the 'X and Y' theories to explain why workers become more cooperative when given greater responsibility for their workplace activities.[7] In each case, extensive empirical evidence has been obtained to suggest that workers possess a strong innate desire to retain some control over their worklives.[8]

One mechanism for providing this control is to develop organisations which can represent workers in their dealings with employers – usually, but not necessarily, trade unions. By representing workers in bargaining for the establishment of wages, working conditions, promotion and layoff regulations, leave provisions, and grievance procedures, these organisations create the conditions in which each worker feels that his views about the way in which his workplace should be operated are taken into

16   Rethinking labour–management relations

consideration. As Professor Cyril Grunfeld of the London School of Economics said about the union to which he belonged:

> I think that, except in the odd, exceptional case, individuals are pretty helpless in any organisation of any size. This union, the Association of University Teachers, represents the things I am interested in, and I feel a little more secure in it.[9]

It might be argued that these results could be obtained without the use of collective bargaining, through discussions between employers and individual employees. If employee productivity is reduced because workers are unhappy with their lack of control over the workplace, there is no reason why employers could not approach those workers on an individual basis and offer to negotiate wages and working conditions with them. But, that this technique is available does not necessarily imply that it would be superior to collective negotiations. First, it is only in exceptional circumstances that workers could be expected to be open and frank with their employers concerning their work-related grievances. Most such grievances represent direct criticisms of the policies of the employer and workers would be extremely reluctant to raise these criticisms with the employer for fear of inciting reprisals. Furthermore, the 'discipline' of the market place would normally be inadequate to constrain employers from taking these reprisals. Although firms with reputations for dealing unjustly with their employees could expect to encounter difficulty attracting new workers, most applicants for vacancies will not have sufficient information to rank firms according to the fairness of their dealings with their employees. And even if applicants were able to obtain such detail about firms' past practices, that would not necessarily provide accurate information about future practices. Finally, the profit-maximisation goal will not, by itself, induce employers to introduce grievance procedures or other elements of industrial democracy if those practices do not increase worker productivity. Yet many theories of worker alienation suggest only that workers will feel a greater sense of satisfaction if they obtain increased control over their worklives – not that they will necessarily become more productive. That is, in these theories, worker control is seen as an end in itself – an end, therefore, which may be of little direct benefit to the employer.

Alternatively, the government might attempt to obtain a

reduction in worker alienation through the introduction of various forms of legislation. In Britain, for example, the Employment Protection (Consolidation) Act 1978 requires that employers establish grievance procedures and that they follow a particular set of provisions with respect to redundancy payments. It is submitted, however, that although it may be preferable to offer the protection of legislation of this type than to provide workers with no protection at all, statutory regulations are inferior to agreements negotiated freely between employers and worker organisations.

With respect to grievance procedures, for example, Section 1(4) of the Employment Protection (Consolidation) Act requires that the employer must provide the employee, within thirteen weeks of the commencement of employment, with a statement which specifies the person to whom the employee can apply if he is dissatisfied with any disciplinary decision relating to him and to whom he may seek redress of any employment grievance. But such requirements only mimic the form of a collectively negotiated grievance procedure – they cannot reproduce its substance. The reason for this is that the collectively negotiated procedure contains, as a central element, protections to ensure that no reprisals are imposed upon the griever as a result of his action. The griever appealing to a company-initiated administration has no such protection. Indeed, in terms of its ability to deal with worker feelings of alienation, an employer-operated grievance system is virtually indistinguishable from no system at all. Whether the employee lodges his complaints with an individual who has been formally designated as the recipient of such complaints or whether he lodges them with an informally selected member of management, the employee is likely to experience the same feeling of insecurity.[10]

The provisions concerning redundancy payments in Section 96(1) of the Employment Protection (Consolidation) Act demonstrate another way in which legislation may be inferior to collective bargaining as a mechanism for regulating employment relationships. One of the arguments made above was that the industrial revolution had induced in workers a feeling that they had lost some control over their working lives. This feeling can only be overcome if workers are given a direct say in the creation of their own firms' employment policies, not if the government

18 Rethinking labour–management relations

paternalistically imposes those policies upon them. Furthermore, if workers' preferences with respect to redundancy payments vary across occupations or industries, government policies, no matter how well intentioned, will be unable to take those variations into account.

Coordination

Although the workers within a single unit of the firm share common working conditions, fringe benefits, and employment practices (e.g. promotion procedures), they do not all share the same preferences with respect to these factors. Accordingly, if employee satisfaction is to be maximised, for any given expenditure by the firm, methods will have to be found to identify what individual employees' preferences are and to select from alternative policies when it is found that employee preferences are not consistent with one another.[11] It is possible that this type of information could be collected by management. But if workers are concerned that information released to the firm may not be used to their advantage, the firm may find it difficult to obtain all the facts concerning its employees' true preferences. To the extent that an employee organisation, such as a trade union, has the confidence of its members (or, at least, greater confidence than the firm's managers would have), it may be able to act as a clearing house for information which is beneficial to both sides but which would not otherwise have been available.[12]

Information gathering

As well as gathering information from employees for presentation to the employer, a union may be able to gather information from the employer and from outside the firm which will be of value to the employees. This will particularly be true with respect to information which is of value to a large number of employees simultaneously. For example, all workers within a unit will have the same interest in information concerning the following: workplace air pollution, the profitability of the employer, and the wages and fringe benefits being paid to comparable workers in other firms. Whereas the cost of collecting this information may exceed the benefit gained by any individual worker, the benefit to a group of workers may be sufficient for that group to consider the investment in information collection to be justified. Trade unions can provide a method of organising this investment.

Long-term contracting

Increasingly, it is being recognised that many workers remain with one employer for most of their working lives.[13] These long-term relationships allow employers and employees to enter into agreements – often referred to as *implicit contracts* – which would not be available to them in a more casual market for labour. A number of examples of these agreements have been given in the economics literature: (i) Many workers accumulate a considerable amount of training 'on-the-job'. As their output is usually reduced while the training is being provided, the firm will often find it profitable to offer workers a reduced wage during that period. In compensation, the firm will, implicitly, contract to pay its workers an increased wage once the training has been completed.[14] (ii) A number of authors have suggested that employers might wish to use long-term contracts in order to induce employees to work harder. For example, employers might offer relatively low starting salaries combined with relatively high rates of promotion in order to discourage employees from 'shirking.'[15] (iii) Because workers in primary and secondary sectors are generally assumed to be risk averse, they might be willing to enter contracts in which they agreed to accept relatively low wages during boom periods in return for the promise that they would not be laid off during recessionary periods.[16]

In each of these cases, and in many others which have been discussed in the literature, workers are asked to make some sacrifice today in return for the promise that a benefit will be provided in the future. But these promises are often extremely difficult to enforce formally. How, for example, would a court interpret the promise to promote an employee 'relatively quickly' if he was not found to be 'shirking'? Instead, informal enforcement mechanisms often have to be relied upon. One such mechanism is to have in place an employee organisation, such as a union, which has the power to 'punish' the firm if it fails to live

20 Rethinking labour–management relations

up to its promises. This approach would be superior to reliance upon the marketplace to enforce promises as new entrants to a firm would generally not have sufficient information to determine which firms were the most likely to uphold their agreements, particularly when firms were just starting up. Thus, applicants would be unable to select firms with good reputations in preference to those with poor reputations.

Empirical evidence

Many of the arguments made in this section have been supported by empirical findings. Duncan and Stafford,[17] for example, have found that unionisation was most likely in those industries in which coordination of worker preferences was most important. Hundley[18] found that unions were more successful in industries with on-the-job training, hazardous working conditions, interdependent work relations, and large (impersonal) workforces. And Farber[19] found that the factors which non-union workers found most attractive about unions included job security and promotion fairness. In sum, it appears that both the modern theory and the empirical evidence support the view which many labour economists have held for quite some time – that collective bargaining is concerned with workers' 'security, status and self-respect – in, short, their dignity as human beings.'[20]

EFFICIENCY

In the last decade, a considerable amount of research has been conducted into the effects which trade unions have on the productive capacity (efficiency) of the economy. Four factors have been investigated in this research, namely the effects of unions on productivity, profits and investment, employment and unemployment, and inflation. The findings with respect to each of these effects will be discussed here in turn.

Productivity

The public perception of unions, fed by the well-publicised British examples of the print and dockworker unions, is that they act to reduce labour productivity by restricting employers' ability to introduce new technology and by insisting that inefficient numbers of workers be employed ('featherbedding'). More recently, the collective voice literature (discussed on p. 14, above) has argued that unions *increase* labour productivity by providing a conduit through which workers' concerns are relayed to management. In particular, it is argued that unionisation may increase productivity through reduced labour turnover, increased worker willingness to accept on-the-job training, improved morale (resulting from greater security and from the provision of grievance procedures), and altered management practices in response to union demands for higher pay (the 'shock effect').

Davies[21] has recently shown that the former of these hypotheses, that unions retard the introduction of technological change, is not supported by the evidence. The express goal of the Trades Union Congress (TUC), for example, is not to resist change, but to encourage its member unions to obtain agreements which include:

- status quo and mutuality clauses, so that major change will not be introduced unilaterally.
- a guarantee of full job security for the existing workforce.
- guarantees to workers, whose pay and status is lowered through job reorganisations that their individual earnings and status will be maintained.
- adequate redundancy provisions, with continuing earnings-related payments to redundant workers rather than lump sum payments.
- a reduction in working time with priority given to the 35 hour week; to reducing overtime; and to providing opportunities for time off for public and union duties.
- earlier retirement for older workers on improved pensions.[22]

In most cases unions fail to realise even this limited goal. In a review of British studies of unions, Davies found 'very little evidence that worker resistance to change [was] a major obstacle to technological progress'.[23] Indeed, most of the authors she surveyed concluded that unions had been 'largely unsuccessful in securing an equitable share of the benefits from new technology in these agreements'.[24] Furthermore, Caves found that differences in productivity between British and American industries were not related to differences in unionisation.[25]

Rather, it appears that if unions have had any role in the

22 Rethinking labour–management relations

introduction of new technology, it has been to act as a means by which workers can be informed about, and prepared for, that introduction. In a study of technological change in the oil industry, for example, Gallie[26] found that worker disaffection was greater in French refineries, where firms had jealously guarded their prerogative to manage change, than in British refineries, where a full set of negotiations concerning change had taken place with the unions. Similarly, Cooke,[27] in a study of 111 American manufacturing companies which had union–management collaborative programmes, found that the greatest productivity gains had been made in those companies which had the highest degree of unionisation.

During the 1980s a considerable amount of research has been conducted in order to determine whether the 'collective voice' role of trade unions has led to an improvement in labour productivity. The evidence has not been kind to this theory. Most studies have found that productivity either is the same in union and non-union firms or is only slightly higher in union than non-union firms. Furthermore, it appears that the source of those productivity differentials which do exist do not derive from collective voice. Rather, the best evidence suggests that most of the differential arises from the so-called 'shock effect'. That is, as unions are generally successful in raising wages, management finds that it must become more productive in order to remain competitive and it is 'shocked' into seeking ways to reduce costs.[28]

Profits and investment

It is usually assumed that when unions are successful in raising wages, they must also reduce employers' profits and discourage investment. There are circumstances, however, in which this assumption may not be correct. Some theories of imperfectly competitive industries, for example, predict that firms will set their prices by adding a 'markup' to their average costs. When unions press up wages in these firms, the resulting cost increases are simply passed on to consumers and have little or no effect on profits. Furthermore, among those firms that previously enjoyed profit rates which were higher than were necessary to attract investors, a reduction in profits need not imply a reduction in investment. If, for example, investors are willing to supply funds when the rate of return is 15 per cent, a reduction in the firm's rate of profit from 20 per cent to 17 per cent will not significantly affect that firm's ability to raise investment capital. Thus, the question of whether unions can be expected to reduce profits and investment cannot be answered by theory alone. Reference must be made to the empirical evidence.

With respect to profitability it is clear that, on average, trade unions reduce firms' profits. Both Addison and Hirsch[29] and Freeman and Medoff[30] conclude that profits are lowered by as much as 10 to 20 per cent in industries which are highly unionised. Furthermore, there is some evidence to suggest that this effect on profitability is lower, the higher the firm's market share (i.e. the greater the employer's degree of monopoly power). Clark[31] found, for example, that unions reduced the profits of low-market share firms by as much as 40 per cent, whereas they had no statistically significant effect on the profits of high-market share firms.

The evidence with respect to the effect on investment is less clear. On the one hand, most research finds that unions capture some of the returns on research and development expenditures[32] and that investments in capital and in research and development are lower, the greater an industry's level of unionisation.[33] On the other hand, it has also been found that productivity is no lower in unionised firms than non-unionised (see above, p.21), and that there is no significant difference between the growth rates of unionised and non-unionised firms.[34] The most plausible explanations for these results are that either the reduction in investment expenditures in unionised industries is not sufficient to lead to a reduction in growth or that the productivity of union members increases sufficiently to counterbalance the negative effect which unions have on investment. In either case, the evidence which is currently available suggests that unions are able to transfer income from employers to workers without reducing industrial growth significantly.

Employment and unemployment

Until recently, it was generally assumed that if unions were successful in raising wages, employers would respond by reducing employment. This assumption was based upon the observation

24 Rethinking labour–management relations

that demand curves for labour are downward sloping; that is, on the observation that as wages fall firms are able to charge lower prices and sell more output, thereby requiring more workers (and conversely that as wages rise prices will rise, causing output and employment to fall). It has been realised in recent years, however, that there are circumstances in which unions can be expected to bargain for increases in both wages *and* employment. Thus, the effect of unions on employment and, therefore, unemployment is no longer as certain as it once appeared. Again, resolution of this uncertainty requires appeal to empirical evidence.

Research conducted during the 1980s points to two conclusions. First, the majority of studies have found that unions in Britain and the United States bargain over both wages and employment. Unions do not merely set the wage rate and allow employers to select whatever employment level they wish. Instead, it has been found consistently that unions demand that employment levels be set above those which would have maximised the firms' profits. In Britain, for example, Carruth *et al.* found that unions in both the steel and mining sectors were interested in maintaining employment levels.[35] Similar results have been found in the United States with respect to the International Typographical Union[36] and with respect to data aggregated across the entire economy.[37] Second, some studies which have relied on data from the United States have found that although union-induced wage increases generally produce reductions in employment, those reductions are very small. Allen,[38] for example, found that the wage elasticity of demand (the percentage change in employment resulting from a given percentage change in the wage rate) was very much lower in unionised construction firms than in non-unionised; and Montgomery[39] found that employment in the city with the highest union/non-union wage differential was only 2 per cent less than in the city with the lowest differential, after all other factors had been taken into account.[40]

Contrary to the 'received' view, the empirical evidence suggests that unions are concerned about the employment prospects of their members. They do not merely raise wages and hope for the best as far as employment is concerned. Rather, they press for employment levels which exceed those which would have been chosen by profit-maximising firms and may even, in some circumstances, attempt to raise employment levels above those which would have resulted in the absence of unionisation. Although this new characterisation of union behaviour does not go so far as to argue that unions, on average, raise employment, it does suggest that unionisation is not a major cause of unemployment.

Inflation

It is commonly argued that unions may cause inflationary pressures in two ways. First, they may set off a round of inflation by pushing up their wages relative to the wages and prices of all other factors of production. We will refer to this as the inflationary initiation hypothesis.[41] Second, once inflationary pressure has been put into place (regardless of the source), unions may act to prolong the cycle of inflation by insisting that their wages rise in accordance with the preceding period's increase in prices. We refer to this as the inflationary continuation hypothesis. Neither view receives strong support from the data.

The most compelling evidence derives from the following observation. Acording to both views of union inflationary pressure, one would expect to find that union wages were rising relative to non-union over time. In the inflationary initiation hypothesis, each round of inflation is set off by an increase in the wages of unionised workers relative to all other workers.[42] Hence, as inflation has been endemic to all developed countries over the last forty years, this hypothesis requires that the union/non-union wage differential must have risen a number of times over that period. Similarly, the inflationary continuation hypothesis requires not just that union wages rise in response to increases in prices, but also that non-union wages rise *less* than union — otherwise it would have to be concluded that it was not unions, but simply the normal operation of the competitive labour market, that was 'continuing' inflation. Thus, like the inflationary initiation hypothesis, this hypothesis leads us to expect that the union/non-union wage differential would have risen over the entire post-war period (as that period was one in which prices virtually never fell).

What the data indicate, however, is that the union/non-union wage differential has not risen appreciably over the post-war

26 Rethinking labour–management relations

years. The conclusion of most authors who have reviewed the (now extensive) literature on this subject is that this differential has remained relatively stable in the long-run – at approximately 20 per cent in Britain[43] and at approximately 15 per cent in the United States.[44] Furthermore, even in those short periods during which union wages *have* increased relative to non-union, it has often been shown that that increase could not have accounted for a significant portion of the overall rate of inflation. To understand this it is only necessary to recognise that the overall increase in wages can be decomposed into the rate of increase enjoyed by all workers (both union and non-union), and a further, incremental increase enjoyed only by that percentage of workers who are unionised. When this decomposition was carried out for the 1967–1973 period, Ashenfelter[45] found that in the United States only 1.2 per cent of the overall 44 per cent increase in wages could be accounted for by union action; and Mulvey and Gregory[46] found that in Britain only 10 per cent of an overall 170 per cent increase in wages could be accounted for in that way.

Also, it has often been reported that short-run changes in the union/non-union differential are countercyclical – decreasing in boom periods and increasing in recessions.[47] As boom periods are invariably periods of inflation, this observation directly contradicts the inflation continuation hypothesis which argues that unionised workers are more successful at protecting themselves from the effects of inflation than are non-union workers.

Finally, a number of studies have reported evidence to suggest that union action during the early 1970s was inflation initiating. One particularly noteworthy example, by Layard *et al.*,[48] showed that the union/non-union differential in Britain had remained relatively constant over the period 1961–1968 but had then risen significantly by 1975.[49] As unemployment and inflation also rose significantly in the latter period, Layard *et. al.* concluded that the change in the union/non-union differential had contributed to the inflationary pressure of that period. But this finding, and others like it, are subject to a number of unresolved criticisms which make their conclusions suspect.[50] First, none of these studies have been able to explain why union militancy suddenly increased at the end of the 1960s. Second, the beginning of the 1970s was

'Perfect' collective bargaining   27

marked by a major increase in world oil prices, which would have been predicted to increase inflation and unemployment simultaneously – precisely what was observed. Third, inflation increased in all countries of the industrial world at the same time. Thus, a model of union 'pushfulness' would have to suggest that unions in all of these countries chose simultaneously to become more militant. Given the heterogeneity of the cultures and of the types of union structures involved, a more plausible explanation would appear to be that all of these countries were being subjected to the same exogenous pressures – those resulting from the oil price shock, for example.

In short, we find only limited evidence, at best, to support the view that trade unions in the industrialised countries have had a major effect upon inflationary pressures. Rather, the best evidence suggests that, although union wages tend to rise relative to non-union in recessions and to fall relative to non-union in booms, in the long-run union and non-union wages tend to move in concert. On this basis, we believe that it can be concluded that union effects on inflation do not represent a significant argument either for or against the use of collective bargaining to establish wage rates.

Summary

The purpose of this section has been to review the theoretical and empirical literatures with respect to the effects which collective bargaining has upon the overall performance of the economy. Four sets of arguments have been considered. These are that collective bargaining increases worker productivity, reduces firms' incentives to invest, increases unemployment, and adds to inflationary pressures. Although each of these arguments has strong intuitive appeal and each has gained considerable popular support, we find that the most reliable, rigorously prepared empirical studies are unable to find strong evidence for any of them. The most that can be said is that some of these arguments may be correct but that further study will have to be conducted before a definitive answer can be reached. As we have no reason to believe that these results would not also apply to a society in which all workers were to be covered by collective bargaining, we conclude that arguments concerning efficiency do not provide a

EQUITY

It is clear that one of the most important roles ascribed to collective bargaining, in both popular and scholastic writing, is the redistribution of income. The purpose of this section is to enquire whether a system of perfect collective bargaining could be expected to effect a redistribution which can be considered to be desirable. The first step in this enquiry will be to enunciate a set of criteria against which one can measure the success or failure of any such redistribution. Rather than adopting an existing set of criteria, such as those contained within the utilitarian or equalitarian models, we have chosen to use the Rawlsian approach to develop criteria which we believe are particularly adapted to the issues raised by collective bargaining. We then apply these criteria to question whether perfect collective bargaining can be expected to produce a distribution of income which is superior to that produced by individual bargaining between employees and their employers. At each stage, we summarise the available empirical data, most of which provide support for our theoretical arguments.

In his seminal work, *The Theory of Justice*,[51] John Rawls confronted the problem that individuals, as participating members in particular societies at particular points in history, find it difficult to divorce themselves entirely from their own preferences when constructing models of 'ideal' distributions of income. The rich may place a different value upon equality than the poor, for example, and men may place a different value than women. Freedom may be valued differently by slaves and citizens; medical care may be valued differently by the healthy and the sick; and freedom of speech may be valued differently by conformists and dissidents.

In an attempt to prevent contamination of philosophical ideals by these personal biases, Rawls suggested that equity criteria be established by individuals who imagined themselves to be in a state in which they had no knowledge about their own positions in society – a state which he called the 'original position'. Specifically, philosophers were to ask themselves what their views concerning equity would be if they were to be denied information concerning 'their place in society, their class position or social status, their place in the distribution of natural assets and abilities, their deeper aims or interests, or their particular psychological makeup'.[52] In pragmatic terms, individuals were to imagine that a 'veil of ignorance' had been placed in front of them. Only after they had made their decisions concerning the ordering of social institutions was this veil to be removed; and only at that time would individuals discover which position in society they were to fill. In short, at the time of the selection of the equity criteria, each individual in the original position was to believe that he or she had an equal chance of becoming any one of the members of society – young or old, male or female, rich or poor, healthy or sick, black or white.

Applying this approach, Rawls concluded that the following principles would be selected:

1 Each person [is to have] an equal right to the most extensive scheme of equal basic liberties compatible with a similar scheme of liberties for all.
2 Social and economic inequalities are to meet two conditions: they must be
> (a) to the greatest expected benefit of the least advantaged members of society (the *maximin* equity criterion) and
> (b) attached to offices and positions open to all under conditions of fair equality of opportunity.[53]

Of these, conditions 1 and 2(b) are commonly accepted and appear to us to require little additional comment. Condition 2(a), the 'maximin' criterion, however, is not only unique to Rawls but has been the subject of much controversy.[54] Accordingly, some discussion of this criterion is in order.

In terms of the evaluation of industrial relations systems, what the maximin criterion suggests is that those systems are to be contrasted solely on the effect which they have upon the 'least advantaged members of society'. When stated in this way, two weaknesses of the maximin criterion become apparent. First, it is not unlikely that two quite different industrial relations systems could have the same impact upon the least advantaged members of society. Assume, for example, that the least advantaged group consists primarily of individuals who are not members of the labour force. In this case, quite dramatic changes in the

30 Rethinking labour–management relations

employer–*employee* relationship could take place with little or no effect upon the least advantaged. Implicitly, the maximin criterion would conclude that society would be indifferent to all such changes. As this conclusion is not the one which one would expect individuals in the original position to choose, we propose to add the following criterion: that if the least advantaged members of society are not made worse off, a change from one industrial relations system to another will be considered to be socially desirable if it reduces inequality in the distribution of income.[55] That is, as individuals tend to be risk avoiders when they are behind the veil of ignorance (and do not know at which end of the income spectrum they will find themselves once the veil is lifted) they will be willing to trade off a reduction in the highest income which they could potentially earn in return for an increase in the lowest income.

Second, it seems unlikely that individuals in the original position would select a criterion which concentrates solely upon the least advantaged. Rawls's argument that the maximin criterion will be selected appears to be based upon the assumption that individuals behind the veil of ignorance would be extremely risk averse. When presented with a selection of income distributions, they would concentrate their attentions exclusively on the lower end of those distributions, saying to themselves, in effect, 'although I have an equal chance of finding myself at each position in the distribution of income, I would be willing to give up all possibilities of gain in every position in order to obtain even the smallest of gains at the lowest position'. Our view is that most individuals are much less risk averse than this. There are some redistributions of income which they would consider to be sufficiently beneficial that, in order to obtain these redistributions, they would be willing to accept the risk of a small loss in the worst case situation.

For example, assume that individuals in the original position are offered the choice between the two distributions of income represented in the following way:

Income group	Distribution I (£)	Distribution II (£)
Non-employed	10,100	10,000
Workers	30,000	40,000
Capitalists	90,000	80,000

'Perfect' collective bargaining   31

Assume also that individuals in the original position are told that, when the veil of ignorance is lifted, there will be a one-third probability that they will find they belong to the non-employed group, one-third to the worker group, and one-third to the capitalist group. In this circumstance, to say that individuals are risk averse means that they would be willing to accept a decrease of £10,000 from the potential income of the capitalist in return for an increase of £10,000 in the income of the worker. The explanation which is generally given for this is that £10,000 added to £30,000 is perceived to be of greater value than £10,000 added to £80,000 (or deducted from £90,000). Thus, if non-employed workers were to be left equally well off in both Distributions I and II, it would be predicted unambiguously that risk averse individuals would prefer Distribution II. But if a redistribution of income from capitalists to workers represents a clear gain (from the perspective of the original position), then it must be possible that that gain would be large enough to compensate for a reduction in the income enjoyed by the non-employed. That is, individuals in the original position might well express a preference for Distribution II over Distribution I even though selection of the former would leave them slightly worse off in the one-third of the occasions in which they found that they were members of the least advantaged group. We conclude, therefore, that the Rawlsian maximin criterion must be modified to allow for the possibility that redistributions among all other groups in society could be considered to be so favourable that individuals in the original position would be willing to countenance a reduction in the welfare of the least advantaged.

What this discussion suggests, we submit, is that when equity considerations are employed to rank industrial relations systems, the following criteria should be applied:

1 Preference is to be given to those systems which provide individuals with the most extensive scheme of equal access to basic liberties compatible with a similar scheme of liberties for all. [This is merely a restatement of Rawls's first criterion, as applied specifically to industrial relations systems.]

2 Systems which reduce the dispersion of income are to be preferred if they do not make the least advantaged members of society worse off; and *may* be preferred if they obtain a

32 Rethinking labour-management relations

significant reduction in dispersion at the cost of a minor worsening of the position of the least advantaged.

3 Industrial relations systems must not interfere with the general principles of:

(a) *horizontal equity:* equally qualified workers under otherwise identical contracts should receive equal remuneration; and

(b) *vertical equity:* differences in remuneration should be based, as much as possible, upon differences in the disutilities attached to employments – for example, upon differences in risk, in educational requirements, in effort required, and in responsibility.[56] [These criteria we suggest may be derived from Rawls's criterion 2(a), on p. 29.]

We now turn to an application of these criteria to the question of whether a system of perfect collective bargaining can be considered to be more equitable than a system of individualised bargaining. We do this by considering, in turn, each of the three sets of criteria outlined above.

Equal access to basic liberties

We believe that a strong case can be made for the argument that collective bargaining provides workers with access to a much more extensive set of basic liberties than does individual bargaining. The history of the trade union movement (see Chapter 1), suggests that the strongest impetus to the development of institutions of collective bargaining was the depersonalisation of the workplace. Whereas, prior to the nineteenth century, workers had been able to maintain an element of control over the pace of their work, the quality of their product, and (to a lesser extent) their rates of remuneration, the industrial revolution removed much of that independence. The increased mechanisation of the factory floor meant that workers became adjuncts to their machines – mere factors of production instead of individual human beings – and the increased scale of production meant that the economic power of employers rose dramatically, leaving workers much less able to influence the courses of their own working lives.

The first way in which collective bargaining may have been said to have increased workers' access to basic liberties was to return some of this power and control to workers. With the support of their fellow workers behind them, individuals felt much freer to complain about unfair or unsafe work practices; they obtained a new ability to recommend changes in the workplace; and they were able to obtain agreements which improved their security of employment. Furthermore, the increased incomes which unions were able to obtain increased workers' abilities to save and, therefore, their abilities to withstand periods of unemployment. Accordingly, workers were provided with greater freedom to quit their jobs if they felt dissatisfied and to look for alternative employment elsewhere.

Collective bargaining also acted to increase liberties in an indirect manner. Because institutions of collective bargaining provided forums for workers to raise social and political issues, those institutions increased the control which workers had over the political process. This gave them a stronger voice in supporting political initiatives to improve the position of the common man – such as the introduction of universal suffrage and free education, for example.

On the other hand, it may also be argued that collective bargaining imposes some limited constraints on individual freedoms. The most important of these derives from the necessity that all workers within a unit bargain together. Inevitably, this implies that the wishes of some workers will be subjugated to those of the majority. To the extent that workers bargaining individually with their employers would have been able to obtain contracts which reflected closely their own preferences and requirements, this subjugation represents a constraint on individual liberty. Set off against this potential constraint, however, are a number of realities which were discussed on pp. 14–20 of this chapter: individual workers are less able than groups of workers to obtain information about firms' reputations, working conditions, and profitability; individual workers generally have much less bargaining power than do groups and, therefore, are less able to induce employers to agree to their terms; and individual workers are less able to protect themselves against employer breaches of implicit agreements than are workers acting in concert. Thus, in all but the most exceptional circumstances, it can be expected that the contracts which are reached through collective action will be preferred by even the

34   Rethinking labour–management relations

minority members of the workplace to those which individual workers could have reached on their own.

Redistribution of income

It can be said with certainty that collective bargaining acts to redistribute income from capital to labour. Extensive evidence has been collected in both the United States and Britain to indicate that unions raise the wages of their members by between 15 and 20 per cent relative to those of non-union workers; and that unions raise the value of the fringe benefits received by their members by an even larger percentage.[57] At the same time, the evidence surveyed on pp. 22–3 of this chapter revealed that unions reduce the rate of profit by as much as 20 per cent. We conclude, therefore, that if all workers were to be covered by collective agreements, (as we assume in the idealised model we call 'perfect' collective bargaining), the redistribution of income which would result would be perceived to be desirable *provided that the least advantaged were not harmed* (in a significant way) by that redistribution.

Thus, it must be asked how collective bargaining affects the least advantaged. This first requires that we identify who the least advantaged are. They are *not* workers, as we have assumed that all workers are covered by collective bargaining agreements; they are not the dependent children or spouses of workers; nor are they workers who have retired. All of these groups will have gained either directly from the increased wages and fringe benefits (including pensions) won by collective action or will have gained indirectly from the gains shared with them. The least advantaged must be individuals (or their dependants) who, over the greater part of their lives, have little or no attachment to the labour market. Are these individuals made worse off by collective bargaining? We think not. Indeed, we believe that it can be argued that these individuals may well be made better off.

Our primary argument is based on the observation that the gains in both economic and political power which the collective organisation of workers brings about allows workers to obtain legislative changes. In many cases, these changes can be expected to benefit those who are outside of the labour force. Workers, for example, can be expected to seek improved health care, unemployment insurance benefits, welfare payments, and public education among a host of other factors which can all be expected to benefit the public at large, not just those who work. Thus, the strengthening of the *working* classes which is brought about by collective bargaining may well contribute to the well-being of those who do not work. Evidence of this effect has recently been obtained in two studies conducted using data drawn from the United States. Both Rubin[58] and Caniglia and Flaherty[59] found that an increase in unionisation had a significant, positive effect on the share of total income received by individuals in the lowest quintile (the bottom 20 per cent) of the income distribution; whereas unionisation had no significant effect upon the share of total *earnings* received by individuals in that quintile. These data suggest that unionisation has very little effect upon the ability of the least advantaged to earn incomes, but that unions use their political power to press for increased government transfers to those who are outside the labour force.

Furthermore, collective bargaining does not appear to have a significant, negative effect on the non-employed in other spheres. The evidence which we presented on pp. 23–7 of this chapter, for example, suggests that, at worst, collective bargaining has only a minor impact on inflation, unemployment, and economic growth. Accordingly, it does not have a significant effect on the prices paid by those outside of the workforce, on those individuals' prospects of employment, nor on the size of national income which is available to be divided among citizens. On these bases, therefore, we conclude that collective bargaining does achieve its intended effect – of redistributing income in a manner which is consistent with the rules of equity which would be selected by individuals who were 'divorced from that information about themselves which might distort their views of distributional equity'.

Horizontal and vertical equity

We have less reason to be sanguine about the impact of bargaining on horizontal and vertical equity. With respect to horizontal equity, the ability of unions to raise wages at any particular place of employment will be constrained by factors such as the employer's ability to pass on increased costs to customers, to substitute capital for labour, and to absorb increased wages in

36 Rethinking labour–management relations

the form of reduced profits. The less competitive the market in which the company is selling its products, the more favourable all these factors can be expected to be to the union. Accordingly, unions which deal with monopolistic or monopsonistic employers, will be able to obtain higher wages for their members, all else being equal, than will unions which deal with competitive employers. Even under a system of perfect collective bargaining, therefore, unions may increase wage differentials among otherwise equivalent workers – they will *reduce* horizontal equity.[60]

There is also evidence to suggest that union activity reduces vertical equity. Most studies find that unions act to reduce wage differentials between skilled and unskilled unionised workers. The explanation which is commonly given for this is that, in unions which are composed of both types of workers, the unskilled usually outnumber the skilled. Thus, the preferences of the former predominate over those of the latter. If this explanation is correct, it implies that the motivation for altering the skilled/unskilled wage differential is unrelated to issues concerning the 'appropriate' compensation of workers for the relative disutilities associated with their various employments. Accordingly, it would be only a coincidence if that alteration had improved vertical equity. On the other hand, this observation suggests that an 'optimal' system of collective bargaining might be one which facilitated the organisation of bargaining units along craft, rather than industrial, lines.

Summary

In this section, we have employed Rawls's concept of the original position to construct a number of measures of distributional equity. When these have been contrasted with the predicted and actual effects of collective bargaining, we have concluded that a system of perfect collective bargaining can generally be expected to improve equity. In particular, we have argued that collective bargaining provides workers with increased control over their working lives; it gives them a greater voice in the political arena; and it allows them to alter wages and public expenditures in such a way that there is a reduction in the inequality of income distribution. On the other hand, collective bargaining may also

'Perfect' collective bargaining 37

reduce both horizontal and vertical equity; although neither effect appears serious, particularly as techniques for avoiding the effect upon vertical equity could be devised.

LEGAL STRUCTURING

The relationships between employers and employees are governed to a large extent by the rules of statutory and common law.[61] In an interesting and provocative article, Marc Galanter[62] has argued that, relative to those parties which have only occasional recourse to the courts – in his terminology, *one-shotters* – parties who are engaged in many similar litigations over time – *repeat players* – will have a distinct advantage in shaping the laws to their own ends. The repeat player, for example, has much more at stake in any particular statutory or common law than does the one-shotter. Therefore, the repeat player will be willing to spend more to ensure that statutory rules are favourable to his position; will enjoy economies of scale in litigation; will be able to adopt strategies which maximise gain in the long-run, even where this involves the risk of maximum losses in individual cases; and will be able to settle cases out of court where he expects unfavourable outcomes,[63] allowing only those cases to go to trial in which he expects a favourable precedent to be established.

One example of a situation in which a one-shotter faces a repeat player is that in which the employee of a large firm has a dispute with his employer. In Galanter's model, the employee is at a disadvantage in this situation for a number of reasons. First, whereas the employee is only interested in the outcome of his current case, the employer will be interested in the effect which that decision will have on his relations with all of his other employees. Therefore, the employer will be willing to spend more on that case to ensure that he wins a favourable decision than will the employee. Similarly, if the employer faces a number of similar cases he and his solicitors will develop legal expertise which will make it less expensive for him than the employee to litigate any single case.[64] Finally, because employers face similar cases many times over, there are greater benefits to them than to individual employees to ensure that both statutory and common law rules are favourable to them. Thus, it can be expected that even if the employer has no financial advantage (over the employee) in

38 Rethinking labour–management relations

pursuing a particular case, he will have a legal advantage arising from the fact that the rules which will be applied will, over time, have become biased in his favour.

Galanter's argument also suggests that, as employers will have command over greater financial resources than will their employees, they will have a correspondingly greater influence over statutory law. Individual employers, for example, may be able to hire lawyers to draft sample legislation for them,[65] employ professional lobbyists to press their case with legislators, and take out advertisements to influence public opinion – options which will not generally be available to the individual employee.[66]

Galanter concludes from his analysis that if the courts and the legislatures are to behave in a manner which is consistent with general notions of 'justice,' one-shotters will have to be aggregated into repeat players. One method which he suggests for doing so is to aggregate employees into trade unions (and, by implication, to aggregate small firms into employer associations).[67] Clearly, the system of perfect collective bargaining being discussed here would be consistent with Galanter's recommendations.

CONCLUSIONS

The purpose of this chapter has been to review the major arguments which have been raised for and against the use of collective bargaining *in principle*. In order to avoid confusing the arguments about particular institutions of collective bargaining, such as the use of pickets or strikes, with arguments about the general concept of collective bargaining, we have directed our discussion to the analysis of an idealised form of bargaining which we call 'perfect' collective bargaining. The primary characteristics of this form are that *all* workers are presumed to be represented collectively in their negotiations with their employers; and that the inducements required to encourage employers and workers to bargain with one another are presumed to be costless. Under these idealised conditions, we have investigated four categories of arguments which have been put forward with respect to collective bargaining.

Collective voice

We have argued that collective bargaining can play an important role in providing workers with a sense that they have some control over their working lives; in bringing the concerns of workers to the attention of their employers; in gathering information of common concern to groups of workers to their employers; and in monitoring the provisions of implicit contracts which long-term employees have with their employers. In each case, we have suggested that it need not be found that any of these benefits increases worker productivity or reduces costs of production before it can be concluded that this function of collective bargaining is desirable. Rather, when it is recognised that workers are human beings, and not simply 'factors of production', the maximisation of their mental well-being becomes a worthwhile goal of the industrial relations system. Collective bargaining has shown itself capable of furthering this goal in a way that could not be reproduced by individualised bargaining or by legislative intervention.

Efficiency

It has variously been argued that collective bargaining leads to: increases in worker productivity, decreases in worker productivity, reductions in economic growth rates, increases in unemployment, decreases in employment, and increases in the rate of consumer price inflation. Our extensive review of the empirical findings in both Britain and North America suggests that none of these arguments receives strong support. The message which one obtains from this literature is that both internal (political) and external (economic) constraints act on most unions to prevent them from taking positions which would seriously jeopardise productivity, employment, or inflation, and that union provision of collective voice is not a sufficiently important factor to allow for significant gains in worker productivity. Instead, 'perfect' collective bargaining is predicted to have only a minor effect on most measures of economic efficiency.

Equity

Employing a set of criteria derived from Rawls's theory of justice, we have concluded that collective bargaining is generally conducive to the improvement of equity. Bargaining provides workers with greater control over their lives, both at work and away from it; it increases the incomes of workers relative to employers; and it may be a factor in the improvement of the well-being of those who are outside of the labour force. It was found that bargaining may, however, result in some horizontal inequities in the distribution of income if some employers are better able to pay increased wages than are others; and it may result in some vertical inequities in those cases in which majority groups within unions are able to impose their preferences upon minority groups. We do not believe that these latter problems outweigh the advantages of collective bargaining. Accordingly, we conclude that bargaining has the potential to act as a positive force in the redistribution of income.

Legal structuring

Finally, we have argued that the trade union role in representing workers in court and at legislatures is unambiguously positive. Left to their own devices, workers are at a severe disadvantage relative to employers when dealing with the legal system. It cannot be denied that some redress of this imbalance is desirable.

Summary

The arguments presented in this chapter suggest that an idealised form of collective bargaining, which we called 'perfect' collective bargaining, could be considered to be superior to a system of individualised bargaining – that is, to the free operation of the market system. What we wish to ask now is whether this conclusion can be extended to any of the 'real world' systems of bargaining which are available to our society. It is to this question that we turn in the remaining chapters of this book.

Chapter 3

The strike-based system

In Chapter 2 we argued that a system of 'perfect' collective bargaining would provide sufficient benefits to workers that it could be considered to be superior to a system in which workers were left to bargain their employment contracts individually. What we wish to initiate in this chapter is the search for a practical form of collective bargaining which approximates the idealised form as closely as possible. This we do by reviewing the various advantages and disadvantages which have been claimed for the most commonly employed form of collective bargaining – the strike-based system.

Our argument proceeds in six parts. In the first of these we define what we mean by a 'strike-based system' and describe how such a system can be expected to operate. In the next four sections, we apply each of the four criteria developed in Chapter 2 – collective voice, efficiency, equity, and legal structuring – to the identification of the advantages and disadvantages of this system. In the sixth section, we discuss the argument that workers have a fundamental, or constitutional, right to strike. Finally, we summarise the main arguments of the chapter.

THE CHARACTERISTICS OF A STRIKE-BASED SYSTEM

Definition

In general, a 'strike-based system' is any system of collective bargaining in which a group of workers induces its employer(s) to bargain over the terms of employment by threatening a collective withdrawal of labour. Conceptually, therefore, a strike-based system of collective bargaining may be thought to differ very little

42 Rethinking labour–management relations

from a system of individualised bargaining between workers and their employers. Whereas individuals, when attempting to bargain a contract of employment between themselves and their respective employers, may threaten to take their services elsewhere – to 'withdraw' their services – if a satisfactory agreement is not reached, trade unions, when attempting to obtain an agreement, threaten that their members will withdraw their services collectively. That is, a strike *may* be seen as simply the collective equivalent of a threat which is open to any party which is attempting to bargain an agreement – withdrawal from the negotiations.

For the purposes of this chapter, however, we wish to make a much clearer distinction between strike-based and individualised bargaining. First, most modern legal systems enjoin individuals from 'combining' to employ monopoly power to extract concessions from other economic actors. Although a strike-based system of collective bargaining *could* survive were these laws to be applied to it (after all, that was generally the situation when the trade union movement first arose during the nineteenth century), it would be dramatically weakened. In particular, all collective withdrawals of labour – strikes – would be considered to be contrary to the public interest and workers would not be protected from either the civil or statutory sanctions associated with anti-combination laws. Accordingly, we extend our definition to include the assumption that a strike-based system offers immunity from the provisions of anti-combination laws.

Second, whereas the threat by an individual worker to withdraw his labour can generally be presumed to imply a threat to take his labour elsewhere; we will presume that the threat by a union to withdraw its members' labour implies a threat to withhold that labour from the employer only until an agreement is reached. That is, we will presume that collective bargaining differs from individualised bargaining in that whereas the latter may well end in no agreement being reached between the bargaining parties, in the former the parties will generally agree to *some* resolution of their dispute.

Finally, in individualised bargaining, the firm is free to attempt to reach agreement with any worker that it wishes. Thus, failure to reach agreement with any particular worker does not imply that production will cease. In collective bargaining, on the other hand, the union's membership may include a large percentage of the workers required for the firm's production; or the union may be able to block the employer's access to alternative workers through the use of tactics such as picketing or calls for 'worker solidarity'. In both cases, if the employer fails to reach agreement with the union, its ability to produce will be impaired. Thus, it will be our assumption that whereas an individual withdrawal of labour will have little or no effect on production, a collective withdrawal – a strike – will result in curtailment of production, at least over the duration of the withdrawal.

The bargaining process

Before one can understand fully how a strike-based system of collective bargaining can be expected to operate, it is first necessary to develop an understanding of the manner in which bargaining between the union and management will proceed. The purpose of this section will be to review the elements of a bargaining model which has been variously attributed to Chamberlain[1] and to Zeuthen and Harsanyi.[2]

In this model, it is assumed that bargaining behaviour will be governed by the trade-off between the cost to the bargainer of conceding to his opponent's demands – the cost of agreeing – and the cost to him of failing to reach agreement – the cost of disagreeing. In particular, Chamberlain argues that if there are two bargainers, A and B, the 'bargaining power' of A is measured by the ratio of B's costs of disagreeing to B's costs of agreeing. That is, A can be said to be in a strong bargaining position if the cost to B of disagreeing is high, relative to its cost of agreeing. The reverse will then be true for B's bargaining power.[3] Thus, the bargaining powers of the union and the firm can be represented by:

Bargaining power of the firm =

$$\frac{\text{Cost to the union of disagreeing with the firm}}{\text{Cost to the union of agreeing with the firm}}$$

Bargaining power of the union =

$$\frac{\text{Cost to the firm of disagreeing with the union}}{\text{Cost to the firm of agreeing with the union}}$$

The importance of bargaining power in Chamberlain's model is that the party with the lesser power is assumed to be forced to

44 Rethinking labour-management relations

make a concession on its position to its opponent. In doing so, the party making the concession reduces its opponent's cost of agreeing (with its demand), thereby increasing its own bargaining power relative to that of its opponent. If the concession is large enough, the party making the concession will be able to increase its bargaining power sufficiently that its opponent will become the weaker party and the opponent will be forced to make the 'next' concession. In this way concession will be followed by counter-concession until agreement is reached.

For example, in the case of union-firm bargaining, the cost to both sides of disagreeing – the cost of failing to reach agreement – will be the cost of a strike; the cost to the union of agreeing will be the cost of accepting the firm's last offer (rather than gaining acceptance of its own offer); and the cost to the firm of agreeing will be the cost of accepting the union's last offer. Thus, if we assume, for simplicity, that the two sides have the same strike costs (costs of disagreeing), then it is the side which has made the most 'reasonable' offer which will have the greater bargaining power. That is, if the union has opened bargaining by making a demand which is totally unacceptable to the firm, whereas the firm has made an offer which is close to the offer the union is seeking, the cost to the firm of agreeing with the union will be much greater than will be the cost to the union of agreeing with the firm. In this case, the union would have little to gain from a strike, as it has already received a 'reasonable' offer from the firm, whereas the firm might consider the risk of a strike to be worthwhile. Therefore, according to Chamberlain, it is the firm which will have the greater bargaining power and it is the union which will make the first concession. In making such a concession, however, the union may reduce the firm's costs of agreeing to such an extent that it would now be the union which would be most willing to accept the risk of a strike and it would be the firm which would have the lesser bargaining power. Thus, the outcome of bargaining will be determined by the costs of agreement and disagreement to the union and the firm, respectively.

The costs to the union of agreeing will depend upon the determinants of the wage rate which it feels it is justified in asking for – its 'preferred' wage – and upon the loss of utility resulting from acceptance of a lower wage rate. That is, the greater is the difference (measured in terms of utility)[4] between the wage offered by the firm and the union's preferred wage, the greater will be the cost to the union of accepting the firm's last offer. In turn, the value of this preferred wage will be determined primarily by changes in consumer prices and changes in the wages of comparable workers; for, in general, workers feel strongly that their wages should not fall behind either the rate of inflation or the wages of workers performing similar tasks. (Consider, for example, the Ambulance Service industrial action of 1988/89 in Britain.) In addition, workers may attempt to obtain compensation for reductions in their 'take-home' pay caused by changes in deductions for items such as income taxes and unemployment insurance. However, failure to obtain the wage rate to which they feel 'justly' entitled may be ameliorated to some extent if alternative sources of income are available – from second jobs, overtime, or promotion. Finally, union costs of agreeing may be altered by political factors internal to the union. For example, during an election of union officers, candidates may use promises of higher wages in their election platforms, thereby raising the expectations of the membership and making bargaining concessions more costly.

The firm's costs of agreeing will be determined by the loss of profits involved in raising the wage rate above the profit-maximising rate (that is, the wage rate which it would have established in the absence of a union). The first determinant of this cost will be the price elasticity of demand for the firm's product.[5] The less elastic is demand, the greater will be the firm's ability to pass on its wage increases to its customers in the form of price increases. Second, the reaction of the firm's labour market rivals to an increase in its wages will also be important. If its rivals do not follow its wage increases, the firm will be able to attract the best-qualified workers in the market. The increased productivity of these workers may 'pay' for a portion of the higher wages being paid to them. On the other hand, if the firm's labour market rivals emulate its wage increases, it will gain no relative advantage from those increases. Finally, wage increases will be less costly the more easily the firm can substitute capital for labour.

In pecuniary terms, the union's costs of disagreeing consist of the wages lost during a strike. The impact of this loss will be determined by the amount of unavoidable expenses incurred by the workers during the strike and by the sources of income

46 Rethinking labour–management relations

available to them at that time. In addition to expenditures on food, heat, and shelter, unavoidable expenditures during a strike may also include payments for contractual obligations such as mortgage payments and repayments of personal loans. Sources of funds during a strike will include personal savings, income from part-time work and from other family members, retail credit, union strike funds, welfare payments, and loans to the union from financial institutions and other unions. Some of the costs of disagreeing may be made up following a strike if the workers are able to obtain extra overtime.

Finally, the costs to the firm of disagreeing will depend upon the effect of the firm's inability to produce during a strike. If the firm has built up stocks of its product before a strike occurs, those stocks may be used to supply customers, thereby resulting in a situation in which the strike has no cost to the firm. For example, this has been the policy of both British Coal and the Electricity Generating Board since the miners' strike of 1973. However, if the firm does not have stocks of its product, the effect of a strike will depend upon the time-specificity of demand for that product. That is, some firms' customers can afford to wait until a strike is over and then make up for consumption lost during the strike. For example, most potential purchasers of new automobiles would be willing to postpone consumption for a few months. Therefore, if automobile manufacturers were able to make up lost production at the end of a strike, their strike costs would be minimised. But other consumption activities cannot be postponed. Airline passengers cannot wait until January to fly home for Christmas, newspaper readers cannot be induced to buy April's news in May, and consumers of natural gas cannot postpone their demand for home heating fuel from winter until summer. In each of these cases, sales lost during a strike cannot be recovered by the firm after the strike has ended.

From this brief discussion, we can identify a number of strategies which will be of importance in the bargaining process. Because the outcome of bargaining is predicted to be dependent on the relative bargaining powers of the two sides, each bargainer will attempt to convince his opponent of his own bargaining power – by increasing his opponent's costs of disagreeing and reducing his opponent's costs of agreeing – while attempting to belittle the bargaining power of his opponent – by reducing his own costs of disagreeing and increasing its own (perceived) costs of agreeing. For example, the union may be able to increase the firm's costs of disagreeing by delaying negotiations until a period of peak demand for the firm's product; while the firm may attempt to increase the union's costs of disagreeing by choosing to hold negotiations at a time when unemployment is high (and striking union members would find it difficult to obtain part-time jobs). The union may also be able to increase its bargaining power by reducing the firm's costs of agreeing, for example by arguing that a wage increase would attract better-qualified workers, reduce absenteeism, or increase worker productivity; while the firm may be able to reduce the union's costs of agreeing by pointing to comparable unions which have accepted relatively low wage increases.

In addition, each side may attempt to reduce its opponent's bargaining power. For example, the firm may be able to reduce its own costs of disagreeing by stockpiling inventory or by gearing-up for extra production in its foreign subsidiaries; while the union may be able to reduce its costs of disagreeing by arranging a loan to be used as strike pay. And the firm may be able to increase its own (perceived) costs of agreeing by announcing that its negotiators will lose their jobs if they agree to an increase of more than x per cent; while the union negotiators may respond by announcing publicly that they would resign if the settlement fell below y per cent.

Finally, the Chamberlain model allows us to compare bargaining situations in order to identify those factors which will determine the relative strengths of various unions. We consider seven of the most important factors here:

a) *Percentage of costs accounted for by labour:* If two unions are otherwise identical, it is the union whose wages represent the smaller percentage of its employer's total costs that will have the greater bargaining power. The reason for this is that, of the four costs which determine bargaining power – the two parties' costs of agreement and their respective costs of disagreement – the share of wages in total costs has an effect only upon the firm's costs of agreement. In particular, as this share increases, the cost to the firm of agreeing to a particular percentage increase in the wage rate will also increase. For example, a wage increase of 10 per cent will increase total costs by 6 per cent if wages account for 60 per

48 Rethinking labour–management relations

cent of costs; whereas it will increase total costs by only 0.5 per cent if wages account for 5 per cent of the firm's costs. As the firm can be expected to be more concerned to oppose the latter than the former, it is predicted that unions which represent small but crucial groups of workers will be relatively successful in obtaining their demands. On this ground, one would expect airline pilots and longshoremen to be more 'powerful' than restaurant workers or government office workers, for example.

b) *Employer's ability to influence price:* The better able is the employer to 'pass on' wage increases as price increases without there being a significant effect upon demand for the firm's product, the lower will its costs of agreement be and the stronger will the union's bargaining position be. Two arguments have been made in this respect. First, it has been suggested that unions in 'essential' industries will be relatively powerful because customers will continue to purchase those industries' products even when wage increases have induced employers to raise prices.[6] Second, it has been argued that unions will have greater bargaining power, the more concentrated is an industry's production in the hands of a small number of firms. The argument suggests that, as concentration increases, the union's ability to organise all firms will also increase. Accordingly, whereas in low concentration industries, customers will be able to turn from unionised to non-unionised producers when union wage increases lead to price increases; in highly concentrated industries, customers will have only the choice of not buying the product when prices have been forced up.

c) *Ease of product storage:* If a firm can store its product for sale during a strike or if customers can 'store' their demand for the firm's product until after the strike is over, a strike may have relatively little effect upon the firm's profitability. However, if neither the product nor its demand can be stored, profits will be reduced both by the effect of the reduced sales during the strike and, potentially, also by the effect of customers diverting their purchases to other producers after the conclusion of the strike. Thus, firms which cannot store their product will have relatively high costs of disagreement and the unions which face them will be relatively powerful. For example, on this basis, newspaper unions would be expected to be stronger than automobile manufacturing

The strike-based system 49

unions; and airline unions would be at their most powerful during the peak seasons, such as school holidays.

d) *Concentration of union membership:* Unions will find it more difficult to maintain cohesion during a strike, the more their members are dispersed across locations. Members will not know each other, communications will be difficult across distances, and employers may be able to prey on small groups to divide the union into weak factions. Union solidarity can be expected to be at its peak, therefore, and unions will be able to impose the highest costs of disagreement upon employers, when most of their members work in single plants, or small groups of plants. It has often been suggested that this factor was important in determining the timing of the birth of trade unionism – during the growth of the factory system in the industrial revolution – and in discouraging the growth of unionism in the retail and service sectors.[7]

e) *Worker attachment to the labour force:* The cost to any individual union member of a concesssion on the union's wage demands will be greater, the longer the worker expects to experience the effects of that concession. An agreement to accept a 1 per cent reduction in the union's wage demand will be felt more keenly by those workers who expect to work full-time over the duration of the collective agreement than by those who expect to work only part-time for a few months. Thus, the workers who have the greatest attachment to the labour force and to the particular employer with whom they are bargaining will have the greatest amount to lose by agreeing to a concession. That is, it is expected that union bargaining power will be greater among full-time workers than among part-time workers and among workers with long-term attachments to their occupations than among workers who move often from employment to employment.[8]

f) *Union 'control' over available workers:* The union will be able to impose higher costs of disagreement on the firm, the more successful it is in restricting the firm's ability to operate during a strike. This success will primarily be linked to its ability to prevent the firm from hiring replacement workers ('scabs') during a strike. Thus, unions will have greater bargaining power: (i) the greater is the percentage of workers which they have organised; (ii) the greater is the freedom which the law provides them to use

50 Rethinking labour–management relations

picketing as a means of discouraging replacement workers; (iii) the stronger are the laws which prohibit use of replacement workers or require that union members be rehired following the conclusion of a strike; and (iv) the lower is the degree of substitutability between the firm's employees and potential replacement workers.[9]

g) *Government support for strikers:* The union's costs of disagreement will be reduced and, therefore, union bargaining strength will be increased if the government provides unemployment insurance or welfare payments to union members and their families during the course of a strike.

UNION VOICE

The first advantage which is attributed to collective bargaining, (see Chapter 2, pp. 14–20), is that trade unions provide a means through which individuals can 'voice' their concerns about their workplaces without fear of reprisal from their employers. There is some suggestion in this argument that some workers might find the provision of a collective voice to be of lesser importance than might others. Individuals whose jobs gave them great control over their day-to-day work patterns, such as managers or university professors for example, might feel less need to use collective voice to combat feelings of alienation than would individuals who worked on assembly lines. Similarly, individuals whose skills were in short supply might possess sufficient bargaining power with respect to their employers that they would be less concerned about employer reprisals than would other workers.[10] Nevertheless, there is reason to believe that all but the tiniest minority of workers will find it to their advantage to have their views represented collectively. For example, although university professors are given the greatest possible leeway in the operation of their individual work relations, thereby reducing their feelings of alienation virtually to a minimum, there is still a strong demand by professors for unionisation, largely to combat feelings of insecurity when dealing with their employers.

On this basis, we submit that an important criterion by which any industrial relations system may be measured is the percentage of workers to whom it provides collective representation – the larger that percentage, the more desirable the system. With respect to this criterion, the strike-based system does not acquit itself very well in either Britain or North America. Only (approximately) 50 per cent of wage and salary earners are unionised in Britain, 40 per cent in Canada, and 20 per cent in the United States.[11] More importantly, many of those who are not represented by unions are among those who would benefit most by unionisation. Among those groups which are relatively underrepresented include women,[12] part-time workers,[13] employees of small firms,[14] and individuals with relatively little specific occupational training.[15] Yet women are, arguably, more in need of the benefits of collective voice than are men because of the discrimination which they feel in the labour force; part-time workers and individuals with only general skills generally feel less secure and, therefore, are less likely to mount individual challenges to their employers than are other workers; and employees of small firms may feel less freedom in expressing their views about their workplaces than employees of large firms because they stand out more.

Furthermore, we submit that the failure of trade unions to organise many of these groups is largely attributable to the union movement's reliance upon the strike threat. The reason for this is that the strike threat acts as a means for ensuring that the employer gives serious attention to employee demands only when the union is able to mount an effective work stoppage. But, as we argued on pp. 48–50, there are many industries and occupations in which such a stoppage may not represent a significant threat to the employer. In particular, unions can be expected to encounter difficulty mounting a strike in industries in which workers are dispersed among a large number of small firms and in which workers are reluctant to shoulder the expense of a work stoppage because they work only part-time or have a weak attachment to the labour force. Also, a work stoppage will impose lower costs on an employer, the less costly the storage of the product (or the demand for the product) and the easier it is for the employer to continue operating while the union is on strike; and the employer will be more willing to oppose a union's demands, the greater the percentage of the firm's costs which is made up of wages. In each of these cases, the impotence of the strike threat makes the opportunity to form a union a hollow right. Before workers in industries characterised by these weaknesses can be said to have

52 Rethinking labour–management relations

been provided with a 'collective voice' they will have to be offered a means of obtaining employer acquiescence other than through the strike threat.

EFFICIENCY

In Chapter 2 it was argued that a system of perfect collective bargaining would have only a limited impact on worker productivity, inflation, unemployment, and investment. There is no reason to believe that those conclusions would differ if perfect collective bargaining were to be replaced by strike-based bargaining. (Indeed, the empirical observations upon which we relied in Chapter 2 to support our arguments were all drawn from countries in which bargaining is based upon the strike threat.) However, there is another sense, not considered in Chapter 2, in which a strike-based system may introduce inefficiencies into the economy; namely, that production generally ceases (or is significantly reduced) during the course of any work stoppage. Accordingly, unless those reductions in output can be recovered without cost at some other time, strikes themselves will produce inefficiencies. The question arises, therefore, as to whether strikes result in significant reductions in gross national product (GNP). We consider four major arguments in this context:

a) *Incidence of work stoppages:* During the decade 1979–1988 an average of 9,747,600 days were lost to strikes each year in Britain.[16] While these strikes were in progress, production was halted. Thus, that output which could not be made up from stockpiled inventories or which could not be recouped when the strikes were completed – for example, by operating plants overtime – was lost and the incomes of both employers and workers were reduced accordingly.[17]

It has been argued that the cost of this strike record, when averaged across the entire workforce is insignificant. Ten million working days per annum, for example, represents approximately half a day per employed person. Thus, even if none of the production lost during those strikes could be recouped,[18] the direct cost of strikes was equivalent to only 0.2 per cent of annual production.[19] However, strikes do not affect all segments of the workforce equally. Of the 781 strikes which occurred in Britain in 1988, for example, only 45 lasted for more than 20 working days (approximately one month); yet those strikes accounted for 43 per cent of the 3,702,000 days lost through all stoppages.[20] Furthermore, not only are most losses concentrated in the longer strikes, but the incidence of strikes is concentrated in particular industries and even in particular firms. In 1988, for example, four industries in Britain averaged more than two days lost per worker. These were (with days lost in brackets): motor vehicles (2.165), 'other' transport equipment (3.188), sea transport (9.500), and 'other' transport (2.350) (see Table 1). [21] A survey which was taken in the engineering industry in 1968 showed that 'under 1 percent of the establishments had over 40 percent of the stoppages and 5 percent had 65 percent of the stoppages.'[22] Three exceptionally strike-prone establishments accounted for 41 per cent of the strikes recorded. Thus, even though output lost during strikes may not significantly affect *national* output, it may have a dramatic effect on the output of individual firms and industries.

b) *Effects on productivity:* In some industries, long-run levels of production are not seriously affected by work stoppages because it is possible to build up stocks of inventories which can be sold during those stoppages. Nevertheless, such a policy is not costless. It is generally cheaper to maintain a constant level of production than to have periods of high production (while building up stocks) followed by periods of no production (during work stopppages) and it is generally expensive to maintain warehouse facilities for the storage of products. Furthermore, it is not only those firms which will have strikes that might find it advantageous to build inventories, but all firms which believe that they, or their suppliers, *might* be subject to a strike. Thus, in a strike-based system, inventory costs can be expected to be increased in all unionised firms (and for their customers) for which it is technically possible to carry inventory.

Richard Caves[23] has presented evidence to suggest that the greater incidence of strikes in the United Kingdom than in the United States is one of the major contributing factors to the lower level of productivity in the former than the latter. Furthermore, the evidence in his study also suggested that the relative levels of productivity in the two countries were *not* related to their relative levels of unionisation. That is, his study provided evidence for the general hypothesis that it is not unionisation *per se* which affects productivity, but the use of the threat of a work stoppage.

54 Rethinking labour–management relations

Table 1 Incidence rates from stoppages of work in progress: Britain, 1987 and 1988

Industry group	Working days lost per employee*	
	1988	1987
Agriculture, forestry and fishing	—	—
Coal extraction	1.691	1.413
Extraction and processing of coke, mineral oil and natural gas	0.001	—
Electricity, gas, other energy and water	0.053	0.030
Metal processing and manufacture	0.067	0.065
Mineral processing and manufacture	0.030	0.053
Chemicals and man-made fibres	0.069	0.028
Metal goods not elsewhere specified	0.119	0.085
Mechanical engineering	0.066	0.223
Electrical engineering and equipment	0.041	0.052
Instrument engineering	0.013	0.033
Motor vehicles	2.165	0.652
Other transport equipment	3.188	0.255
Food, drink and tobacco	0.086	0.070
Textiles	0.318	0.075
Footwear and clothing	0.050	0.104
Timber and wooden furniture	0.008	0.007
Paper, printing and publishing	0.007	0.036
Other manufacturing industries	0.020	0.018
Construction	0.016	0.021
Distribution, hotels and catering, repairs	0.001	0.001
Railways	0.088	0.017
Other inland transport	0.073	0.201
Sea transport	9.500	0.109
Other transport and communication	2.350	3.204
Supporting and miscellaneous transport services	0.071	0.056
Banking, finance, insurance, business services and leasing	—	—
Public administration, sanitary services and education	0.064	0.243
Medical and health services	0.027	0.005
Other services	0.016	0.032
All industries and services	0.164	0.162

*Based on the latest available mid-year (June) estimates of employees.

Source: Employment Gazette, July 1989

c) *External costs:* Strike losses are not confined to workers and employers. The consumers of the commodities whose production is disrupted also suffer losses. The extent of these losses depends upon the necessity of the commodities, the availability of substitutes, and the time-specificity of demand. In general, disruption of the supply of such necessary commodities as ambulance services and the supply of natural gas for home heating will produce greater losses to consumers than will disruption of the supply of such luxury goods as theatre productions and restaurant meals. Furthermore, if there are no close substitutes for the commodity being affected by a strike and if consumption cannot be delayed until the strike is over, losses will be higher than if consumption can be delayed or transferred to a similar product. For example, although flour may be considered by some to be a necessity, during a strike of one flour-producer consumers may simply switch to a second producer or may use up stores of flour set aside before the strike.

d) *International trade:* In those cases in which consumers find themselves severely inconvenienced by a strike, or series of strikes, they may transfer consumption from one producer to another, thus reducing long-term demand for the product of the firm which has been struck. The 1988 Post Office strike in Britain is an example. Firms were encouraged to seek alternative means of delivering mail, including couriers and fax machines, and they continued to use these after the strike ended. Clearly, the potential damage to the firm so affected is much greater than the costs of forgone production which result from the strike itself. Furthermore, these indirect costs will be greatest in those industries which trade internationally. If one milk producer has a worse strike record than another, causing consumers to switch from the former to the latter, employment and production will merely transfer between them. There will be no overall reduction in the country's GNP. But if the firm with the better strike record is situated in a foreign country, the transfer of demand will reduce both employment and GNP in the country with the poor strike record. This effect will be particularly pronounced in industries which are highly competitive in world markets. Yet it is precisely those industries in which Britain faces the greatest international competition – manufacturing and engineering – which have the worst strike records. In the words of T.G. Whittingham and B. Towers:

56 Rethinking labour–management relations

> [The] centre of gravity of strike incidence [in Britain] is in 'key' export industries and in industries which compete at home with imports: mechanical and electrical engineering and motor vehicle production. [Furthermore, these industries are] image-makers and may influence the psychology of decision-making in markets for British exports.[24]

In short, although the number of man-days lost through work stoppages is not large, the costs of these stoppages may be significant as (i) they tend to be concentrated in particular firms and industries; (ii) they reduce productivity; (iii) they disrupt production of necessary commodities; and (iv) they are often localised in industries which compete in international markets.

EQUITY

In Chapter 2 we argued that the following criteria should be applied to determine whether the effects of an industrial relations system could be said to be equitable:

1 Preference is to be given to those systems which provide individuals with the most extensive scheme of equal basic liberties compatible with a similar scheme of liberties for all. [This is merely a restatement of Rawls's first criterion, as applied specifically to industrial relations systems.]
2 Systems which reduce the dispersion of income are to be preferred if they do not make the least advantaged members of society worse off; and *may* be preferred if they obtain a significant reduction in dispersion at the cost of a minor worsening of the position of the least advantaged.
3 Industrial relations systems must not interfere with the general principles of:
   (a) *horizontal equity:* equally qualified workers under otherwise identical contracts should receive equal remuneration; and
   (b) *vertical equity:* differences in remuneration should be based, as much as possible, upon differences in the disutilities attached to employments – for example, upon differences in risk, in educational requirements, in effort required, and in responsibility. [These criteria we suggest may be derived from Rawls's criterion 2(a), see p. 29, above.]

It can be argued that an industrial relations system which is

The strike-based system 57

based upon the strike threat fails to meet at least three of these criteria (considering 3a and 3b to be separate criteria).

Equal access to basic liberties

A strike-based system fails to provide workers with equal access to basic liberties in at least three important senses. First, reliance upon the strike threat to press worker demands makes it very difficult to organise some groups of workers. Individuals who have a weak attachment to the labour force, such as part-time employees, are often unwilling to employ the strike threat because they find that the benefits obtained do not exceed the costs of the strike; and individuals who work in decentralised workplaces find it difficult to maintain the cohesion which is necessary to mount a successful strike. These workers, therefore, are denied equal access to the use of collective bargaining to obtain security in, and control over, their places of employment.

Second, even among those who have been successful in organising trade unions there is unequal access to liberty because the strike-threat system provides much greater bargaining power to some unions than to others. Those unions which produce 'essential' products or services, those which control a significant portion of the workers required by an industry, and those which deal with firms whose wages represent a small percentage of total costs all enjoy a relatively high degree of bargaining power, allowing them to obtain concessions from their employers which would not be available to other unionised workers. Thus, even within the union movement, the strike threat may not allow for equality of access to 'basic liberties'.

Finally, even if unions are democratic, it is likely that the views of some workers will not be represented adequately by their unions in the collective bargaining process.[25] The reason for this is that in a democracy, it is the candidate, or party, whose platform most closely reflects the views of the majority which can be expected to win election. But this means that the views of the minority will often be ignored or, at least, given relatively little weight. This is particularly true with respect to that large percentage of collective bargaining issues concerning which the union must select only one position. For example, whether the union bargains over an issue explicitly or not, the decisions made by the union can lead to only one level of employment by the firm. Therefore, if one group of workers prefers a high-employment policy and another prefers a low-employment policy, at least one group must 'lose'. (A compromise position would represent a 'loss' for both groups.) Similarly, as many fringe benefits, such as pension plans, and workplace policies, ranging from grievance procedures to safety practices, apply equally to all members of large groups of workers, no individual member of any group can expect to have his or her preferences fully reflected in the demands of the union.[26]

No system of collective bargaining can fully overcome this problem. (Indeed, in Chapter 2 we identified this as one of the few disadvantages to 'perfect' collective bargaining.) Nevertheless, some elements of the lack of individual control over the policies of the trade union could be overcome if each union were to represent a relatively small, homogeneous group of workers;[27] for, in such a situation, it could be expected that workers would share similar views concerning the optimal policies of their unions and, accordingly, the numbers of 'dissident' workers would be minimised.[28]

We submit, however, that the use of the strike threat as the means of encouraging collective bargaining acts to discourage the formation of small unions and, therefore, inhibits the development of truly 'representative' policy-making bodies. There are two reasons for this. First, large unions are much better able than small unions to organise and mount successful work stoppages. They can accrue large strike funds, they can strike one portion of an industry while continuing to collect dues in another, and they can benefit from economies of scale in the leadership function while trying to maintain the cohesion which is essential to the operation of a successful work stoppage. Second, in a strike-based system it can be extremely inefficient to allow the development of a large number of small unions within a single establishment. If each union selects a separate timetable for negotiations with the employer, it is possible that the same firm could experience strike action many different times each year, resulting in losses in production which would far exceed those that would arise were all workers to act in concert. These factors place great pressure on workers to combine into monolithic unions, for economic advantage, even though that action significantly reduces the ability of unions to take into account the diversity of opinions among their members.

To summarise, it is seen that use of the strike as the means of inducing employers to engage in collective bargaining does not provide all workers with equal access to the 'most extensive scheme of basic liberties'. Those workers who are able to organise successful unions will be in a better position than those who are not; those who belong to unions with strong bargaining power will be in a better position than those who belong to unions with weak bargaining power; and those individuals who belong to unions in which they share the majority position will have their views better represented than those who belong to unions in which they are part of a minority.

Redistribution of income

The evidence which was summarised in Chapter 2 indicated that trade unions achieve their desired effect with respect to the redistribution of income. They increase the incomes of their members at the expense of those who are wealthier than themselves while having little discernible effect upon those who are less advantaged than themselves. (See pp. 34–5 of Chapter 2 for the detailed argument.)

Horizontal equity

Horizontal equity requires that equally qualified workers, under otherwise identical contracts, should receive equal remuneration. It is clear that the distribution of income which is produced by a strike-based industrial relations system violates this principle.[29] First, the bargaining powers of otherwise identical unions will differ if they face employers whose ability to pay wage increases or to absorb the costs of a work stoppage differ. That is, as the bargaining power of the union depends upon the costs to the firm of agreeing with the union's demands, relative to its costs of disagreeing with those demands (see pp. 43–50 of this chapter), unions' abilities to obtain wage increases will be affected by factors which are not only beyond their control, but which are also unrelated to any considerations of horizontal equity. It is inconceivable that individuals behind the Rawlsian veil of

60 Rethinking labour–management relations

ignorance would select a distributional criterion which suggested that workers' relative wages should be proportional to the difficulty which their employers encountered in storing output; or inversely proportional to either the percentage of the firms' total costs which are accounted for by wages or the employers' ability to substitute capital for labour. Yet, under a strike-based system, these factors are of great importance in determining unions' abilities to obtain wage increases from their employers.

Second, unions' abilities to obtain their demands will also depend upon characteristics which vary among the unions themselves (as opposed to characteristics which vary among employers). We have argued above, for example, that a union whose membership is concentrated in a small number of workplaces will be more powerful than one whose membership is dispersed; that a union which represents full-time workers will have greater bargaining power than one which represents part-time workers; and that a union which 'controls' a large portion of the workers required to produce an industry's output will be more successful in obtaining its demands than will a union whose members can be replaced easily during the course of a strike. Again, however, under no reasonable assumptions would we expect that individuals behind the veil of ignorance would select any of these characteristics as determinants of an equitable distribution of income. Thus, once again, the conclusion must be that use of the strike threat cannot be expected to produce horizontal equity.

Finally, because many workers will not be able to mount a successful strike – often because potential union members are geographically dispersed – many industries and occupations will not be unionised. Workers in these sectors will be denied the ability to use collective bargaining to raise their wages and, hence, their wages and working conditions can be expected to fall behind those of otherwise identical workers who work in industries in which it is possible to organise successfully. As the ability to organise a successful work stoppage is not necessarily related to the factors which determine equity in the distribution of income, this factor also can be expected to reduce the level of horizontal equity.

To summarise, the theoretical arguments presented here suggest that the use of the strike threat will provide some workers with an advantage over others in raising wages, thereby reducing horizontal equity. The empirical literature provides ample support for this proposition. All empirical studies of sector-by-sector union/non-union wage differentials find that unions are much more able to raise wages in some sectors than in others. In the most detailed survey of this literature yet published, Lewis[30] reported that in the United States the union/non-union differential was higher in small cities and firms than in large ones and that it was higher for labourers than operatives, for operatives than for craftspeople or service workers, for private sector workers than for public, and for construction workers than for non-manufacturing workers. Similar, though less detailed, results have been obtained using data from Britain and Canada.[31] All of these results, both empirical and theoretical, point to the conclusion that the strike-based system has a negative impact on horizontal equity.

Vertical equity

Vertical equity requires that differences in remuneration should be based, as much as possible, upon differences in the disutilities attached to employments – for example, upon differences in risk, in educational requirements, and in responsibility. The primary manner in which trade unions can be expected to affect these differences is through their influences on *intra* union wage relativities. As we argued above, the most that can be asked of internal union democracy is that it induces union leaders to follow the wishes of the majority among their electorates. In general, the wishes of those who are in a minority will be given relatively little weight; and where the union must make an either/or choice among policies, minority views may be ignored altogether. According to this model, it would be expected that industrial unions would increase the wages of unskilled and semi-skilled workers relative to skilled members (because the latter would be in a minority); and that most unions would raise the wages of young workers relative to older workers (again, because the latter would represent a smaller percentage of most workforces than the former). These hypotheses are supported by the empirical evidence. Lewis,[32] for example, found that unionisation had generally benefited blue-collar workers more than white-collar and that young workers had gained more than older workers from unionisation. And Ashenfelter[33] found that unionised labourers and operatives had made greater gains, relative to non-union workers, in manufacturing industries (where they could be expected to dominate) than in construction (where skilled workers could be expected to dominate).

These findings do not necessarily suggest that the strike-based system of collective bargaining is inferior to other forms of collective bargaining with respect to vertical equity. Any situation in which a union bargains for a large number of heterogeneous workers is bound to favour those workers who form its majority over those who represent minority positions. Nevertheless, we have argued above (see pp. 49–52 and 58–9 of this chapter), that the strike threat is most powerful when wielded by unions composed of large numbers of workers. For this reason, a collective bargaining system which did not encourage the formation of large unions could be expected to produce a distribution of income which was vertically more equitable than one which relied upon the strike threat.

LEGAL STRUCTURING

One of the advantages which has been claimed for trade unions is that they can act as worker representatives in disputes which have gone to the courts or tribunals and as worker lobbyists with legislative bodies.[34] The argument is that changes in the law, either through the courts or through the legislature, may have a major impact when aggregated across all workers even if they have only a minor impact on any individual worker. Thus, although no individual worker may find it worthwhile to expend the resources required to obtain a change in the law, if workers could band together they might find it in their collective interests to devote sufficient resources to that action. Trade unions provide a means of organising workers for this purpose.

As there is no reason to believe that some groups of workers will benefit from legal representation more than others, an ideal system would provide all workers with equal ability to organise for the purpose of obtaining such representation. Generally, the benefits from legal representation will not be sufficient to cover all of the costs of organising a worker coalition – a union.

Therefore, it will only be in situations where there are other benefits from unionisation that workers will be able to organise (i.e. through collective bargaining). The most important of these benefits is the ability to obtain improved wages and working conditions. But the strike-based system does not offer all workers equal bargaining power for these purposes. Indeed, some workers would have so little bargaining power that the costs of organisation cannot be justified. Such workers, therefore, will find it much more difficult to obtain legal representation than will workers in occupations and industries in which unions have considerable bargaining power. Thus, a criticism of the strike-based system is that, because it provides some groups of workers with inadequate incentive to organise, it constrains those workers' abilities to participate fully in the legal system.

THE RIGHT TO STRIKE

It is commonly suggested, in defence of the strike threat, that use of the strike is a fundamental right.[35] It is so important to the functioning of a democratic society that no argument to the contrary can be strong enough to justify removal of that right. Before this position can be subjected to rigorous analysis, it is necessary to define what is meant by a 'fundamental' right. Thus, in this section, we first review a categorisation of rights developed by Dworkin[36] and then employ that categorisation to enquire into the nature of the 'right to strike' in a democratic society.

Dworkin identifies two types of rights: constitutive and derivative. The first of these, constitutive rights, are rights which are valued for their own sake. Thus, except in those (limited) cases in which they conflict with one another, these rights may be considered to be inviolable – they are the kinds of rights which a democratic society might wish to enshrine in a written constitution, for example. In countries with a common religion, these rights may be derived from the teachings of that religion. In mixed societies, however, for a right to be considered inviolable it must be seen to be 'axiomatic' or 'self-evident'. Clearly, there are very few propositions which meet this stringent test. Some such propositions might include that individuals (i) have the right to pursue their own happiness, (ii) have the right to freedom of speech; or (iii) have the right to freedom of worship (in each case,

64 Rethinking labour–management relations

subject to the condition that pursuit of these objectives does not infringe upon the rights of others).

The second type of rights in Dworkin's typology are those which derive from the constitutive rights. These derivative rights differ from constitutive, or fundamental, rights in that, being a means of achieving the constitutive rights, rather than an end in themselves, it is often possible to substitute one such right for another. Derivative rights are of the type which might be formalised in legislation, rather than in constitutional form. Of particular importance in this context are the so-called 'economic rights' such as the right to own property. These rights are left to legislative rather than constitutional statement because it is often possible to achieve the same end by substituting one such right for another. For example, in capitalist societies the constitutive right to pursuit of happiness is generally held to require that individuals be given the right to hold private property. But there are many communal (and not necessarily communist) societies in which the right to a 'fair' share of the communal property is substituted for the right to private property. As both rights (may) achieve the same goal, neither can be said to be constitutive, or fundamental.

In terms of Dworkin's typology, before it can be argued that the right to strike is inviolable, it must be shown that that right is constitutive and not derivative. The argument that the right to strike is constitutive is generally based upon the Benthamite postulate of the freedom to dispose of one's labour, as in the following quotation from Otto Kahn-Freund and Bob Hepple:

> The case for freedom to strike can . . . be put in terms of social ethics. If people may not withdraw their labour, this may mean that the law compels them to work, and a legal compulsion to work is abhorrent to systems of law imbued with a liberal tradition, and compatible only with a totalitarian system of government.[37]

But this argument does not provide sufficient justification to classify the right to strike as a constitutive right. First, as Kahn-Freund and Hepple recognised, it is possible to discourage the use of strikes without forcing individual strikers to return to work. Instead, fines and other sanctions can be levied against the union's leadership or against the union as a corporate body.

The strike-based system   65

Second, a ban on strikes does not necessarily condemn individuals to work for a particular employer. If they are dissatisfied with their current terms of employment, they are free to attempt to find employment elsewhere. Third, a ban on strikes does not necessarily remove workers' power to bargain with their employers. If alternative means of achieving this end can be devised, the right to strike may be seen to be only a derivative, and not a constitutive right. Finally, one of the characteristics of a constitutive right is that it must be seen to be axiomatic. We submit that the right to strike cannot be considered to meet this criterion, primarily because opposition to the use of strikes is too widespread.[38]

The analysis of this section leads us to question the proposition that the right to strike is a fundamental, or constitutive right. The force of this conviction would become compelling if it could be shown that alternative industrial relations systems were capable of providing workers with the same processes of collective bargaining as are provided by the strike-based system. In that case, we would be forced to conclude that the right to strike was a derivative right and, therefore, the proper subject of speculation concerning the advantages and disadvantages which it offered to society.

SUMMARY

In Chapter 2 we argued that an idealised system of collective bargaining would be superior to a system of individualised bargaining between employees and employers. Recognising that one could not expect to obtain such a perfect system in practice, however, we began in this chapter a review of the alternative systems of industrial relations which have been suggested by analysing the advantages and disadvantages of the strike-based system. It was our finding that, relative to the idealised model discussed in Chapter 2, the strike-based system suffers from the following deficiencies:

1   Many workers are unable to organise unions under the strike-threat system because they lack the degree of centralisation required to mount a successful strike; or find that organisation is too costly relative to the benefits because the strike provides them with very little bargaining power. These workers are denied two of unionisation's most important functions: the

provision of a collective 'voice' in dealing with their employers; and the development of economies of scale in dealing with the legal system.

2 Strikes in themselves can be inefficient if they disrupt production in industries in which output cannot be stored or recouped; if they induce firms to devote resources to producing and storing excessive inventories; or if they encourage producers to situate in foreign countries.

3 Because the strike-threat system provides some workers with more bargaining power than others, and because those variations in bargaining power are uncorrelated with general notions of equity, the strike-threat system reduces horizontal equity.

4 Because the strike-threat system encourages the formation of large unions composed of heterogeneous workers, it contributes to the situation in which the views of some groups of workers are given less consideration by their unions than would occur were unions smaller or more homogeneous. When it is older or more skilled workers who find themselves in the minority, this implies that vertical equity may be inhibited.

That the strike-based system suffers from these deficiencies leads us to conclude that the search for an alternative industrial relations system would be justified. This we do in the remaining six chapters of this work.

Chapter 4

Possible modifications to the strike-based system

In Chapter 3 we argued that the strike-based system, as it currently functions in most industrialised countries, suffers from a number of defects. Primary among these are: that it provides so little bargaining power to many workers that they are unable to obtain the benefits of collective bargaining; that it distributes bargaining power very unevenly among those workers who do manage to organise; and that it restricts production in those industries which are most sensitive to the effects of work stoppages. These findings led us to suggest that it would be worthwhile to search for alternative systems of collective bargaining. In this chapter we propose to initiate such a search by reviewing four suggestions which have been made to modify the existing strike-based system. These proposals concern: employer use of replacement workers during strikes; union boycotts of strike-hit firms' customers and suppliers; changes in the degree of union internal democracy; and substitution of the strike by the 'statutory' strike.

REPLACEMENT WORKERS

Laws concerning employers' ability to employ *replacement workers* or 'scabs' during a strike vary widely among jurisdictions. In Britain, the function of the law with respect to strikes is primarily to protect the union and its leaders from actions in tort – for example, conspiracy, intimidation, and inducement of breach of contract – and criminal law – such as trespass and criminal conspiracy.[1] The law provides virtually no protection for individual union members. In particular, under British common

68 Rethinking labour–management relations

law an individual who refuses to work because he is on strike is considered to be in fundamental breach of his contract with his employer, thus entitling the employer to dismiss him summarily[2] or (in theory) to sue the employee for damages.[3] The employer is free to treat the contract as at an end[4] and may hire replacement workers with (legal) impunity.[5] Furthermore, on this interpretation of the basis of the law relating to strikes, it is seen that there is no requirement that, following the cessation of a strike, the employer must rehire workers who have been on strike.[6]

The striking employee is slightly better off in the United States than in Britain. In the United States, the striking employee is not held to have breached his contract. Instead, until he obtains other and substantially equivalent employment he is considered to remain an 'employee'. Furthermore, the striking worker is entitled to reinstatement following the cessation of a strike either (i) if the employer has not replaced the worker during the strike; or (ii) if the employer has replaced the worker but the replacement worker has left the job.[7]

Finally, the employer's rights are even further constrained in Canada. There, it is generally the rule in the English-speaking provinces that the worker may be replaced during the strike but that he is entitled to be reinstated following the cessation of the strike. In Quebec, the legislature has gone even further, prohibiting the use of replacement workers entirely.[8]

We believe that adoption of the Quebec approach, to ban the use of replacement workers, can meet some of the objections to the use of the strike-based system which were raised in Chapter 3. First, a ban on replacement workers will increase the power of those unions which are currently relatively weak because they have no 'control' over the labour force from which the firm draws its employees. In this way, the horizontal inequity which results from imbalances in power among unions would be reduced. Second, many workers currently experience difficulty organising into unions because they have insufficient bargaining power. To the extent that their bargaining power would be increased by a ban on replacement workers, such a ban would allow for the spread of the benefits of collective bargaining to a much wider group of workers than would otherwise be possible.

On the other hand, tightening of the rules concerning

replacement workers might have a number of negative effects. For example, a ban on replacement workers could be expected to increase the bargaining strengths of many unions who are already relatively powerful, thereby exacerbating those inequities in the distribution of income which currently exist. Furthermore, such a ban might fail to meet some of the criticisms which have been levied against the strike-based system. The reason that many workers are unable to organise under that system is not that they are unable to prevent employers from hiring replacements, but that they are too decentralised to be able to maintain the cohesion necessary to mount a successful work stoppage. And other workers, who have been able to organise and do have control over their labour markets, have relatively weak bargaining power for reasons unrelated to the hiring of replacement workers, such as the employer's ability to sell inventories during a strike or to make up lost production after the strike has concluded. These workers could not be expected to benefit from a ban on the hiring of replacement workers and would, therefore, suffer a reduction in their standards of living relative to those workers who did benefit from such a ban. On these bases, we conclude that although manipulation of the employer's right to hire replacements might remove some of the inequities in the current system, it would not be a panacea for all of that system's faults.

SECONDARY INDUSTRIAL ACTION

In order to make a strike or other industrial action more effective, a common tactic widely used by trade union officials is to extend the action to various third parties.[9] By so doing, it is hoped that pressure will be exerted upon the employer in dispute. The provisions of s.17(3) of Britain's Employment Act 1980, were, before they were repealed by the Employment Act 1990, typical in this regard. That section specified that a union official acting in contemplation or furtherance of a trade dispute was immune from liability if (and only if) two conditions concerning secondary action were met. These were, first, that if he organised secondary industrial action, such as blacking or a sympathy strike, the principal purpose of that action had to be to interfere with goods and services which were traded between the employer with whom there was a dispute and that employer's *first* supplier or customer;

70 Rethinking labour–management relations

and, second, that there was a reasonable likelihood that the secondary action would have had its intended effect. In terms of the analysis of Chapters 2 and 3, rules concerning secondary action are designed with two competing ends in mind. Extensions to those rules (i.e. allowing workers to pursue secondary actions against additional firms), act to increase union bargaining strength; whereas contractions in those rules protect innocent third parties from the effects of strike action. We consider each of these effects in turn.

There are many situations in which the purpose of an industrial action may be defeated if the union is unable to restrict the activities of firms which do not have a direct relationship with their employer. Such a situation is exemplified by the House of Lords case of *Merkur Island Shipping Corporation* v. *Laughton*.[10] The plaintiffs in this case were shipowners who had registered their ship, the *Hoegh Apapa*, under the Liberian flag of convenience. A sub-charterer of the ship had contracted with a tug company to assist the *Hoegh Apapa* leave dock at Liverpool. At that port, however, the International Transport Workers' Federation (ITWF) was campaigning against ships which used flags of convenience. As part of the campaign, the ITWF called upon tugmen to refuse to handle the *Hoegh Apapa*. The plaintiffs sought an injunction to restrain the ITWF from interfering and succeeded, on the ground that the shipowners, against whom the ITWF's industrial action was directed, had no contractual relationship with the tugowners. Clearly, in this case, and in others like it, the employers were able to frustrate the goal of the industrial action through the simple expedient of sub-contracting the work in dispute. This implies that unions will be weaker in industries in which this expedient is available than in those in which it is not. Thus, failure to allow secondary action beyond the employer and, as was the law before 1991, its immediate customers and suppliers may produce an inequitable distribution of income among union members.

At the same time, the further the law allows a union to carry its dispute, the more severe will be the effects of strike action upon the nation's productivity. For example, if the right to secondary action were to be extended in such a way that unions could shut down six firms where they had previously shut down only two, the number of days lost to strike activity could triple overnight; and strike activity, which had previously had only a minor impact on production, could become of such major importance that the efficacy of the strike-based system would be called into question.

In short, under the strike-based system, all changes in legislation concerning secondary action have costs as well as benefits. Extensions of the right to engage in secondary action benefit those unions which would otherwise experience difficulty mounting a successful work stoppage and, therefore, allow for reductions in the inequity of income distribution. But those same extensions may also increase the costs of work stoppages substantially, particularly as they will apply equally to all unions and not just to those in industries in which work can be subcontracted. Conversely, therefore, restrictions on the right to engage in secondary action must have a positive impact on third parties but a negative impact on many unions. For this reason, changes in legislation concerning secondary action cannot produce a significant improvement in the net social benefits which derive from the strike-based system.

UNION DEMOCRACY

We have argued above that one of the deficiencies in the strike-based system is its failure to provide a mechanism by which the preferences of all union members can be taken into account equally. To a certain extent it might be argued that this problem could be overcome if legislation were to be passed increasing the requirements for internal union democracy.[11] Some such legislation which has recently been introduced in Britain is among the strictest in the western world. In this section, we first review this legislation and then ask whether it, or any other similar enactment, could be expected to overcome the drawbacks to the strike-based system which we identified in Chapter 3.

The most recent manifestation of union democracy in Britain can be found in the Trade Union Act 1984, as amended by the Employment Acts 1988 and 1990. The spirit of this legislation is to democratise unions, i.e. to 'give unions . . . to their members'.[12] It is the membership which elects its principal executive, which votes for strike action, and which decides on whether or not there is to be a political fund.

In the case of the election of the principal executive committee (i.e. the governing body of the union), a duty is imposed on the

72 Rethinking labour–management relations

union to hold a secret postal ballot of its membership for purposes of electing[13] or re-electing every five years[14] all members on the committee. Provisions exist to ensure that the statutory provisions on elections are not contracted out of[15] and that any union rules which restrict an entitlement to vote are void.[16]

For the purposes of proper and effective representation, stringent provisions are laid down by the Act in connection with elections to the principal executive committee in that entitlement to vote must be given to all. Indirect election by a trade group or a regional group executive which chooses members of the executive as delegates is prohibited. The method of voting must be secret and by the marking of a ballot paper and must be free from interference. So far as is reasonably practical, every person must be sent a voting paper by post and must be given a convenient opportunity to return the voting paper by post without incurring any cost. The results must be determined solely by counting the number of votes cast and the count must be accurate.[17] Prior to the Employment Act 1988, workplace and semi-postal ballots were provided as alternatives to postal ballots,[18] but the new legislation is so concerned that unions be representative of their members and, therefore, democratic that it provides for postal ballots only.[19]

The provisions for secret ballots before taking official industrial action equally show that the union is expected to act as the democratic representative of its members. Before official industrial action is taken, a secret ballot must be held showing a majority in favour.[20] Stringent requirements on the ballot,[21] similar to those already discussed, apply equally in the case of industrial action. For meaningful democracy to operate, *nonmembers* who are within the group subject to potential industrial action are also to be balloted.[22]

Can legislative changes, such as these, overcome the criticisms of the strike-based system which we raised in Chapter 3? We submit that not only do they not achieve this goal, but that they *cannot*. The reason for this is that even in the most enlightened democracy, the views of the majority must predominate with respect to those issues concerning which the union can take only one position. The clearest example of such a situation occurs with respect to the strike ballot. Union members have only two choices: they can vote either to call all of their members out on strike or to encourage all of their members to remain at work. No effective system of industrial relations could be founded upon the principle of each worker following his own preferences as to whether he wished to engage in industrial action. Such action is only effective if it is 'all or none'. Accordingly, the wishes of those who are in the minority *must* be subjugated to those of the majority.[23]

The way to avoid this conundrum is not to alter the techniques for registering worker preferences, for these problems arise in even the most democratic of unions. Rather, the solution is to provide an industrial relations system in which it is not disadvantageous to form unions small enough that most workers within each union could be expected to share common preferences. We have argued that the strike-based system is not such a system. The reasons for this are: first, that it is inefficient to have many unions in the same workplace all setting their own timetables for strike action. Under this circumstance, the number of work stoppages would increase dramatically relative to the number already experienced. Second, there are often 'economies of scale' in the execution of strikes which make it desirable to organise as many workers as possible into the parent union. We submit, therefore, that the strike-based system necessarily limits the extent to which the goal of true workplace democracy can be achieved.

STATUTORY STRIKES

The primary function of the strike is to impose costs of disagreement on the parties – in the form of lost wages and forgone profits – in order to induce them to reach a settlement. But strikes also have a secondary, unintended effect; that is, as they disrupt production, they impose 'external' costs on the consumers of the product and on the suppliers of the inputs into the production process. In order to avoid this problem, while maintaining the parties' incentive to reach settlement, a number of writers have attempted to devise industrial relations procedures in which the costs of disagreement to the disputants were retained but in which external costs were avoided.

One such procedure is commonly referred to as the *statutory strike*.[24] Under this system, when a bargaining impasse has been reached, the government orders the parties to continue production. However, in order to induce the parties to reach agreement, the workers are not allowed to collect wages and the firm is taxed an amount equal to the profits which it would have lost had a strike occurred. Thus, while suppliers and consumers are not inconvenienced, the parties to the dispute suffer the same costs of disagreement as they would have under a traditional strike.

The statutory strike has failed to gain acceptance for three main reasons. First, although it may be possible to force employees to continue working, it is not possible to control the quality and intensity of their work effort. Second, it proves extremely difficult to construct non-controversial measures of the effect which strikes have on employers' profits – particularly when the employer is a government agency[25] or when the effects on profits are felt well after the strike has ended. Finally, although the use of the statutory strike may avoid interruptions in production, it does not provide a means by which the bargaining power provided by the strike threat can be equalised across employee groups.

CONCLUSION

The purpose of this chapter has been to review a number of proposals to modify the strike-based system in order to determine whether implementation of those proposals would overcome the criticisms which have been levied against that system. Our conclusion in each case is that although some minor improvements could be achieved, the most important criticisms would be left undisturbed. For this reason, we believe that the search for alternative collective bargaining techniques must cast its net beyond the constraints of the strike/lockout nexus.

It is our view that most of the advantages of the strike-based system could be retained, and most of the disadvantages avoided, if a system of compulsory arbitration of labour disputes were to be employed. Not only does arbitration provide a means by which all workers can be represented equitably without the necessity of resorting to strikes, but it also gives workers and employers a direct say in the establishment of the wages and working conditions which apply to them. Because of the promise which we feel arbitration holds for the resolution of the problems facing industrial relations, it is proposed to consider this proposal in much greater detail. This we do in the chapters which follow.

Chapter 5

Arbitration systems: a taxonomy

Before one can begin to discuss the merits of arbitration, it is first necessary to specify how arbitration systems can be expected to function. As a great variety of such systems have been suggested or put into practice, it would be inappropriate simply to identify one such system as being 'the' system of arbitration. Rather, recognition must be given to the wide diversity of approaches which are possible. In order to provide the reader with some insight into the differences among alternative approaches, and to set the stage for our analysis of the relative merits of each, in this chapter we identify seven separate characteristics of arbitration systems and discuss the alternatives which are available within each such characteristic.

TYPE OF DISPUTE

Traditionally, a distinction has been made between arbitrations which deal with *rights* disputes and those which deal with *interest* disputes. In terms of union–management relations, a rights dispute is a disagreement over the interpretation of a section of an *existing* collective agreement. Thus, arbitration hearings in this type of case tend to take on a legal-judicial aura. An interest dispute, on the other hand, concerns disagreements which arise during the negotiation of a *new* collective agreement. The arbitrator's role in this case is not one of interpretation but of construction of the agreement. Much more than in the case of rights arbitration, his role is to search out a solution which will be acceptable to both parties.

Although a very clear distinction is made between rights and interest disputes in North America, the differentiation is much less

76 Rethinking labour–management relations

clear in Europe. This contrast between the two continents is the result of differences in the locus of bargaining power. Whereas each local of an American or Canadian union enters into its own agreement with its employer, European unions often reach national, general agreements with employers' associations and then allow their locals to work out details appropriate to their specific circumstances. Thus, European, and particularly British, unions often find that local disputes involve elements of both 'rights' – interpreting the national agreement – and 'interests' – developing special provisions for the local situation – a possibility which would not normally arise in the less centralised North American system.[1]

THE LEGAL STRUCTURE

Foundations

Arbitration systems may be said to be based on one of two models – the 'private law' and the 'public law' models. In the first of these, the parties agree voluntarily to submit their disputes to binding arbitration and choose for themselves the type of arbitration procedure to be followed. In the labour relations field, the private law model has traditionally been applied primarily to rights disputes; however, instances certainly exist in which unions and management have voluntarily agreed to send their interest disputes to binding arbitration. In Britain, for example, the Electrical, Electronic, Telecommunications and Plumbing Union (the EETPU) has recently reached a number of such agreements;[2] and Rico, writing about the EETPU, has commented that 'recently reported collective bargaining innovations and experiments that constitute the 'new industrial relations' in the United States closely resemble many of the developments . . . in the British electronics industry'.[3] In addition, private legal structures have also been developed to handle disputes as disparate as complaints of unfair political campaign tactics,[4] claims of medical malpractice,[5] division of marital property in divorce cases,[6] patent infringements,[7] and financial services complaints.[8]

Under the 'public law' model, the legislature introduces laws which require that certain groups of disputants submit unresolved disagreements to binding arbitration. As a rule, these laws also specify the procedures to be followed, although this is not universally the case (as our references to Britain will show).

Although it will be argued in Chapter 7 that voluntary, private arbitration is in many senses preferable to publicly imposed, compulsory arbitration, very few examples can be found of private arbitration of interest disputes. Some of the reasons why this procedure has failed to develop are historical and institutional. But the most formidable obstacle is the fact that the distribution of bargaining power under arbitration will generally be different from that experienced under a strike-based system. Under most circumstances one of the parties will find that a move to binding arbitration will reduce its relative bargaining power. Thus, it has been very unusual for labour and management to agree voluntarily to arbitrate their interest disputes; and where interest arbitration has been considered to be (socially) advantageous it has almost always been introduced through 'public law', that is through legislation which compels the parties to submit their disputes to binding arbitration.[9]

Coverage

With the notable exception of Australia, most arbitration legislation applies to workers in activities which are considered 'essential' to consumers, such as fire, police, and health services. An advantage of the Australian system, in which all sectors are subject to arbitration, is that large numbers of arbitrations are held, giving arbitrators the opportunity to develop expertise in selected fields. Also, universal coverage ensures that all weak employee and employer groups have access to the added bargaining power which arbitration can provide; and that strikes are deterred in sectors of industry in which disruption would be harmful to international trade. On the other hand, there may be many sectors in which labour–management relations are sufficiently well-developed that arbitration procedures are unnecessary. If there is concerted opposition to the use of arbitration it may well be advisable to exclude these groups from any initial attempts to introduce compulsory arbitration.

A second aspect of coverage concerns the unionisation of the employees to whom arbitration is to relate. Whereas many Canadian employee groups covered by arbitration agreements

78 Rethinking labour–management relations

are not unionised – police associations and university academic staffs are common examples – the British arbitration legislation of 1940–1959 applied only to unionised workers. This aspect of the British legislation has often been criticised as it has been argued that one of the functions of arbitration is to increase the bargaining power of otherwise weak groups, which, of course, will include the non-unionised.

ARBITRATORS

Number

Normally, there is either one, three, or five persons on an arbitration panel. The one-person system is used more often for rights disputes than for interest disputes; but in America the states of Nevada and Wisconsin have provision for one person in the latter case. The primary advantages of a single person are speed and flexibility – a time for the hearing can be chosen more quickly if only one person's timetable has to be met and one person can reach a decision much more quickly than can a group.[10] The tripartite system does, however, offer a number of advantages, particularly for complex issues, such as those generally found in interest arbitration.[11] As members can be chosen for their knowledge of economics and industrial relations as well as labour law, a tripartite board helps to avoid excessive legalism. If the union and management each select one of the arbitrators, a tripartite board offers the psychological advantage that each side will know there is a member of the panel who will see that their arguments are given full and fair consideration. Thus, it increases the probability that the parties will find the arbitration award to be acceptable. Furthermore, it has practical advantages in the sense that 'the parties have the benefit of the experience and judgement of three people with different industrial relations backgrounds, which should ensure a well-balanced award'.[12] Finally, the five-person system is usually considered to be unwieldy and tends to be used only in arbitration systems in which the arbitrators are permanent employees operating in an industrial court setting.

Selection

The most common system for selecting arbitrators (where more than one is to arbitrate), is for each of the parties to select its own representative – often known as a 'sideman', a 'side member', or 'wingman' – and for those representatives to choose a chairman. No constraints are set on the choice of the sidemen other than that they are usually required to have no pecuniary (or other personal) interest in the dispute. The main advantages of this system are that the parties can be certain that at least one of the arbitrators is familiar with, and sympathetic to, their case and that both parties can ensure that the chairman is impartial. The most important disadvantage is that, as the sidemen appear as representatives of the parties, they cannot be expected to act in an unbiased manner. This particularly becomes a problem when they attempt to select a chairman. Often the two sidemen are so determined to choose a 'favourable' chairman that they are unable to agree. Thus, a procedure is necessary for making such a selection in the event of an impasse. The most common procedure is to refer the matter to a government body, such as the Department of Labour.

A second method of selecting arbitrators is to assign the decision entirely to the government. In the United States and Canada, the government will often make an *ad hoc* selection, but in other jurisdictions the arbitrators are selected either from boards of government employees or from panels, which often have been constructed upon consultation with labour and management beforehand. In Britain, for example, ACAS maintains lists of arbitrators who include academics, lawyers, and retired conciliation officers. (ACAS officials do not act as arbitrators.) The primary advantage of these systems is that, as the arbitrators are not seen to be representatives of the parties, their impartiality is not compromised.

Finally, in some jurisdictions the parties may assign the selection of an arbitrator to an impartial, third party. In the United States, for example, this role is played by an independent, non-profit making organisation of professional arbitrators, the American Arbitration Association. The AAA's usual selection procedure is to send a list of potential arbitrators (along with a brief description of the qualifications of each) to both disputants. Each party then crosses off those arbitrators who are deemed not satisfactory and ranks the remainder in order of preference. The

AAA then selects an arbitrator (or panel of arbitrators) from those who have not been eliminated.[13] In Britain, the Chartered Institute of Arbitrators also maintains a list of arbitrators – although private labour arbitration is less common in Britain than it is in North America.

Payment of the arbitrators' fees

Under most existing arbitration systems the arbitrators' fees are paid by whoever selects the arbitrators – usually the government or the disputants. But it would also be possible for the government to subsidise the fees of those arbitrators who had been chosen by the disputants or for the disputants to be charged for the services of government-provided arbitrators.[14] In Britain, ACAS pays the fees and expenses of arbitrators who have been selected through its procedures.[15]

ROLE OF MEDIATION

Most industrial relations systems require that disputes go to *conciliation* or *mediation* before they proceed to the arbitration stage.[16] In this process, the role of the independent is to attempt to bring the parties to a voluntary agreement, the belief being that voluntary agreements are likely to be more satisfactory to both sides than are agreements which are imposed by a third party (an arbitrator).[17] It has been argued that mediation is particularly useful in interest disputes, as these disputes often involve a very large number of issues (the entire collective agreement may be under consideration). If mediation can encourage the parties to settle on the less contentious of these issues, the complexity of the arbitrator's job may be reduced dramatically.[18] It has also been argued that mediation may be more important when the parties face 'pendulum' (or 'final offer') arbitration than when they face 'conventional' arbitration. In the former, the arbitrator is asked to select the final offer of either the union or management; whereas in the latter, he may construct his own award, based upon his interpretation of the facts of the case. A common objection to pendulum arbitration is that the arbitrator may find that he is forced to choose between two offers, each of which he considers to be unreasonable. A mediator may help to avoid this dilemma by providing the parties with independent advice concerning the acceptability of their demands.[19]

An important question which arises in this situation is whether the mediator should also act as arbitrator if mediation fails to bring about an agreement.[20] The most important disadvantage of a fusion of mediation and arbitration is that the failure of a mediator to obtain agreement may taint his ability to produce a satisfactory agreement as an arbitrator. On the other hand, such a fusion may be advantageous if mediation efforts fail and the arbitrator is called upon to give a ruling, for he will have a far more detailed and intimate knowledge of the issues than would a freshly constituted arbitration panel.

INFORMATION [21]

'Official' data sources

In general, the parties to an arbitration are left to obtain their own information. This creates a number of problems: the arbitrator may be confused by conflicting statistics; much of the arbitration hearing may be wasted while the parties debate the relative merits of different statistical sources; and, because statistical 'support' can be found for virtually any position, each party may be encouraged to take an extreme position. In some systems, therefore, a government agency has been established to provide statistical data to the parties to an arbitration.[22] The disadvantage of this system is that if the parties are allowed to 'supplement' the official statistics with their own the confusion is merely compounded; whereas if they are prevented from providing supplementary information, errors and biases in the official statistics cannot be challenged.

Information about the arbitrator's preferences

When the parties are bargaining with one another prior to entering arbitration, an important determinant of their behaviour will be the information which they possess about the arbitrator's preferences. Assume, for example, that they know with certainty that the arbitrator has a strong preference for an award of a 10 per cent wage increase and a reduction of the

82 Rethinking labour–management relations

workday from 8 hours to 7. It is clear that this knowledge will cause the parties to approach their negotiations in a different manner than if they knew that the arbitrator preferred a 5 per cent wage increase and no change in the length of the workday, or if they knew nothing at all about the arbitrator's preferences. Existing and proposed arbitration systems can be divided into three (rough) categories according to the amount of information which they provide about the arbitrator's preferences: full-information, limited-information, and no-information.

a) *Full-information arbitration*: There are a number of ways in which the parties can be informed about the outcome which will be preferred by the arbitrator. First, rigid rules may be set down to *specify* precisely how the arbitrator is to reach his decision. To our knowledge, this system has not been employed anywhere. Second, arbitration tribunals could be instructed to follow *precedents* closely. Again, this system has not been employed, although precedents do play an important role in Australia. Third, it should be possible for *bargaining* to take place *after* the arbitrator has announced the award which he intends to make – we might refer to this as arb–med (arbitration–mediation), as opposed to the normal med–arb. There exist at least three jurisdictions in which arb–med is employed: the Australian federal arbitration system, in which the arbitrator is expected to make a broad statement of his views *before* the arbitration hearings take place and to encourage the parties to reach their own agreement at that time;[23] the state of Michigan, in which the parties are given the opportunity to 'receive some indication of the neutral's views through their appointed representative to the [tripartite arbitration] panel'[24] *after* the arbitration hearing has been held but *before* the award has been officially announced; and the British Central Arbitration Committee (CAC), under which the following *problem solving* approach is sometimes followed:

> At the first stage at an informal hearing, the case is examined and discussed and the issues and problems are identified. An indication can then be given that the CAC would be prepared to proceed to an award along certain general lines but that it would be much more preferable for the parties, during an adjournment of appropriate length, to tackle the problem themselves.[25]

b) *Limited-information arbitration*: More commonly, the parties to a dispute have only limited information concerning the likely behaviour of the arbitrator. This information is drawn from previous decisions of the same arbitrator, loosely written arbitral rules,[26] loosely followed precedent, the statements of Ministers of Labour, etc.

c) *No-information arbitration*: If arbitrators act rationally and consistently, the only way to produce a situation in which the parties have no information about the arbitrator's preferences is to introduce an element of randomness into the selection of those preferences. One method for doing so would be to announce that the arbitrator's *award* would be chosen at random from a specified, pre-selected set of outcomes. A less drastic method, however, would be to select the *arbitrator* at random. This process was followed at the University of Lethbridge in Alberta, Canada, for example. In that situation, each of the parties put forward a panel of potential arbitrators before negotiations began and if an impasse was reached one arbitrator was chosen at random from the combined panels.

The primary advantage which has been claimed for full-information arbitration is that it induces the parties to reach their 'own' agreement. That is, if the parties know that the arbitrator prefers a package incorporating a 10 per cent wage increase and a 7 hour workday and if both parties would prefer a 12 per cent wage increase and a $7\frac{1}{2}$ hour workday, we can expect that, in order to avoid imposition of the arbitrator's preferred outcome, the parties will reach their own agreement. Whereas if they had been uncertain about the arbitrator's preferences (as they would be under limited-information arbitration) they may have each formed over-optimistic views concerning those preferences, thereby preventing them from reaching agreement voluntarily.

On the other hand, it is seen that full-information arbitration will constrain the scope of bargaining severely. If the parties expect the arbitrator to select a 10 per cent wage increase and a 7 hour workday, for example, it is highly unlikely that the employer would agree voluntarily to a 13 per cent wage increase and a $6\frac{1}{2}$ hour workday, regardless of the social desirability of such an outcome. Yet, if the arbitrator's preferences are constrained by

84 Rethinking labour–management relations

rules and precedents, it is quite possible that the outcome he prefers will be wholly inappropriate to the case at hand.

Perhaps surprisingly, no-information arbitration also provides an incentive for the parties to reach their own agreement. For, when the outcome is to be chosen at random, each side will consider there to be a strong possibility that the outcome will be completely unacceptable. In this case, risk avoidance may induce the parties to reach agreement. The primary disadvantage of no-information arbitration is that if agreement is not reached – for example, because one of the parties has publicly committed itself to the attainment of a particular outcome – the randomly selected outcome may prove to be wholly inappropriate.

SELECTION PROCEDURE

In the last two decades the academic literature on compulsory arbitration has concerned itself primarily with the method by which the arbitrator selects an outcome. The two major techniques which have been considered are *conventional* arbitration and *final-offer* arbitration.

Conventional arbitration

Under conventional arbitration, the parties present their cases to the arbitrator and the arbitrator then chooses whatever outcome he deems appropriate. Implicitly, therefore, the arbitrator's role is to interpret society's welfare function and to act in such a way as to maximise that function with respect to the dispute before him.[27]

Conventional arbitration is subject to two well-known criticisms. First, as the parties are not responsible for the outcome selected under conventional arbitration, they have no incentive to place a damper on the militants within their ranks. Thus, unreasonable offers may be made and expectations raised to unrealistic levels. When these expectations are not realised, morale within the workplace may be compromised. Second, as arbitrators are not omnipotent they may resort to short-cuts to resolve difficult disputes. It has often been argued, for example, that arbitrators simply 'split the difference' between the final positions of the two sides. If the union asks for a 12 per cent wage increase and a 7 hour day, while management offers an 8 per cent wage increase and an 8 hour day, the arbitrator will award 10 per cent and $7\frac{1}{2}$ hours. The danger of this approach is that it induces the two parties to take increasingly extreme positions, simultaneously discouraging the voluntary settlement of disputes and obscuring the issues for the arbitrator. It should be noted, however, that experienced participants in the conventional arbitration process[28] and impartial researchers[29] have concluded that there is no evidence to support the contention that arbitrators 'split the difference'. Furthermore, the available evidence suggests that what tendency there is to 'split the difference' declines as the parties' positions become further apart from one another.[30]

Final-offer arbitration

In order to avoid the propensity of parties to take extreme positions, as in conventional arbitration, it seemed advisable to develop a new arbitration system in which the parties would be penalised for failing to make compromises. This system is generally known in North America as final-offer arbitration and in Britain as pendulum arbitration. Four variations of this system will be considered.

a) *Single package*: In the original version of final-offer arbitration each side was to make known to the arbitrator the final package of offers which it had made at the time that negotiations had reached an impasse. Argument was then to be heard with respect to these packages and the arbitrator was to choose one or the other of the two packages.

Assuming that the arbitrator's preferences are known to the parties, the theoretical effect of this selection procedure is clear. Returning to the bargaining power model outlined on pp. 43–50 of Chapter 3, it is seen that for either of the parties the 'cost of disagreement' under this form of arbitration is the cost of having its opponent's final package chosen rather than its own. For example, if the union's final offer lies 'closer' to the outcome known to be preferred by the arbitrator than does management's final offer, the union will expect to have its offer chosen and its costs of disagreement will be zero. If management wishes to prevent the arbitrator from selecting the union's final offer, therefore, it will be forced to offer concessions which will make its offer more attractive to the arbitrator than is the union's offer. But, if it does so, the union's bargaining power will be driven down and it will be induced to make further concessions. This process can be expected to continue until one of the parties has been induced to offer the outcome which is preferred by the arbitrator.

The British Advisory, Concilliation, and Arbitration Service (ACAS) has offered strong support for final-offer arbitration, concluding:

> One result of this process . . . is that parties are encouraged to modify their collective bargaining stances and to pitch their claims and offers at a reasonable level: because final offer arbitration lies at the end of the procedure both sides tend to move into the middle ground and, because this narrows the gap at the negotiation stage, agreement is made easier without necessarily requiring third party involvement.[31]

Two major criticisms have been levied against the single package form of final-offer arbitration. First, as has just been seen, when the parties know what the arbitrator's preferred outcome is, they are virtually forced to approach that outcome (or one 'near' it), regardless of the extent to which that outcome may be seen to be inefficient. Second, when the parties are uncertain about the arbitrator's preferred outcome, incentive for them to reach agreement will be reduced and impasses may occur. In these cases, the arbitrator will be forced to choose one package or the other. But this may create serious problems for the arbitrator if both parties have made extreme offers or if one (or both) has embedded an unreasonable demand within an otherwise reasonable package. In this circumstance, final offer may 'give a clear cut result but may not stand the test of fairness or improve relations in the longer term'.[32] Arbitrators themselves are particularly unhappy with final-offer arbitration on this ground.[33]

In order to combat these problems, a number of variants on single-package, final-offer arbitration have been devised. We consider three of these.

b) *Multiple offer:* In Eugene, Oregon, the municipal government sends disputes with its employees to arbitration.[34] In that system, each side offers *two* 'final offers' to the arbitrator, and the arbitrator chooses the one which he prefers. The advantage claimed for this system is that it reduces the probability that the arbitrator will find all of the offers facing him to be unacceptable.

In a similar vein, C.B. Donn[35] and V.P. Crawford[36] have suggested a system in which each party offers a large number of packages (say, five or six) and the arbitrator chooses not the package which he prefers but the party whose *set* of packages he prefers. The second party is then asked to select one package from that set. Not only does this system reduce the probability that all offers will be unacceptable, but it also increases the probability that the package selected will be acceptable to both parties. The main drawbacks to their multiple-offer system are its complexity and the difficulty which the two sides will have constructing more than one or two alternatives.

A third form of multiple-offer, final-offer arbitration is employed in the states of Iowa and Massachusetts. There, the recommendations of a 'fact-finder' (a form of mediator), are made available to the arbitrator as a third package from which he may choose. Rehmus has reported that this system encouraged the parties to settle on the fact-finder's recommendations in approximately 70 per cent of the situations in which it was employed; and that in 75 per cent of the unresolved disputes, the arbitrator selected the fact-finder's recommendations.[37] The primary drawbacks to this system are: (i) that it drives the parties to select the fact-finder's recommendations even when they consider those recommendations to be undesirable; and (ii) that it requires the imposition of a second, costly, level of neutral hearings.

c) *Multiple issue*: Instead of having the arbitrator choose between packages of final offers it should be possible to have him select between final offers on an issue-by-issue basis.[38] In this way the arbitrator would not be faced with the problem of choosing between packages which each contained unacceptable elements. Furthermore, the parties might be encouraged to settle as many individual issues as possible before entering arbitration. On the other hand, multiple-issue, final-offer arbitration presents the arbitrator with the problem of choosing a settlement package when he is unfamiliar with the preference functions of the parties to the dispute. It is quite possible that he could choose a combination of issues which was unacceptable to both sides.

88 Rethinking labour–management relations

d) *Revised offers:* In most discussions of final-offer arbitration, it is assumed that the offers which are to be presented to the arbitrator are the offers which were 'on the table' at the cessation of negotiations. Recently, John Magenau[39] has investigated the implications of a system in which the parties were free to revise the packages which they submitted to the arbitrator in any way which they wished. He found that the probability of negotiated settlement was significantly higher under this system than under a final-offer system in which the parties were tied to their last negotiation offers. His explanation for this observation was that when revisions were permitted both parties faced the possibility that their opponents would secretly make substantial concessions on their final demands in order to 'win' the arbitration. The parties 'may have tried to reach agreement to avoid the uncertainties of arbitration or may have made last-minute concessions in an effort to match any concessions their opponent might make'.[40]

THE SETTLEMENT

Selection

If there is more than one person on the arbitration panel, it is necessary to decide whether the final decision should require approval by a majority of the panel members or approval by only the chairman.[41] When making this decision it must be recognised that the meeting of the arbitrators will become a mini arbitration hearing of its own. As the sidemen generally represent the interested parties they will press their parties' cases much as they were presented in the formal hearing. Thus, to require that the final decision be agreeable to the majority of the panelists necessitates that the chairman select an outcome which is acceptable to one of the sidemen. In effect, in this situation, the selection procedure used by the arbitrators themselves is forced into the final-offer mould, as the chairman is forced to select either the outcome preferred by the union's representative or that preferred by management's representative. Thus, if conventional arbitration is preferred to final-offer, the chairman must be allowed to select an outcome alone.

Publication of the rationale for the decision

Whereas it has sometimes been argued that no rationale should be provided for arbitral decisions, arbitrators in most jurisdictions summarise the reasoning which led to their awards, much in the same way as common law judges indicate the reasoning behind their decisions.[42] The relative desirability of these two approaches will be discussed in detail in Chapter 7 of this work.

CONCLUSION

The purpose of this chapter has been to identify, illustrate, and, where appropriate, analyse the characteristics of various arbitration schemes. Given this basic understanding of the nature of arbitration we now turn to the question of whether an arbitration system can be devised, employing these characteristics, which would prove superior to the current, strike-based industrial relations system. That will be the purpose of Chapters 7 and 9.

Chapter 6

The role of arbitration

The purpose of this chapter is to analyse the various advantages which have been claimed for arbitration, and the disadvantages which have been charged against it, in much the same way that the strike was analysed in Chapter 3. For this purpose, the chapter has been divided into six sections. In the first of these, we adapt the model of union–employer bargaining, developed in Chapter 3, to the case of bargaining in the face of compulsory arbitration. The next four sections analyse the four major characteristics of collective bargaining that were introduced in Chapter 2 – collective voice, efficiency, equity, and legal structuring. Finally, the sixth section reviews a number of practical difficulties which might arise from the use of an arbitration system.

THE NATURE OF THE BARGAINING PROCESS IN COMPULSORY ARBITRATION

The general model of union–employer bargaining power which was developed in Chapter 3 to describe negotiations conducted in the face of the strike threat can equally be applied to negotiations conducted in the face of the threat of compulsory arbitration. In that model, the bargaining powers of the union and the firm were represented by the formulae:

Bargaining power of the firm =
$$\frac{\text{Cost to the union of disagreeing with the firm}}{\text{Cost to the union of agreeing with the firm}}$$

Bargaining power of the union =
$$\frac{\text{Cost to the firm of disagreeing with the union}}{\text{Cost to the firm of agreeing with the union}}$$

The role of arbitration   91

In both the strike-based and arbitration models, the union's costs of agreeing are determined by the wage rate which it feels it is justified in asking for – its 'preferred' wage – and upon the loss of utility resulting from acceptance of a lower wage rate. Similarly, in both models, the firm's costs of agreeing will be determined by the loss of profits which result when the wage rate is raised above the profit-maximising rate (that is the wage rate which the firm would have established in the absence of a union). Where the models diverge is with respect to the determinants of the costs of disagreeing. Whereas these costs are determined by the strike in the strike-threat system, they are determined by the arbitrator's decision in the arbitration-threat system.

The nature of arbitration ensures that the costs of disagreement are symmetric between the two parties. The most important costs are the salaries of the arbitration panel and the parties' respective representatives at the arbitration hearing; and the loss of either utility or profit which is experienced if the arbitrator's decision differs from the outcome which the respective parties would have preferred. As both parties can be expected to pay roughly the same salaries to the arbitrator and to their representatives, their costs of disagreement on this ground will be approximately the same. Furthermore, if the arbitration system is established in such a way that the arbitrators' decisions can be expected to be 'fair', both sides will have approximately the same probability of 'winning' and, hence, approximately the same cost of disagreeing.

These considerations allow us to identify a number of factors which will be of importance in the determination of the relative success of the firm and the union. We identify four such factors below. As the first two of these derive from differences in the costs of agreeing, they do not differ between the arbitration model and the strike-based model.

a) *Percentage of costs accounted for by labour:* If two unions are otherwise identical, it is the union whose wages represent the smaller percentage of its employer's total costs which will have the greater bargaining power. (For further discussion of this issue, see pp. 47–8 of Chapter 3.)

b) *Employer's ability to influence price:* The better able is the employer to 'pass on' wage increases as price increases without

92 Rethinking labour–management relations

there being a significant effect upon demand for the firm's product, the lower will its costs of agreement be and the stronger will the union's bargaining position be. (See pp. 43–8 of Chapter 3.)

c) *Impartiality of the arbitrator:* If the arbitrators are not expected to be impartial – if they are expected to favour one party's position over that of the other – the costs of disagreement to the favoured party will be lower than those of its opponent. Accordingly, the bargaining power of the party preferred by the arbitrator will be higher than that of its opponent and it will be able to obtain favourable agreements even where they are reached 'voluntarily' between the parties.[1]

d) *Government regulations:* In many jurisdictions, government regulations constrain the scope of arbitration. To the extent that these regulations increase the probability that one party will have its position adopted by the arbitration board, the bargaining power of the 'favoured' party will be increased relative to its opponent.

Equally, the replacement of a strike-based system by an arbitration-threat system will remove many sources of bargaining power differentials. In particular, whereas ease of product storage, concentration of the union's workforce in a small number of locations, government support for strikers, and union control over potential replacement workers ('scabs'), all influence the relative costs of disagreement in the strike-based system, they are of little or no importance in arbitration. Furthermore, whereas the attachment of workers to the labour force is expected to influence their willingness to strike – those workers who expect to remain with the firm for the greatest amount of time will be best able to recoup the considerable costs of a strike – this factor can be expected to have little effect upon their willingness to enter arbitration – as the costs of arbitration are so low that most workers will be able to recoup those costs within a very short period of time.

COLLECTIVE VOICE

One of the most important roles of collective bargaining is the provision for workers of a 'collective voice' – a way in which they can express their views concerning their workplaces without fear of retribution from their employers. Trade unions can provide the

The role of arbitration   93

benefits of 'voice' in a number of ways: (i) they can reduce workers' feelings of alienation from the production process and increase feelings of security by speaking to the employer collectively instead of individually; (ii) they can coordinate workers' representations to their employers; (iii) they can take advantage of economies of scale in the collection of information about factors such as workplace safety, working conditions in other firms, and trends in the economy; and (iv) they can monitor and enforce the provisions of long-term contracts between workers and employers.

Once a union has been organised, each of these roles can be fulfilled as well by a union which faces the strike as by one which faces arbitration. Where the two systems differ is with respect to the effects which they have upon workers' ability to organise into a union. The strike-based system discourages workers from organising if they are unable to mount a succesful strike. These workers include those who have little control over substitute workers ('scabs'), who have little attachment to the labour force, who are widely dispersed among employers and geographic locations, and who deal with employers who can easily store their products. In each of these cases, workers find that it is difficult to organise under a strike-based system and, accordingly, they are denied many of the benefits of the collective voice mechanism. Under arbitration, on the other hand, workers can impose compelling sanctions on their employers without concern for substitute workers or for the firm's ability to store its output; and those sanctions can be imposed at sufficiently low cost that organisation of geographically dispersed members and part-time workers does not pose an insurmountable problem. Accordingly, an arbitration system provides a means through which many more workers can be provided with a collective voice than would be possible in a strike-based system. As we have argued that this role is socially desirable, on this ground arbitration must be seen as being preferable to the strike.

EFFICIENCY

In this section, we show that, according to two measures of efficiency, an arbitration system can be expected to be more effective than a strike-based system; and we offer evidence that

94 Rethinking labour–management relations

the two systems will have approximately the same effect upon a third measure of efficiency. We also introduce a measure of efficiency that was not considered in previous chapters – *Pareto efficiency in exchange* – according to which arbitration may be inferior to the strike.

Productivity

Under a strike-based system, unions may find it advantageous to encourage anti-management feelings among workers in order to prepare them psychologically to strike. This anti-management bias must certainly be further developed during strikes and (especially) lockouts. By avoiding the need for work stoppages, arbitration may be able to provide an industrial relations setting which is more conducive to the improvement of worker morale than is the strike-based system.[2]

Loss of production and third party effects

One of the most important criticisms of the use of the strike is that it disrupts production. This reduces the incomes of both management and workers, it can have serious effects upon the consumers of the product (particularly if the product is an 'essential service'), and it may reduce GNP if foreign buyers are discouraged from purchasing the products of strike-prone industries. There is now considerable evidence to show that, by reducing the incidence of work stoppages, arbitration is able to minimise these costs.[3]

Inflation

In Chapter 3 we presented evidence to suggest that collective bargaining had not introduced a significant inflationary bias into the economy. Recent evidence has shown that wage agreements reached in the face of arbitration, or which have been handed down by arbitration boards, result in wage increases which are approximately equal to, or slightly lower than, those which would have been obtained through use of the strike threat.[4] These findings suggest, therefore, that arbitration does not have a significant negative effect upon inflation.

Pareto efficiency in exchange

A labour contract may be said to be Pareto inefficient in exchange if there exists a second contract which is preferred to the first by both the union and management. For example, referring back to the hypothetical example given in chapter 5 (p. 81–3), if we were to assume that an arbitrator has awarded a 10 per cent wage increase and a reduction in the workday from 8 hours to 7, but that both the union and the firm would prefer a 12 per cent wage increase and a reduction of the workday to only $7\frac{1}{2}$ hours, the arbitrated settlement in this case would be said to be Pareto inefficient.

This source of inefficiency has been said to arise in two situations in an arbitration system. First, as arbitrators can generally be presumed to be less knowledgeable concerning the preferences of the parties to a dispute than are those parties themselves, outcomes chosen by arbitrators can be assumed to be Pareto inefficient more often than are agreements reached voluntarily. That is, it is commonly argued that whereas labour and management would not agree between themselves to a contract which could be altered in such a way as to make them both better off, a third party, being unfamiliar with the details of their positions, might impose such a contract upon them.

This criticism can, we believe, be easily met. First, if arbitration-mediation (described in Chapter 5 of this study) is provided, the parties can renegotiate any inefficient, arbitrated outcome.[5] Second, if the arbitrator is chosen for his expertise in the industry with which the arbitration is concerned, he should be able to produce an outcome which does not differ significantly from the set of Pareto efficient outcomes.[6] Indeed, a third, impartial party may be better able to reach a satisfactory solution than would the parties involved, as the latter will be unable to take unbiased views of the arguments of their opponents. Finally, the efficiency of the arbitrator's award will be improved if he is not constrained to follow rigidly defined precedents or a detailed set of legislated rules.

Furthermore, there is empirical evidence to indicate that in countries with a long experience of compulsory arbitration, very few disputes reach the arbitration stage. In Australia, which has had compulsory arbitration for over eighty years, 90 per cent of federal civil service negotiations during 1960–1970 were settled without arbitration;[7] and in New Zealand, which has had

96 Rethinking labour–management relations

compulsory arbitration for a similar length of time, 96 per cent of disputes were settled without arbitration between 1965 and 1977.[8] Even in North America, with its much shorter experience of interest arbitration, it is unusual for more than 30 per cent of the negotiations which arise in a particular jurisdiction to result in an arbitration award;[9] and in Britain fewer than 10 per cent of the cases conciliated by ACAS in 1978 eventually went to arbitration.[10]

A second situation in which it has been argued that an inefficient outcome will be obtained is that in which the parties reach a voluntary agreement in the face of full-information, final-offer arbitration. As we argued in Chapter 5, one of the parties in such a situation will be induced (eventually) to offer the outcome which is preferred by the arbitrator. Vincent Crawford[11] argues that the second party will then be forced to accept this outcome, as no other outcome would be selected by the arbitrator. Thus, to the extent that the arbitrator's preferred outcome is inefficient, the parties will be induced to accept an inefficient outcome 'voluntarily'.

It can easily be seen, however, that Crawford's argument requires extremely naive bargainers.[12] Assume, for example, that the union has offered the outcome which is preferred by the arbitrator and that that outcome is Pareto inefficient. As long as management believes that the union's offer is inefficient, it can improve the expected outcome of the bargaining process by attempting to find a counter-offer which is preferred by both it and the union. If it succeeds, it can expect that the union would accept that offer (or make a counter-offer in an attempt to move the final agreement closer to the set of Pareto efficient outcomes), in which case it will be better off than if it had simply accepted the union's initial offer (of the arbitrator's preferred outcome). Whereas if the union refuses to concede to its initial position, the arbitrator will select the union's offer and management will be no worse off than if it had simply accepted the union's position. In this way, it can be anticipated that even if full-information, final-offer arbitration is employed the parties will be able to reach an efficient agreement.

Thus, to conclude, we do not accept the contention, commonly made in the literature, that agreements reached under arbitration need to be inefficient. Simple adjustments to existing systems of arbitration should be sufficient to overcome this problem.

EQUITY

In Chapter 2 we suggested that the following criteria should be applied to determine whether the effects of an industrial relations system could be said to be equitable:

1 Preference is to be given to those systems which provide individuals with the most extensive scheme of equal basic liberties compatible with a similar scheme of liberties for all.
2 Systems which reduce the dispersion of income are to be preferred if they do not make the least advantaged members of society worse off; and *may* be preferred if they obtain a significant reduction in dispersion at the cost of a minor worsening of the position of the least advantaged.
3 Industrial relations systems must not interfere with the general principles of:
(a) *horizontal equity:* equally qualified workers under otherwise identical contracts should receive equal remuneration; and
(b) *vertical equity:* differences in remuneration should be based, as much as possible, upon differences in the disutilities attached to employments – for example, upon differences in risk, in educational requirements, in effort required, and in responsibility.

We shall argue that, with respect to each of these criteria, an arbitration system can be expected to prove superior to a system based upon the strike.

Equal access to basic liberties

It was argued in Chapter 3 that a strike-based system fails to provide workers with equal access to basic liberties in at least three important senses. First, reliance upon the strike threat to press worker demands makes it very difficult to organise some groups of workers – particularly those who have a weak attachment to the labour force, such as part-time employees. Second, even among those who have been successful in organising trade unions there is unequal access to liberty because a strike-based system provides much greater bargaining power to some unions than to others. Finally, even if unions are democratic, it is likely that the views of some workers will not be represented adequately by their unions in the collective bargaining process. The reason for this is that in a democracy, it is the candidate, or party, whose platform most

98 Rethinking labour–management relations

closely reflects the views of the majority which can be expected to win election with the result that the views of the minority will often be ignored or, at least, given relatively little weight.

With respect to the first two of these factors, we submit that an arbitration system is clearly superior to a strike-based system. The reason that individuals who are working part-time or who have only a weak attachment to the labour force will often be unwilling to strike is that they do not expect to be able to recoup the wages which they have forgone during the strike. As the costs of arbitration are significantly lower than the costs of strikes, however, these individuals can be expected to be much less reluctant to use the arbitration threat than the strike threat. Accordingly, more individuals will be given the power to protect their basic liberties in an arbitration system than in a traditional industrial relations system. Furthermore, whereas the strike provides more power to some unions than to others, arbitration provides the same bargaining power to all unions. The ability to protect basic liberties, therefore, will be more equitably distributed among those workers who have managed to organise unions when the dispute resolution system is based upon arbitration than when it is based upon the strike.

Finally, although no democratic organisation can entirely overcome the problem that individual members will have only limited control over the policies of the organisation, we submit that arbitration offers greater scope for unions to deal with this problem than does the strike.[13] Our reasoning is based upon the assumption that individual preferences are most easily taken into account in relatively small, homogeneous groups of workers; for, in such situations, it is expected that workers will share similar views concerning the optimal policies of their unions and, accordingly, the numbers of 'dissident' workers will be minimised. Therefore, if arbitration is more conducive to the formation of small unions than is the strike, the former will be better able to represent the views of individual workers than the latter. Both theory and empirical observation lead us to conclude that arbitration will enjoy this advantage.

First, as we noted in Chapter 3, use of the strike threat encourages the formation of large unions, both because such unions have an advantage in organising and mounting successful work stoppages and because it can be extremely inefficient to allow the development of a large number of small unions – each of which can shut down the entire plant – within a single establishment. Second, neither of these factors is relevant to the use of arbitration. Although a certain minimum size is required in order to raise the funds to employ an arbitrator, the financial requirements to undertake arbitration are far less severe than those required to mount a successful strike. And because the arbitration of disputes between one set of workers and the firm does not interfere with the production of other employees of that firm, arbitration does not discourage the formation of a number of unions within a given workplace. On both counts, it can be expected that much smaller unions could survive and prosper under arbitration than could be expected to develop under a strike-based system. Finally, the experience of the Canadian public sector offers some evidence that arbitration does provide the means for small unions to survive, as is predicted by theory. In particular, in that sector, unions are given the choice of resolving their bargaining impasses through the use of the strike or through the use of arbitration. Many commentators have noted that a strong dichotomy has developed – the larger unions have predominantly chosen the strike route while the smaller unions have relied primarily upon arbitration.[14]

To summarise, it is seen that use of arbitration as the means for inducing employers to engage in collective bargaining is better able to provide workers with equal access to the 'most extensive scheme of basic liberties' than is the use of the strike. Arbitration allows more workers to organise successful unions than does the strike; it provides greater equality of bargaining power across unions; and it is better able to ensure that unions will be composed of workers who share common views and goals.

Redistribution of income

The evidence which was summarised in Chapter 2 indicated that trade unions achieve their desired effect with respect to the redistribution of income. They increase the incomes of their members at the expense of those who are wealthier than themselves while having little discernible effect upon those who are less advantaged. (See pp. 34–5 of Chapter 2 for the detailed argument.) Furthermore, if the use of arbitration makes it easier

100   Rethinking labour–management relations

to organise workers than does use of the strike, arbitration will allow for an increase in the size of the union sector relative to that of the 'less advantaged' group. Thus, not only will some members of the less advantaged – those who move from that group into the union sector – suffer no negative effect from collective bargaining, they will gain from that bargaining.

Horizontal equity

Horizontal equity requires that equally qualified workers, under otherwise identical contracts, should receive equal remuneration. In Chapter 3 we argued that the distribution of income which is produced by a strike-based industrial relations system violates this principle. Under such a system, the abilities of unions to obtain their demands vary according to criteria which would not, under any reasonable set of assumptions, be selected by individuals behind the Rawlsian veil of ignorance (see pp. 59–60). In particular, under a strike-based system the bargaining powers of otherwise identical unions will be directly proportional to the difficulty which their employers encounter in storing their output and inversely proportional to the percentage of the firms' total costs which are accounted for by wages and to the employers' ability to substitute capital for labour. Furthermore, unions whose mem- bers are concentrated in small numbers of workplaces will be more powerful than those whose memberships are dispersed; unions which represent full-time workers will have greater bargaining power than those which represent part-time workers; and unions which 'control' large sections of the workforce required to produce their industries' output will be more successful in obtaining their demands than will unions whose members can be replaced easily during the course of a strike. Finally, because many workers will not be able to mount successful strikes – often because potential union members are geographically dispersed – workers in many sectors will be denied recourse to the collective bargaining system.

Many of these impediments to horizontal equity could be overcome, we submit, if the strike was replaced by arbitration. In particular, under arbitration, bargaining power would not vary across industries and occupations according to the company's ability to store its product; the percentage of the workforce which was 'controlled' by the union; or the ability of the union to mount a strike.

Furthermore, it would be less important in an arbitration-based system than in a strike-based system that workers be concentrated in one geographic locality or that they be full-time workers with a long-term commitment to a single employer or industry. Many groups who currently choose not to unionise, either because they abhor the use of the strike or because they feel that the strike provides them with very little bargaining power, may choose to organise if provided with the power to impose arbitration upon their employers. McCarthy has found, for example, that the 'great majority of cases' heard before the (former) British Industrial Disputes Tribunal 'concerned comparatively weak groups'.[15] He also reported that the earlier National Arbitration Tribunal was used by the local government worker's union, NALGO, as the means to force employers to bargain with it and, thereby, to allow it to increase its membership and create an effective national bargaining machinery.[16] In this sense, therefore, arbitration may be better able than the strike threat to improve the distribution of income in the Rawlsian sense.

For each of these reasons, therefore, it would be expected that arbitration would offer greater equality of bargaining power – and, therefore, greater horizontal equality of income distribution – than does the strike.

Vertical equity

Vertical equity requires that differences in remuneration should be based, as much as possible, upon differences in the disutilities attached to employments – for example, upon differences in risk, in educational requirements, and in responsibility. The primary manner in which trade unions can be expected to affect these differences is through their influences on *intra* union wage relativities. With respect to a given union, it would not be expected that these relativities would differ if a strike-based system of bargaining was to be replaced by an arbitration-based system, as the internal voting mechanism by which union members expressed their preferences would be unaffected by such a change. This presumption is supported by the empirical

102 Rethinking labour–management relations

evidence with respect to both teacher[17] and police[18] salaries in the United States.

Summary

We have argued in this section that an arbitration-based system of collective bargaining can be expected to provide greater equity than can a strike-based system for three major reasons. First, because it is much easier for workers to obtain representation before an arbitration panel than it is to mount a successful strike, it can be expected that access to arbitration will provide more workers with the benefits of collective bargaining than will access to the strike. Second, arbitration can be expected to distribute bargaining power more equally among workers than will the strike. Finally, an arbitration-based system may be better able than a strike-based system to ensure that workers' preferences are reflected in their unions' demands. Whereas the use of the strike makes it imperative that workers be organised into large unions – often of heterogeneous workers – arbitration can be conducted successfully by small organisations consisting of workers with relatively homogeneous preferences.

LEGAL STRUCTURING

One of the advantages which has been claimed for trade unions is that they can act as worker representatives in disputes which have gone to the courts and as worker lobbyists with legislative bodies. An ideal system would provide all workers with equal ability to organise for the purpose of obtaining such representation. But the strike-based system does not offer all workers equal bargaining power for this purpose. Indeed, some workers have so little bargaining power that the costs of organisation cannot be justified. Arbitration, on the other hand, provides equal bargaining power to most groups of workers and, therefore, allows many more workers to be represented in the determination of common and statutory law than does the strike.

OPERATIONAL DIFFICULTIES

In this section, we consider a number of practical difficulties which

The role of arbitration 103

would arise were an arbitration system to be introduced. These include: (i) that arbitrators may not be seen to be impartial and that, therefore, the parties would refuse to submit their disputes to arbitration; (ii) that arbitration may discourage bargaining in 'good faith'; and (iii) that the parties may refuse to accept unfavourable arbitrated decisions.

Lack of impartiality

The first problem with arbitration is that it may be difficult to find arbitrators which both sides consider to be 'fair'. Thus, even if the arbitrator makes an honest attempt to produce an impartial judgement, one of the parties may be unwilling to accept that judgement. This will particularly be true if the party which feels it has reason to question the impartiality of the arbitrator obtains a settlement which is less favourable than it had anticipated. In such a situation, discontent may lead to lower morale, unofficial/illegal work stoppages, or a call for a return to the strike-threat system of bargaining.

This defect can only be overcome if arbitrators can be seen to be truly impartial. There are two ways in which this goal might be attained. First, individuals with experience in labour relations might be encouraged to offer themselves as arbitrators, either on a competitive market basis or through a professional organisation such as the American Arbitration Association or, in Britain, the Chartered Institute of Arbitrators. If the decisions of these arbitrators were made public, the parties to disputes could then use the transcripts of previous cases in order to restrict their selections to arbitrators who had shown themselves to be capable of reaching solutions which were, in general, satisfactory to both sides. Furthermore, in the case of permanent arbitrators, as their livelihoods depended upon the appearance of impartiality, arbitrators could be expected to make every effort, in every case, to produce settlements which both parties considered to be acceptable. Alternatively, the government could establish a panel of arbitrators such as, in Britain, ACAS or the CAC, to be appointed in particular cases as the need arose. The incentive for the arbitrators to act as impartially as possible in such a system would be the government's desire to avoid having to return to a strike-based system.

It may be argued that even the two arbitration systems described here would be insufficient to ensure that arbitrators were seen to be impartial. But there is evidence from existing arbitration systems that arbitrators can act in such a manner as to satisfy most workers *and* managers. For example, Ponak and Wheeler[19] found that Canadian civil servants chose binding arbitration instead of the strike in 79.9 per cent of 682 occasions between 1967 and 1979; that British Columbia police and firefighters chose arbitration in 93.5 per cent of 31 opportunities between 1974 and 1979; and that Wisconsin municipal workers and teachers selected arbitration in all 90 opportunities presented to them in 1978; while Lester[20] found that in New Jersey the percentage of agreements reached with the assistance of a mediator–arbitrator increased over time. Furthermore, when Ontario hospital workers and managers were surveyed, 66 per cent of union members indicated satisfaction with the arbitration awards they had received, while 75 per cent of managers were similarly satisfied;[21] and a number of studies have found that labour and management representatives share many similar views concerning the characteristics which make arbitrators desirable.[22]

In all, it is the general finding of most research that arbitrators are able to behave in a sufficiently impartial manner that a true system of collective *bargaining* can develop in the 'shadow' of binding arbitration. As Richard Lester concluded in his intensive study of interest arbitration in the United States:

> experienced, skilled arbitrators and advocates, together pursuing their common interests, can work out agreed awards by processes that increasingly look like genuine collective bargaining.[23]

Discouragement of bargaining in good faith

K.G.J.C. Knowles[24] has argued that arbitration removes from union officials the necessity to behave in a responsible manner, as the outcome is imposed by a third party. Therefore, the incentive to restrain the demands of union militants is removed and it is these demands which will be put to the arbitrator. In doing so, Knowles implies, the expectations of the union's members are raised unrealistically and worker morale will suffer when these expectations are not met.

But this argument applies only in those situations in which conventional arbitration is employed and arbitrators use a 'split-the-difference' method of determining the final outcome; as in these circumstances the parties are encouraged to take extreme positions. If final-offer arbitration is used, or if arbitrators under conventional arbitration use more sophisticated selection procedures, negotiators will be encouraged to present moderate positions. In the case of final-offer arbitration, a union which presents a militant offer will find that it is the management's offer which is chosen. And in conventional arbitration, if the arbitrator forgoes the 'split-the-difference' selection procedure, the parties will be provided with an incentive to present sound, logical positions, for it is to logic that the arbitrator can be expected to respond and not to militant posturing.

Indeed, a considerable amount of empirical evidence has been collected in recent years to indicate that arbitrators do *not* employ a 'split-the-difference' procedure. A number of studies have found, for example, that arbitrators primarily base their decisions concerning an equitable, or fair, award upon the 'facts of the case' – *not* upon the offers of the two parties.[25] Furthermore, in those studies in which the parties' offers did appear to have some influence over the arbitrator's award, it was found that one party's offer played a greater role than the other's (i.e. the arbitrator did not split the difference between them),[26] and that the influence of the parties' offers diminished the more they diverged from the arbitrator's view of a fair award.[27]

Furthermore, we argue in Chapter 7 that if arbitrators were to 'sell' their services on a competitive market, they would not be selected were they to employ a 'split-the-difference' approach. In a competitive market, unions and employers could be expected to seek out arbitrators who were able to weigh carefully the competing demands of the two sides, to take into account the legitimate goals of the parties, and to match their settlements to the particular circumstances facing them. It would be surprising if an arbitrator who employed gross 'rules of thumb' would survive in such a system.

Problems of enforcement

A drawback to any scheme which requires compulsory arbitration is that such a scheme may be difficult to enforce. It is not sufficient merely to pass legislation instructing labour and management to submit their unresolved disputes to an arbitrator. Those to whom the strike threat offers the greatest relative power will be reluctant to cede that power to a third party and compliance with the government's wishes may only be obtained if suitable penalties can be devised. But most such penalties have been found to be flawed in some way. For example, it has been suggested that supplementary benefits and PAYE (income tax) refunds should be denied to workers who were on strike illegally.[28] But both these penalties would have to be tempered somewhat in a society in which the government was unwilling to allow the families of strikers to starve; and they may have little effect against a union which has a large strike fund.[29] Second, it might be possible to rule that any worker who illegally took strike action would be treated as having thereby terminated his contract of employment; or the government could remove the immunities against common law action which are currently enjoyed by striking workers.[30] However, a strong union might be able to make the waiving of these provisions a condition of its return to work.[31] Third, governments have occasionally tried to force strikers back to work by threatening imprisonment. But when this bluff is called the jails have been found unable to hold all of the members of even a relatively small union.[32]

In the view of most industrial relations experts, compliance with compulsory arbitration legislation is best achieved by establishing a dispute resolution procedure which is acceptable to all sides. Indeed, as we argue in Chapters 7 and 9, if compulsory arbitration is to be imposed upon the industrial relations system, it is *imperative* that the government leave the construction of this procedure to the parties themselves – otherwise, the government will incur a substantial risk that one of the parties will consider the procedures chosen to be inequitable and, therefore, that that party will refuse to participate. In North America, the experience of those jurisdictions in which the parties have not been severely constrained by legislation has been that strikes have become extremely rare.[33] Those strikes which have occurred have generally been attributed to arbitration procedures which (one of) the parties have considered to be inequitable.[34]

However, if penalties are also considered to be necessary, two possibilities present themselves. First, New Zealand has had considerable success with a system in which 'registered' unions are offered legal advantages which are not available to unregistered unions. For example, registered unions are granted 'exclusive representational and bargaining rights'[35] for specific groups of employees and are allowed to impose a union shop.[36] The government is then able to threaten that the use of illegal strikes will be punished by de-registration. Second, it should be possible to design a set of penalties which would have the effect of removing the benefits which had been won through use of an illegal strike or lockout. For example, if a union had used an illegal strike to obtain a benefit which had been denied in arbitration – such as a wage increase or an improvement in fringe benefits – the appropriate penalty would be a tax which was equal (or greater[37]) in value to that benefit, to be imposed on individual workers' post-strike wages.[38] Alternatively, if it proved difficult or expensive[39] to levy such a fine against the union's members, the same purpose would be achieved by imposing the fine on the employer; for that would increase the resolve of the employer to combat illegal strikes. In either event, however, the fine would not be designed to penalise the parties for partaking in an illegal action but to remove from them all of the benefits of such an action (while retaining the costs).

CONCLUSION

Throughout this book we have argued that industrial relations systems should be evaluated according to their performance with respect to four major criteria: union voice, efficiency, equity, and legal structuring. In this chapter, we have contrasted strike-based and arbitration-based systems of collective bargaining with respect to each of these criteria. In each instance, we have found the arbitration-based system to be superior to the strike-based system; or, at least, to be its equal. This conclusion arises for a number of reasons. First, because it is easier to organise workers under arbitration than under the strike, we predicted that more workers would be able to enjoy the benefits of collective bargaining under the former than under the latter system. Second, we noted that arbitration hearings would be much less expensive than strikes. Third, we predicted that arbitration would allow for smaller unions than would the strike and, therefore, would provide workers with a greater feeling of participation in their workplaces. Finally, because arbitration provides all workers with similar bargaining powers, whereas the strike distributes those powers very unequally among bargaining units, we concluded that arbitration would produce a more equitable distribution of income than would the strike. With these conclusions in hand, we now turn to the question of determining which characteristics of arbitration systems will prove to be the most desirable.

Chapter 7

The market for arbitration

In the preceding analyses two major arguments were developed. First, in Chapter 2, it was suggested that a system in which employers and employees bargained with one another collectively would have a number of advantages over one in which the two parties competed freely in the labour market. Second, in Chapters 3 to 6, it was argued that the most desirable form of collective bargaining was that which used binding arbitration as its main procedure for resolving impasses.

In this chapter we propose to proceed from the assumption that these two arguments have been accepted. This will allow us to address the most important question which arises once a decision has been made to implement a system of binding arbitration; namely, how is such a system to be organised? In particular, six aspects of binding arbitration will be identified: (i) the degree to which the arbitration process is to be *voluntary* and whether this degree should vary systematically among bargaining groups; (ii) the extent to which the provision of arbitrators' services is to be left to the *private market*; (iii) the type of arbitration *procedures* which are to be employed; (iv) the question of who pays the arbitration fee; (v) the extent to which the *reasoning* of the arbitrators in reaching their decisions is to be made public, and how that publication should occur; and (vi) the methods by which *penalties* for illegal strikes and lockouts are to be assessed and enforced. Each of these issues will be considered in a separate section in this chapter.

VOLUNTARY VERSUS COMPULSORY ARBITRATION

Compulsion

Assume that it has been agreed that, for a particular group of workers (and employers), binding arbitration is socially superior to the strike threat as a technique for resolving bargaining impasses. Is there any reason why the government should impose arbitration compulsorily? Or will the logic of the situation be such that the parties will reach a voluntary agreement to arbitrate their disputes?

In order to answer these questions it is first necessary to return to the model of bargaining power which was introduced in Chapter 3. According to that model, the ability of either side to extract concessions from its opponent will be an increasing function of the opponent's cost of disagreeing and a decreasing function of its opponent's cost of agreeing. Within an open market, for example, the cost to the employer of rejecting one of its employee's requests for increased remuneration or improved working conditions (the employer's cost of disagreeing) will be a function of either the cost of replacing that employee should he leave or the reduction of morale and productivity should he remain. Within a strike-based system, on the other hand, the employer's costs of disagreement will depend upon the effect, permanent or otherwise, which a strike will have on his profits. And within a system of binding arbitration, the cost to the employer of disagreeing with the union will be a function of the difference in cost between the package of offers which the employer has made and the package which it expects would be imposed by an arbitrator.

Similar differences between these three systems of dispute resolution can also be expected to arise with respect to the union's costs of disagreement and with respect to both parties' costs of agreement. As a result, movement from one system to another will, in all but the most exceptional of circumstances, alter the relative bargaining powers of the two parties, giving one party greater ability to obtain concessions from the other while making the second party less able to win reciprocal concessions. In order to induce the latter to move from one system to another voluntarily, the former would have to offer a 'bribe' equal in value to that of the future stream of reduced concessions. But it would be extremely difficult to raise such a bribe without incurring severe financial penalties – in the form of high interest rates, for example. Furthermore, given the extreme uncertainty about the value of such a bribe, risk averse parties may prefer to continue with their current industrial relations system rather than to gamble on a wholesale change. For these reasons we would predict that very few sets of bargainers would choose to move voluntarily from either a free market situation or a strike-based system to a system of binding arbitration.[1] Thus, if there is to be binding arbitration of interest disputes, that system must be introduced through some form of governmental compulsion.

Coverage

In the preceding discussion we assumed that a choice had been made as to which groups were to be covered by binding arbitration. It is possible, however, that it may be desirable to leave some groups not covered by such requirements. Let us approach this question by first identifying two groups which might reasonably be subjected to the requirement that they use binding arbitration to resolve their disputes.

The first of these are trades and industries in which unions have had difficulty organising or have had very little bargaining power either because the workforce was widely dispersed or because workers did not remain with one employer for a sufficient length of time to make a strike worthwhile.[2] The rationale for extending compulsory arbitration to these groups was discussed in Chapter 2; namely, that collective bargaining reduces worker alienation and increases job security, and that it may have a desirable effect on the distribution of income. (The means by which this extension of bargaining rights would be carried out is discussed in Chapter 9.)

The second group for which it would be desirable to make arbitration compulsory is composed of those trades and industries in which use of the strike will have a serious negative impact on the community as a whole. In particular, we suggest that compulsory arbitration should be imposed on those groups which are of key importance to the country's position in international trade[3] and on those groups which produce 'essential' goods and services. In both cases, a carefully constructed arbitration system[4] would maintain for workers their rights of collective bargaining while simultaneously removing the costs which the strike-based system has traditionally imposed on third parties.

112 Rethinking labour–management relations

This leaves a large 'middle ground' composed of employer/employee groups for which the strike/lockout threat is sufficiently strong that the parties are induced to enter meaningful negotiations, yet not so strong as to impose significant external costs on the remainder of the community. The argument for imposing compulsory arbitration on these groups is much weaker than it is for the two discussed above. For this reason, and because any introduction of compulsory industrial relations legislation is bound to meet concerted opposition, it is our recommendation that groups in this middle ground be allowed to opt out of the binding arbitration system. A method for distinguishing between those groups which should be exempted in this way and those which should not is suggested in Chapter 9.

TYPES OF ARBITRATION PROCEDURES – PRIVATE VERSUS PUBLIC LAW[5]

Once the decision has been made to impose compulsory arbitration on certain groups it must then be decided: (i) how the arbitration procedures (e.g., conventional arbitration versus final-offer selection) are to be chosen; (ii) how the arbitrators are to be selected; and (iii) how the rules for settling cases are to be determined. As each of these decisions requires, to a large extent, that a choice be made between government-made rules (public law) and market-determined rules (private law), much of the analysis to follow will be based on a comparison of the relative advantages and disadvantages of public and private arbitration agencies. We begin this analysis by identifying the criteria which labour and management can be expected to employ when selecting their preferred arbitration system. We then develop theoretical models of the relative abilities of government and private arbitration systems to meet these criteria, and test the predictions of these models against empirical data.

The goals of an arbitration system

There are a number of circumstances in which labour and management may wish to employ an arbitrator. First, the parties may find that they have committed themselves to mutually inconsistent positions. In this circumstance, they can be expected to seek arbitration in order to break the impasse. Alternatively, if an arbitrator has developed a reputation as an expert in a particular industry or occupation, the parties may wish to approach that person in order to obtain suggestions concerning methods of dispute resolution which may not have occurred to them. In addition, if the negotiators have reached an agreement which they feel may be unpalatable to their constituents, they may hire an arbitrator to announce the agreement for them, in order to distance themselves politically from that agreement.

Conversely, there will be a number of circumstances in which the parties will wish to avoid employing an arbitrator. The first of these occurs when the decisions of arbitrators are easily predicted by the parties. If the parties predict that the arbitrator will produce an unacceptable or, in economic terms, 'inefficient' decision, they will prefer to reach their own agreement.[6] Whereas if the parties predict that the arbitrator will produce an efficient decision, they will be able to save themselves time and money by agreeing to that decision themselves. Second, if risk averse parties are unable to predict the outcome of arbitration they may be willing to make significant concessions to their opponents in order to avoid the uncertainty of arbitration. Finally, if an arbitrator is perceived to be biased in favour of one party over the other, the party which is the object of the bias will wish to avoid employing that arbitrator. Thus, if all arbitrators are perceived to be biased against one or the other of the parties, the parties will wish to avoid arbitration altogether.

These considerations suggest that there are four criteria, or goals, against which labour–management negotiators might be expected to measure the success of an arbitration system. The first of these is that arbitrators must be expected to produce decisions which are efficient, or which deviate from the efficient set of decisions by as little as possible. Because the parties could have been expected to select outcomes which did not deviate significantly from the efficient set if they had reached their own decisions, they cannot be expected to employ an arbitration system which produces decisions which are clearly inefficient. Also, whether the parties are able to obtain their own agreements or not, it is tautologically true that they will prefer an arbitration system which produces efficient decisions to a system which does not. Second, an arbitrator who is able to bring innovative ideas to the resolution of contractual disputes may be preferred to one who simply applies the accepted conventions to the selection process. Third, the parties can be expected to seek arbitrators who are considered to be fair, or unbiased. If arbitrators are known to be biased in favour of one party, the other party will use whatever powers it has to avoid going to arbitration – even though it would otherwise find arbitration to be desirable.

Finally, it has often been suggested that the parties will find it beneficial to be informed of the decisions which arbitrators have reached in disputes other than their own. A variety of arguments have been put forward in support of this position. Both Fuller[7] and Eisenberg,[8] for example, argue that when a dispute arises concerning the distribution of income, each party to the dispute will find it to its advantage to couch its arguments in terms of rights and principles. To the extent, therefore, that these rights and principles will be accorded greater respect the more generally have they been recognised, each party will wish to be as well-informed concerning past decisions as is possible. More pragmatically, Landes and Posner[9] suggest that knowledge concerning past decisions will help parties to minimise the expense of arbitration. In particular, if such knowledge allows the parties to agree as to the outcome which an arbitrator would reach in their current dispute, they can generally be expected to be able to employ that information to settle 'out of court'. Furthermore, knowledge of the reasoning employed by arbitrators in previous, similar cases may be useful to bargaining parties if that reasoning 'increases the stock of knowledge and expertise about arbitration'[10] and, thereby, provides insights into the methods by which the parties might settle their own disputes.[11]

Public arbitration

Assume that the government has decided that it is desirable that labour–management disputes be settled through a process of binding arbitration. The government then faces the question as to whether it should provide its own arbitration system or whether it should leave the development of such a system to the private market. If it is assumed that this decision is to be based upon the relative abilities of the two systems to achieve the goals set out on pp. 112–14, above, it will first be necessary to model those two systems in order to predict how they will operate.

For the purposes of this section, we will assume that the public arbitration system is modelled on the court system. That is, we assume that, like judges, arbitrators are employed by the government and are allocated among disputants according to statutory criteria. The reason for adopting this assumption is that many examples of public arbitration (one is the industrial courts of Australia) employ this system. Thus, if public arbitration is modelled as a court-like agency it will be possible to use information from these examples to test the predictions of the theory. We begin our analysis by developing a theoretical model of such an agency.[12]

Since 1970, economists have developed a model which employs standard economic assumptions to analyse the behaviour of government agencies.[13] With only slight modifications, this model can be used to predict the manner in which a government-run arbitration system would operate. In particular, we will assume that there are four groups of actors relevant to such a model: the electorate (voters), elected officials (the government), consumers of the arbitration system's services (consumers), and employees of the arbitration system (government employees). We will first set out a number of assumptions concerning the goals and constraints which face these groups and will then employ these assumptions to predict how a public arbitration service would operate.

We assume that voters will devote very little of their time and money to the monitoring of a public arbitration system, primarily because no individual voter will obtain sufficient gains from any improvement in the functioning of such a system to offset the private costs of monitoring. Accordingly, it will be assumed that voters will possess accurate information about only those aspects of the arbitration service which are observable at little cost. Given this assumption, and further assuming that members of the government are primarily interested in maximising the probability of being re-elected, we assume that the government members responsible for the arbitration service will concentrate their attention upon those aspects of the arbitration service which are easily monitored by the voters. To a certain extent, the consumers of the arbitration service, labour and management, will be able to

116   Rethinking labour–management relations

assist the government in this monitoring by providing information about arbitral decisions. However, the government may not be able to rely on this information as consumers will have an incentive to 'free ride' on other taxpayers by exaggerating the need for improvements in the quality of the public service. The final group of actors in the model is made up of the employees of the arbitration service. Although it is sometimes assumed that these individuals will obtain utility from the efficient operation of their agencies, we will assume that this goal is dominated by their desire to maximise personal utility.

These assumptions lead to a number of well-known predictions about the operation of a public agency – in this case, the public arbitration service. First, because it will be difficult for voters and the government to measure the quality of arbitral decisions, it is anticipated that the salaries of arbitrators will be based upon such easily monitored variables as levels of education, years of experience, and numbers of arbitrations conducted instead of upon direct measures of arbitrator productivity. For a similar reason, it is expected that a ceiling will be placed on the arbitrators' salary scale in order to ensure that arbitrators do not use their superior information about their own productivity to argue for excessively high salaries. At the same time, however, arbitrators may be able to increase their personal utilities by manipulating information concerning activities which voters and the government cannot monitor easily. They may, for example, be able to convince the government that they need large libraries and research staffs, that their offices and arbitration (court) rooms must be oak panelled (to 'maintain decorum'), or that they must attend international conferences in order to improve their expertise.[14]

A further implication of the model of government agencies is that the quality of arbitral decisions can be expected to suffer. If the government experiences difficulty in distinguishing between 'good' arbitral decisions and 'poor' ones, it will be unable to reward the production of good decisions. Accordingly, much of the financial incentive for arbitrators to be innovative and to be responsive to the wishes of consumers will be lost. Furthermore, even if the government is able to make some distinctions among arbitrators on the basis of quality, the incentive to be innovative will be reduced if voters have demanded that a ceiling be placed on the arbitrators' salary scale. If the effect of such a ceiling is to

The market for arbitration   117

reduce the benefits of making good decisions without reducing the costs of making poor decisions, arbitrators might be expected to respond by 'satisficing' – for example, by placing reliance on precedent when making their awards. And in order to ensure that arbitrators did not employ decision criteria which were inconsistent with those which the voters perceived to be desirable, the government might be expected to impose constraints on the factors which arbitrators could take into account when selecting their awards. Because each of these constraints will be based upon imperfect information, they can be expected to introduce inefficiencies into the operation of the arbitration service, relative to the first best level of performance.

A related problem arises when the government uses this uncertainty about the socially desirable set of arbitral criteria to bias its selection of those criteria in favour of one group over another. For example, if there was legitimate public debate concerning the social desirability of a constraint which would favour management, a pro-management government might choose to impose that constraint whereas a pro-labour government would not. In neither case would the government's critics have a strong argument against its decision; yet, in both, the impartiality of the arbitration system would have been brought into question. This problem will become particularly acute when the workers to whom arbitration is to apply are the government's own employees. In this case, the goverment will find it very difficult to convince its employees that it has acted in a completely disinterested manner in the selection of arbitral criteria and, therefore, it will find it difficult to obtain its employee's agreement to enter arbitration.

Finally, the model suggests that voters will demand that the arbitration service be operated as close to full capacity as possible, in order to minimise costs. In particular, the number of periods in which arbitrators are not actively involved in the resolution of disputes must be kept at a minimum. Accordingly, in order to avoid the situation in which some arbitrators are idle while others are overworked, voter preference will be for a system in which consumers (negotiators) are offered only limited ability to select among arbitrators and in which each arbitrator is encouraged to become a generalist, capable of dealing with any type of arbitration submitted to him. If the government had clear evidence that

118 Rethinking labour–management relations

superior decisions would be rendered if consumers could select freely among arbitrators it might not accede to this demand. But, as government members are expected to have imperfect information concerning the quality of arbitral decisions, it will have no basis on which to override the wishes of its electorate.[15]

Private arbitration

As an alternative to the establishment of its own arbitration service, the government could choose to require that the parties to labour disputes seek their own arbitrators. As a first step in predicting how this market might operate, assume that it proved to be highly competitive. In this case, it would be expected that the incomes (including fringe benefits) of arbitrators would not exceed their opportunity costs; that is, arbitrators would be unable to extract significant profits (economic rents) from their customers. Arbitrators who were willing to offer innovative decisions, however, would be able to command sufficient fee premiums to compensate them for the risks (and other costs, if any) associated with that offer. Also, as customers would select among arbitrators on the basis of the merits of the arbitrators' decisions, it is to be expected that age, education, and years of experience would play relatively unimportant roles in the determination of the demands for different arbitrators' services. For similar reasons, arbitrators who produced low-quality decisions would find it difficult to obtain customers; and those who were willing to specialise in the arbitration of disputes in particular sectors would obtain more customers than those who did not specialise – to the extent that the decisions of specialists were perceived to be superior to those of generalists.[16] Finally, no excess capacity would be expected to develop in the market. Profit-maximising arbitration firms would hire workers only to the point where their wages equalled their marginal revenue products, for example; and private arbitration 'courtrooms' would have only that amount of oak panelling for which the arbitrators' customers were willing to pay.

In short, most of the drawbacks to public arbitration which were discussed above could be overcome if a competitive private arbitration system could be put into place. However, there are a number of reasons why the private market for arbitration might not develop in this way. In the remainder of this section we will consider how these imperfections might be expected to influence the manner in which the market for private arbitration functioned.

First, before a competitive market can develop, buyers must be able to distinguish among sellers on the basis of the relative qualities of their products. As the product of an arbitration market is arbitration decisions, it is seen that a necessary condition for such a market to become competitive is that arbitrators' decisions become publicised (either by the arbitrators themselves or by third parties). We believe that sufficient incentives exist that this publication could be expected to occur. On p. 114, we argued that it would be of importance to negotiators that they be able to identify the capabilities of potential arbitrators, *ex ante*, as they would wish to select the arbitrator best suited to their circumstance and as they could always choose to settle their disputes voluntarily if they could not identify a mutually satisfactory arbitrator. Therefore, arbitrators would always find it to their benefit to publicise those of their decisions which were (positively) innovative, or otherwise of high quality. Furthermore, they could expect to be assisted in this process by private publishing houses who would collect and print arbitration decisions in much the same way that court decisions are printed in legal reports today.

In response to this argument, it might be suggested that arbitrators would be reluctant to allow their rivals to gain access to their decisions, as that would allow their rivals to make use of their insights (and, thereby, increase competition in the market). This suggestion fails if any of three conditions is met. First, arbitrators may believe that publication of their innovative decisions will bring sufficient extra business (from customers who expect further innovation) to compensate for the loss of business to rivals who rely on the use of those decisions. Second, labour disputes are often of sufficient complexity that knowledge concerning the manner in which one dispute was resolved may not be of great use to individuals attempting to resolve other disputes. Under this circumstance, in the eyes of the arbitrator, the advertising effect of publication of the decision may well outweigh the increased competition effect.[17] Finally, should either of these conditions be insufficient to encourage arbitrators to

120 Rethinking labour–management relations

allow their decisions to be published, the government would be free to order that those decisions be made public.

Similarly, Landes and Posner[18] have argued that it would be to arbitrators' advantage, collectively, to refuse to make the reasons for their decisions known. This would hamper negotiators in their efforts to resolve their own disputes and force them to turn to arbitrators for assistance. But this argument fails to recognise that it is important to negotiators that they be able to identify the impartiality and competence of potential arbitrators, *ex ante*. If negotiators were unable to do this, they might well choose to settle their disputes 'out of court'.[19] Furthermore, as we noted above, if arbitrators refused, on this ground, to make the reasons for their decisions known, the government could require publication of those reasons. Finally, as Landes and Posner recognise themselves, if the arbitration market contains a large number of competing arbitrators, no individual arbitrator could expect to obtain an appreciable increase in business by obfuscating the reasons for his decisions. Only in a highly imperfect market could the refusal of an arbitrator to publish his decisions be expected to have sufficient impact on the market that he would find it advisable to take that impact into account.

Thus, although competitive markets may fail to develop if arbitrators do not allow their decisions to be published, the theory developed in this chapter – not to mention the empirical observation of how arbitral markets already operate in Canada and the United States – suggests that this should not become a major problem. There are sufficient benefits from publication of decisions that arbitrators in markets which are otherwise competitive will generally be induced to make their decisions public. It is only when the market is already imperfectly competitive, for other reasons, that arbitrators are predicted to withhold information about their decisions. But even then, governments could easily circumvent this problem by ordering that decisions be made public.

Would arbitrators' desire to publicise their 'best' decisions ensure consistency among different arbitrators? Provided only that 'consumers' of arbitral decisions could agree upon a ranking of such decisions by quality, the answer to this question is 'yes'. Consider: if one arbitrator was to announce a decision which all parties agreed was superior to previously announced decisions

The market for arbitration 121

concerning similar disputes, they would, in the future, refuse to employ arbitrators who did not follow that decision. Thus, all arbitrators would find it in their interests to adopt similar reasoning – unless they felt that they could improve even further on the announced decisions. In this way, not only would there be consistency in the short run, but the 'law' would also evolve over time.

The greatest threats to the competitiveness of the arbitration market arise from restrictions on entry and from product differentiation. With respect to the former, it is to be expected that once a number of individuals had established reputations as competent, reliable arbitrators, customers would be reluctant to hire relatively untried newcomers. Again, the reason for this is that most labour disputes involve issues which can have a profound impact on a large number of individuals. Thus, risk averse negotiators can be expected to prefer to entrust decisions about these matters to arbitrators whose capabilities have been proven. Similarly, if negotiators do not share the same preference functions, they will not all demand arbitrators with the same characteristics.[20] That is, arbitrators will become differentiated with respect to the characteristics which are observable by negotiators. For both reasons (restrictions on entry and product differentiation), those arbitrators who manage to establish positive reputations may be able to earn incomes which exceed their opportunity costs by an appreciable margin. Furthermore, if the number of reputable arbitrators is small enough, backlogs of cases may develop – although arbitrators may be willing to use a differential pricing system to determine placing in the 'queue'.

On the other hand, as backlogs and arbitrators' incomes grow, entry into the market will be encouraged. For example, a reputable arbitrator may be willing to take on apprentices, whose work he would guarantee to his customers. This policy would be to the arbitrator's advantage as long as the surplus he was able to extract from the apprentice while he was employed with the arbitrator exceeded the present value of the business which was attracted away by the apprentice once he left the employment of the arbitrator. Also, negotiators could be expected to seek out inexperienced arbitrators, particularly in cases in which relatively unimportant issues were at stake, as backlogs and arbitration fees grew. Thus, a limit on the effects of the barrier to entry would be

122 Rethinking labour–management relations

set. In any event, the preference of negotiators for experienced arbitrators should not have an appreciable effect on the quality of arbitral decisions rendered. If this quality should begin to deteriorate noticeably, negotiators would be induced either to settle their own disputes or to try to attract new arbitrators into the market.

Evidence

In this section, public and private arbitration systems will be contrasted on the basis of four criteria: the extent to which they can be expected to provide consistent bodies of precedent; the quality of the decisions which they can be expected to produce; their costs of operation; and the extent to which they are able to ensure that there will be sufficient numbers of qualified arbitrators. Wherever possible, empirical evidence will be employed to support the theoretical arguments.

(a) *Production of consistent precedent*: Landes and Posner[21]offered three reasons for believing that 'a private market is more likely to emerge in dispute resolution than in rule creation' (p. 240); that is, for believing that private courts would settle disputes but would not produce consistent rulings which could be employed by others. Their reasons were: (i) If a private judge were to 'explain the result in a way that would provide guidance for future parties . . . [that] would confer an external . . . benefit not only on future parties but also on competing judges' (p. 238). (ii) 'If there are many [private] judges, there is likely to be a bewildering profusion of precedents and no obvious method of harmonizing them' (p. 239); whereas harmonization of public decisions could be enforced through the use of an appeal court. (iii) 'Any rule that clearly indicates how a judge is likely to decide a case will assure that no disputes subject to the rule are submitted to that judge . . . [therefore, private judges] will tend to promulgate vague standards' (pp. 239–40).

In our argument above, we developed a number of theoretical arguments in response to Landes and Posner. These arguments suggested that a private arbitration market *could* be expected to produce consistent precedents because individual arbitrators would find it in their interests to advertise their 'best' decisions and because negotiators would refuse to hire arbitrators whose decisions deviated in a significant manner from the best decisions known.

But these theoretical arguments pale in the face of the vast amount of empirical evidence concerning the operation of private arbitration markets in Canada and the United States. That evidence, we suggest, overwhelmingly supports the contention that a private arbitration system is able to produce consistent, precedential rulings. First, that private arbitrators will find it in their interests to publicise their decisions and that publishers will find a market for those decisions is beyond dispute. Two major American publications – *Labor Arbitration Reports* (Bureau of National Affairs) and *Labor Arbitration Awards* (Commerce Clearing House) – have already published thousands of labour arbitration decisions. Canada has at least five publications devoted to labour arbitration decisions.[22] And standard arbitration textbooks in both the United States[23] and Canada[24] contain citations to literally thousands of decisions.[25]

Second, both the demand for 'arbitration law' textbooks (such as Elkouri and Elkouri and Palmer) and the comments of numerous expert arbitrators make it clear that precedents are established and followed in private arbitration markets. Speaking of the Canadian market, for example, Paul Weiler, then Chairman of the Labour Relations Board of British Columbia, argued that:

> Analysis in any arbitration award has to survive in the free market place of ideas; it must persuade through the quality of ideas, not compel by force of authority. But gradually a consensus does emerge as typical clauses are sifted and refined in a series of decisions.[26]

Speaking of the American market, Charles Killingsworth, then President of the National Academy of Arbitrators, argued that the 'greatest accomplishment of [the arbitration process], in my estimation, has been the development of a quite substantial and functional industrial jurisprudence';[27] and Elkouri and Elkouri noted that a 'glance through recent volumes of reported arbitration decisions reveals the very frequent citation, discussion, and use of [arbitral] precedents'.[28] Furthermore, there is now a substantial statistical literature which argues that the decisions of arbitrators can be predicted from information about the facts of

124 Rethinking labour–management relations

the disputes (as opposed to biographical information about the arbitrators).[29] A plausible explanation of this finding is that arbitrators produce consistent decisions because they rely on precedential decisions.

Third, Landes and Posner[30] suggest that the lack of appeal procedures in private judicial markets will mean that conflicting precedents will be established in those markets. We have shown, however, that a high degree of consistency has been obtained in private markets for labour arbitration. That finding suggests that the explanation for the presence of appeal courts in public arbitration systems (such as Australia's[31]) is that such courts act as government 'watchdogs' to monitor the quality of decisions at the 'trial' level. Under this explanation, the general absence of appeal courts in private arbitration systems implies that user-monitoring of arbitration decisions is sufficiently precise that users do not feel the need to establish an appeal procedure.[32] Appeal procedures only need to be used when users are not free to select their own arbitrators and, therefore, inefficient arbitrators are able to survive.

Finally, it should be noted that it is not clear that public arbitrators will produce clear, consistent decisions. Arthurs,[33] for example, suggests that the widespread use of commercial arbitration in the nineteenth century arose, at least in part, from the failure of the common law courts to behave in a predictable manner. And Bonn reports that lawyers experienced in the handling of (commercial) claims in the textile industry found that 'the decision of an arbitrator was by far the "most predictable", that a judge's decision was "predictable at some but not all times", and that a jury's decision was "virtually one of pure chance".'[34]

To conclude, the experience of labour arbitration in North America strongly suggests that private arbitration systems are at least as capable of producing consistent, evolving sets of precedential rules as are public arbitration systems. Thus, if one of these systems is to be proven superior to the other it must be on the basis of a different criterion than the one emphasised by Landes and Posner.

(b) *Quality of decisions*: We argued above that the quality of the decisions rendered by private arbitrators could be expected to be superior to that rendered by the employees of a public arbitration service. Three reasons were offered: First, the government would be less able to monitor the quality of decisions than would the users of arbitral services and, therefore, would be less able to discipline arbitrators who provided low-quality decisions, or reward arbitrators who provided high-quality decisions, than would the market. Second, we argued that voter pressure would force the government to set ceilings on arbitrator salaries, thereby reducing the incentives for public sector arbitrators to be innovative. And, third, as the government would be unable to obtain accurate measures of arbitrator productivity, it could be expected to impose constraints upon the actions of its arbitrators. Although these constraints might act to prevent malfeasance in certain circumstances, it is also possible that they would prevent arbitrators from following the optimal course of action in others.

The ideal test of these hypotheses would be to allow negotiators to choose between private and public arbitrators and then to observe which they selected. Unfortunately, there are very few jurisdictions in which this choice is offered, and most of those contain provisions which introduce biases into the selection process.[35] For example, Hayford and Pegnetter[36] found that in all of the seventeen civil service union contracts which they studied, labour and management had rejected the available government-run appeals procedures in favour of arbitration by jointly selected neutrals. And Brookshire and Rogers[37] found that in a period of forty years the sixteen trade unions and numerous contractors working on Tennessee Valley Authority projects had chosen only fourteen times to have their interest disputes resolved by an arbitrator selected by the Secretary of Labor. In both cases, however, the unions were dealing with a government employer. Thus, their desire to avoid using public arbitrators may have derived more from their fear that the arbitrators had been selected for their pro-government views than from their view that public arbitrators in general would produce inferior decisions. On the other hand, these two experiences suggest that private arbitration may be preferred to public arbitration in that large percentage of cases in which the union represents civil servants.

Labour negotiators are also offered a choice of judicial forums in those cases in which statutory law duplicates the provisions of labour contracts. For example, in the United States, Title VII allows employees to press claims of discrimination in the courts. Yet, in a study of grievance arbitration decisions, Fletcher found

126 Rethinking labour–management relations

that neither 'employers nor unions appear reluctant to use the arbitration machinery [embodied in their contracts] to solve Title VII problems'.[38] Apparently, many employers and unions prefer to pay private arbitrators to hear their discrimination cases rather than to take those cases to a subsidised public court. It is not entirely clear, however, whether this choice is made because the parties preferred the decisions of private arbitrators to public; for, in the same article, Fletcher also notes that a Title VII action 'frequently consumes three years or more' in the public courts.[39]

A less direct measure of the relative qualities of public and private decisions might contrast interest arbitration in North America, where it is conducted by private arbitrators, with that in Australia, where it is conducted by government arbitrators. A number of pieces of evidence suggest that the Australian system may be inferior to the North American. First, although strikes are outlawed in Australia and although the vast majority of strikes which do occur last less than 10 days,[40] the number of days lost to strikes, per worker, is more than twice as high as it is in the United States.[41] The explanation which is universally offered for this phenomenon is that the Australian arbitration courts have consistently refused to introduce a grievance procedure into labour–management contracts.[42] As a result, workers who have a grievance often express their feelings by engaging in short, 'wildcat' strikes. Given the prevalence of these strikes, the strength of the feeling among commentators that most such strikes could be avoided if workers were to have a formal grievance procedure, and the near-universality of such procedures in North American contracts, one is drawn to the conclusion that the failure to provide grievance procedures represents a weakness of public arbitration in Australia.

In a similar vein, Kelsall has argued that the lower degree of strike severity in the Australian state of Victoria than in the state of New South Wales arose from the greater involvement of labour and management in the arbitration process of the former state than in that of the latter.[43] In particular, whereas arbitrators in New South Wales are full-time civil servants, Victorian 'wages boards' are composed of equal numbers of labour and management representatives chaired by a government-appointed neutral. Thus, the Victorian system allows the parties to exercise greater control over the arbitration process than does the New

South Wales system. In turn, the theory developed in this paper would predict that the Victorian system would produce more desirable outcomes and, therefore, fewer strikes than the New South Wales system – precisely the result observed by Kelsall.

Kelsall's result might also be explained by another failing of public arbitration which was predicted by the theory developed above. That prediction was that public arbitrators would not be allowed to specialise and that, as a result, they would produce decisions of lesser quality than would private arbitrators (who would not be so-constrained). In Australia, very little specialisation is allowed in those jurisdictions which rely on full-time civil service arbitrators; whereas those states, such as Victoria, which employ the more democratically oriented wage board system may each have over 200 specialist boards.[44]

Finally, the Australian governments have imposed numerous constraints upon their arbitration systems which can only act to restrict the flexibility of those systems and, therefore, the efficiency of their operations. For example, the qualifications for membership on many of the federal and state courts have been set in such a way that virtually all such members are lawyers.[45] Yet in the United States, where the parties are free to select arbitrators on the basis of perceived quality, only 51 per cent of arbitrators on the US Federal Mediation and Conciliation Service (FMCS) roster included law in their educational background.[46] Conversely, whereas the Australian federal legislation expressly prohibits lawyers from appearing as the representatives of parties at arbitration hearings,[47] Fleming found that in 60 per cent of FMCS arbitrations at least one of the parties was represented by counsel.[48] The Australian legislation also requires that certain cases be heard by a panel of three (or more) arbitrators;[49] whereas North American negotiators have the option of using panels of any size they wish. Finally, whereas Herrick found that 'the great bulk of [FMCS] arbitrators was between 47 and 75 years' old, with one as old as 85;[50] many Australian jurisdictions require that arbitrators retire at the age of 65.[51]

The evidence presented in this section is not conclusive with respect to the relative qualities of public and private arbitration. Nevertheless, it *is* consistent in its findings: that negotiators prefer private arbitration to public when given the choice, that public arbitration decisions in Australia suffer from faults which are not

128 Rethinking labour–management relations

found in less formal systems, and that the Australian government has chosen to impose constraints on its public arbitrators which the open market in arbitration services has not chosen to impose on North American arbitrators. At the very least, these findings are more consistent with the hypothesis that private decisions will be of superior quality to public than they are with the reverse hypothesis.

(c) *Cost*: It is not clear, from the model developed in this chapter, whether or not the public arbitration system will be more costly than the private. On the one hand, the model predicts that the public arbitration system will spend more on its capital budget and support staff than will the private system, as expenditures on these items in the private system will come directly out of the arbitrator-owner's profits. On the other hand, the model also suggests that private arbitrators may be able to command higher personal incomes than will public arbitrators. This results, first, because public sector salaries are easily monitored by both voters and the government. As neither of these groups can easily monitor arbitrator quality, the government can be expected to ensure that salaries do not become 'excessive' by setting ceilings on public sector salary scales. Second, we argued above (p. 121) that the preference which customers would express for arbitrators with established reputations would act as a barrier to the entry of new arbitrators into a private market. This barrier will allow established arbitrators to raise their incomes above their opportunity cost levels.

Considerable evidence is available to suggest that private arbitrators in the United States are paid more than their public sector counterparts. In the calendar year 1984, 1,087 American Arbitration Association arbitrators charged an average of $355.97 per day, which is the equivalent of $81,873.10 for a 230-day year.[52] The New York State Board of Mediation, on the other hand, paid its employees (who also act as arbitrators) $42,000 per year in 1986 – although a spokesman indicated that their arbitrators were relatively inexperienced[53] – and the Federal Services Impasse Panel paid part-time arbitrators only $300 per day (also in 1986).[54] Also, whereas FMCS panel arbitrators' fees averaged $299.62 per day in 1981;[55] the state of New York paid only $150 per day to its part-time arbitrators in 1979.[56]

On the other hand, the fees of private arbitrators include all of their office and secretarial expenses plus their fringe benefits;

whereas those expenses and benefits are incremental to the salaries of full-time government arbitrators. In the 1981 survey of FMCS panel arbitrators, to which we referred above, arbitrators charged their clients only $43.52 per day for expenses – an amount which was less than 15 per cent of their average daily fee. Unfortunately, no information is available concerning the non-salary costs of public labour arbitration services in the United States. However, we do know that the total cost of maintaining a US Federal Court judge is more than three times the cost of the judge's salary.[57] If this ratio should apply to the New York State Board of Mediation's arbitrators, inclusive of salary they would each cost taxpayers more than $126,000. This is well in excess of the $81,873 cost of American Arbitration Association arbitrators cited above, even if 15 per cent is added for expenses.

The evidence of this section suggests that private arbitrators in the United States earn more than their public sector counterparts. Some, but not all of this difference may be accounted for by the greater experience of private arbitrators. There is also some evidence to suggest that the remaining differential between the two groups is attributable to the costs of fringe benefits, office expenses, and support staff which private arbitrators pay from their fees but which are incremental to public arbitrator salaries.

(d) *The supply of arbitrators*: The theory developed above suggested that a private market might experience chronic shortages of qualified arbitrators. Indeed, in the 1960s and 1970s it was a common complaint of industrial relations experts that the United States did not have enough labour arbitrators. Recent evidence suggests, however, that this problem may have been overcome. First, Abernethy has reported that fully one half of those responding to a 1984 National Academy of Arbitrators question-naire had been members of that Academy for eight years or less.[58] Second, indirect evidence of increasing competition in the market for arbitration is provided by the observation that, in the United States, arbitrators' fees rose more slowly than professional incomes over the period 1962–1981. Whereas the average professional income increased approximately 2.75 times[59] over that period, FMCS panel arbitrators' fees rose only 2.30 times.[60] Finally, respected observers of the American arbitration market (for example, Prasow and Peters[61] and Kochan[62]) have recently made it clear that they believe 'the supply problems associated

130 Rethinking labour–management relations

with arbitrator acceptability are not only soluble but are well on their way to being resolved'.[63]

Conclusion

In the introduction to this section, we set out a number of criteria against which the success of an arbitration system could be measured. Specifically, we argued that such a system should encourage the production of settlements which were efficient, innovative, and equitable, and would also be expected to create a body of precedent which could be used by the parties to assist them in reaching their own settlements. Our theoretical and empirical analyses of public and private arbitration systems have led us to conclude that these goals would best be obtained if the resolution of labour–management disputes was left to private arbitrators who had been selected, without any government constraint, by the parties to those disputes.

With respect to efficiency, equity, and innovation, this conclusion was based primarily on the observation that governments are divorced from the milieu in which bargaining takes place. Accordingly, they must be much less competent than the parties themselves to determine what constitutes efficient, equitable, or innovative decisions or to be able to reward arbitrators when they produce such decisions. Furthermore, because governments are commonly perceived to be partisan in their dealings with labour and management, it will be difficult to convince the parties to a labour dispute that a government-directed arbitration service will act impartially.[64] Particularly with respect to government employees, therefore, the parties will prefer to select their own arbitrator rather than use one selected for them by the government.

With respect to the production of precedent, we have argued in this section that private arbitrators will have a strong incentive to allow their decisions to be published and an equally strong incentive to follow the decisions of other arbitrators, where those decisions are perceived to be fair and efficient. Furthermore, we have provided evidence to show that, where private systems of arbitration exist, publishing services have arisen which have made the decisions of arbitrators widely available.

Finally, we have also argued in this section that private arbitration systems cannot be expected to be more expensive than

The market for arbitration 131

public and that it is not likely that there will be a greater shortage of arbitrators in a private system than in a public. Thus, we conclude that the most desirable arbitration system is the one which contains the least government intervention and which offers the parties the greatest freedom to select their own arbitrators.

SELECTION OF ARBITRATION PROCEDURES

In most jurisdictions which impose compulsory arbitration, the government, or one of its agencies, identifies the dispute resolution procedures which are to be followed and will even establish the criteria according to which decisions are to be made. One set of reasons for rejecting this approach was set out in the preceding section where it was argued that public agencies would be less efficient in their operations, and produce outputs (i.e. dispute resolution procedures) of lower quality than private agencies. That argument was based primarily on the hypothesis that public agencies would be subjected to less discriminative monitoring than would their private counterparts. However, a number of additional reasons exist for arguing that private selection of dispute resolution procedures will be superior to the external, centralised imposition of those procedures.

First, as conditions and customary practices vary between sectors it may be desirable to vary dispute resolution procedures also.[65] For example, if an industry has a record of industrial conflict, the parties may consider it necessary to lay out a formal procedure in some detail – in spite of the lack of flexibility which this will provide them – and to impose a set of penalties for failing to reach agreement without the assistance of a third party;[66] whereas an industry with a record of industrial harmony may prefer a more informal procedure, with its greater flexibility and reliance on mutual trust. Similarly, whereas industries which are composed of homogeneous firms may wish to standardise the bases for dispute resolution – through the recognition of arbitral precedent, for example – industries composed of heterogeneous firms may find it necessary to instruct arbitrators to treat each dispute separately. The most direct method of allowing for these types of inter-industry differences is to encourage each industry, if not each firm, to develop its own procedures.

132 Rethinking labour–management relations

Second, if there is an alteration in the conditions governing industrial relations it may be desirable to change the dispute resolution procedure also. For example, an industry which had faced stable markets and little technological change may have developed an informal conciliation system which relied largely on custom. But if competition for markets should increase or if the industry should enter a period in which rapid changes in production methods were taking place, a more formal procedure for resolving disputes might become necessary. Or, if an industry's labour relations should improve it might wish to reduce the formality of its dispute resolution procedure in order to obtain greater flexibility. In these situations, the necessary changes would best be made by the parties involved rather than by a governmental agency both because labour and management would be the first to recognise that circumstances had altered and because the direction which those changes could be expected to take would be more easily recognised by the parties involved than by an external agency.

Third, a number of knowledgeable observers of the industrial relations system have suggested that labour and management will feel a greater responsibility for ensuring that dispute resolution procedures are followed if they have created those procedures themselves than if the procedures have been developed by a third party. For example, A.J. Marsh has argued that

> self-imposed regulation is more reliable in complex industrial relations, than rules which are externally imposed. . . . Decisions arrived at in voluntary procedures are more likely to be kept because only those who are to apply them know where the shoe is likely to pinch; they are thus likely to arrive at decisions which, however imperfect, are workable.[67]

Furthermore, there is some feeling that although a government agency could impose penalties in an attempt to force compliance with the procedures which it had laid down, labour and management would always be able to find ways to circumvent those procedures if they wished to. Clifford Donn, for example, argues that although

> penalties and rewards may be capable of enforcing the *letters* of the rules . . . conformity with the *spirit* of the rules lies beyond such control.[68] (emphasis added)

The market for arbitration   133

Finally, whereas a government agency may find that institutional forces constrain it from introducing experimental alterations in procedures, the large number of different procedures generated by a free enterprise system will provide a natural laboratory from which all parties will be able to select lessons for their own use.

To summarise, it is our view that it would be desirable to leave the parties to select their own dispute resolution procedures. This creates greater involvement in the process by the disputants; it encourages the competitive production of improved procedures; and it allows for greater flexibility within and between industrial sectors. A number of recent developments, in which greater control over choice of arbitration and arbitration procedures has been given to (North American) disputants,[69] provides some confirmation that these conclusions are shared by others.

PAYMENT OF THE ARBITRATION FEE

Under most existing arbitration systems the arbitrators' fees are paid by the party which selects the arbitrators – either the government or the disputants. But it would also be possible for the government to subsidise the fees of those arbitrators who had been chosen by the disputants or for the disputants to be charged for the services of government-provided arbitrators.

In our view the question of who should pay these fees hinges on the extent to which an arbitration award can be expected to provide benefits which cannot be captured by the parties to that award (in economic terms, external benefits). That is, if the parties responsible for the 'production' of arbitration awards are unable to capture the full benefits which those awards impart to society, some awards will not be 'produced' (i.e., the parties will settle voluntarily rather than go to arbitration) even though the social benefits of those awards exceed their social costs. In such cases, economists and lawyers would argue that the parties responsible for the production of arbitration awards should be subsidised in order to induce them to produce the socially desirable number of such awards. One method of providing this subsidisation would be for the government to pay the costs of arbitration.

Thus, three conditions are required before the subsidisation of arbitrators' fees can be considered to be economically justified:

first, arbitration awards must provide external benefits; second, the external benefits provided by arbitration must exceed those provided by the voluntary settlement of disputes; and, third, the parties to disputes must be unable to 'sell' their settlements to third parties. The first of these conditions is met in a number of senses: a particularly insightful decision reached by an arbitrator in one case may be useful in settling conflicts in subsequent, similar cases. Disputants who wish to select an arbitrator who is known to be impartial will be assisted if they are able to contrast the decisions which have been reached by different arbitrators in the past. Furthermore, negotiators who wish to determine whether they should offer concessions on their current positions may find it useful to determine how arbitrators have viewed such concessions in the past.[70]

It is less clear, however, that the second and third conditions will be met. Consider the second condition, that arbitration awards produce greater external benefits than do voluntary settlements. This condition is required because the government would not wish to provide incentives to disputants to enter arbitration if arbitration awards were found to be inferior to the settlements which the disputants would have reached themselves. But the overwhelming consensus of opinion among industrial relations experts is that arbitration awards *are* inferior to voluntary settlements,[71] primarily because arbitrators can never be as well informed concerning the disputants' situation as the disputants themselves. In this case, therefore, the government will not wish to encourage the parties to enter arbitration, but will wish to *discourage* them.

In some cases, however, it is possible that the arbitrator will be able to devise a solution which is superior to that which the parties would have reached themselves. For example, an experienced arbitrator may be able to apply the lessons he has learned from other, similar situations to the resolution of a particularly intractable bargaining problem; or, the antagonism between two parties may be so great that they may be unable to reach a 'responsible' agreement without the assistance of a third party. If the arbitrator's solution to such a problem had application elsewhere, therefore, it would be socially desirable to provide some incentive to the parties to seek arbitration. The question which would remain, then, is whether such an incentive could be provided through the operation of the marketplace or whether it would have to be provided by the government – for example, through government subsidisation of the arbitrators' fees.

It is our belief that the market will operate sufficiently well in this case that government intervention will be unnecessary. There are two ways in which a market for the sale of arbitration awards may be organised. First, if awards could be copyrighted, the parties to a dispute could sell information concerning their awards to third parties directly, or they could sell that information indirectly by offering it to a private company which published a digest of arbitration awards.[72] Alternatively, in a competitive market for arbitration services, an arbitrator who expected to be able to use the reputation he gained from a current decision in order to obtain employment in the future might be willing to offer his services in the current case at a fee which was less than the maximum he could demand. In effect, therefore, the disputants who employed him in the future would 'subsidise' those who employed him at the time he was creating precedent-setting decisions.

To summarise, there is no clear argument for state subsidisation of arbitrators' fees. As it is desirable in most cases that the parties settle their own disputes, any policy which encourages them to enter arbitration will be counter-productive. And in those cases in which the arbitrator is able to produce an award which is superior to that which would have arisen from voluntary settlement of the dispute, arrangements exist through which information concerning that award can be 'sold' to interested parties.[73]

PUBLICATION OF AWARDS

Publication of reasoning[74]

There is some dispute as to whether arbitrators should make public the reasoning behind their judgements. Those who object to publication of this reasoning are primarily concerned that previous decisions will come to be treated as forming *precedents*. It has been argued that the development of a set of such precedents, or case law, is inadvisable for six reasons:[75] (i) arbitrators may be deterred from tailoring their decisions to the disputes at hand;

136 Rethinking labour–management relations

(ii) publication of the arbitrator's reasoning may provide further grist over which the parties could argue, thereby prolonging and exacerbating the dispute; (iii) inappropriate precedents may be transferred from one situation to another; (iv) if the members of an arbitration panel have each supported an award for different reasons, publication of those reasons could confuse the issue and reduce the authority of the decision; (v) employers and workers may be deterred from using arbitration if they know that their disputes are to be 'aired in public'; and (vi) the arbitrator may be deterred from commenting on the issues as he sees fit.

Each of these arguments can be refuted, however. First, the argument that precedent will unduly constrain arbitrators in the making of future decisions represents a misunderstanding of the role which precedent plays in the common law. It is a well-recognised tenet of our legal system that the degree to which a precedent is binding is determined by the level in the decision-making hierarchy at which that precedent was established. Thus, for example, whereas in Canada or Britain a District Court judge or High Court judge respectively would find himself bound by a precedent established by the Supreme Court or Court of Appeal, he would treat a precedent set in another District or High Court as merely advisory. In an arbitration system, as there is normally no provision for the appeal of awards, there will be no hierarchy of 'courts' and, therefore, each arbitrator can be expected to treat the decisions of his fellows as non-binding. Instead, they will primarily refer to precedent in order to obtain information and to help them to crystallise their own thinking about particular issues.[76]

Second, the argument that publication of the reasoning behind an arbitration award will prolong the dispute fails to recognise the role which arbitration awards can play in avoiding future disputes. In many, if not most, disputes brought to arbitration there are a number of bases on which the award could be made. For example, in a dismissal case the arbitrator may decide to reinstate the employee either because the *grounds* for dismissal were found to be insufficient, because the *procedure* for dismissal was improperly constituted, or because the existing procedure was not followed correctly. If management is not informed of the reason for the arbitrator's decision, it could make changes to its hiring practices or dismissal procedures which were found wholly inappropriate.[77]

As a result, further disputes could be expected to arise in the future, which might equally be decided on unclear grounds, leading to even more disputes. Were the arbitrator to specify the reasons for his decision, however, management could alter its rules and procedures in a manner which was seen to avoid the behaviour which the arbitrator found unacceptable, thereby avoiding future disputes. Thus, rather than prolonging disputes, the provision of reasoning can be expected both to

> facilitate the settlement of disputes which had, in fact, occurred [and also to] prevent their occurrence; for the rights of the parties in any matter of difference would thus be indicated from the outset.[78]

Similarly, the argument that the establishment of precedent will lead to the inappropriate transfer of rules from one situation to another proves to be the very antithesis of what centuries of experience with the common law has led us to expect. That is, it is in situations in which *no* reasoning is offered that arbitrators are most likely to make inappropriate transfers of decisions from one situation to another inadvertently; for, in this case, neither of the disputants will be able to challenge the appropriateness of the arbitrator's reasoning. Indeed, the assumption that the potential for challenge from the disputants will avert the inappropriate transfer of precedents is so strong that Lord Amulree felt able to conclude that

> It is important that each case should be considered on its own merits and not by reference to facts and circumstances beyond the interest or concern of the parties. *Where no grounds of a decision are stated* it must often happen that the parties are left with insufficient assurance on this point.[79] (emphasis added)

Finally, each of the three remaining objections prove to be trivial. If publication of the reasoning of each of the arbitrators undermines the force of an award, it is necessary only to have the chairman write the decision alone.[80] Experience with the civil courts has shown that most individuals are not reluctant to discuss legitimate grievances in a public forum; and even if they were, this would merely provide a salutary incentive to them to reach their own agreements. Furthermore, it is not at all clear that it is desirable that arbitrators be encouraged to make statements to

138 Rethinking labour–management relations

unions and employers which could not be repeated in public; and even if such statements were desirable, it would appear preferable that they be made in private correspondence rather than in the arbitration award itself.

In addition to these counter-arguments there are a number of positive reasons why publication of awards would be desirable. First, if the parties to a dispute are to be encouraged to reach their own agreement they must share a common view as to the likely outcome of an arbitration hearing. For example, if each party overestimates the extent of the gain which it will be able to obtain through arbitration, neither side will be willing to make the concessions necessary to reach a voluntary agreement.[81] Therefore, knowledge of the bases on which arbitrators can be expected to make their awards will be essential to the operation of an industrial relations system in which impasses are settled by arbitration. Second, knowledge of the reasoning employed by arbitrators in previous, similar cases may be useful to bargaining parties if that reasoning 'increases the stock of knowledge and expertise about arbitration'[82] and, thereby, provides insights into the methods by which the parties might settle their own disputes. Third, if labour and management are to have confidence that arbitration can provide an impartial resolution of their disputes, they must be able to identify potential biases in arbitrators before the arbitration process begins. This requires that the previous decisions of individual arbitrators be available publicly. Finally, if there is to be competition between arbitrators to provide the best services, not only must they provide evidence of their abilities to produce equitable awards but there must also be enough arbitrators to provide a competitive atmosphere. The latter condition is much more difficult to achieve than it might first appear; for disputants will prefer to choose experienced arbitrators with proven records, thereby deterring the entrance of new arbitrators. One method of expediting this entrance would be to provide a bank of past decisions by respected arbitrators on which novice arbitrators could draw and, more importantly, which they could quote to give greater authority to their decisions.[83]

Payment for publication of awards

In those jurisdictions in which the government provides an arbitration service, the awards made by arbitrators are usually published by a government agency;[84] whereas in jurisdictions in which arbitration is conducted privately, the content of awards is usually released only to the parties concerned. As we argued on p. 138 that the publication of awards will confer benefits on third parties – that is, on future disputants – it might appear that the former practice is preferable to the latter. However, it can easily be shown that government subsidisation of publication costs is unnecessary. For if disputants are sufficiently interested in the reasoning underlying previous awards that the government would be justified in publishing a digest of those decisions, disputants would be willing to pay a private firm to provide such a publication. Furthermore, the amount which the publishers of a private arbitration digest would be willing to pay to obtain the results of a particular arbitration would be determined by the demand which its readers had evidenced for that type of decision. Thus, not only would the private publication of arbitration awards be economically feasible, but private publication would also ensure that excessive funds were not allocated to that activity.

PENALTIES

In this chapter we have argued that labour and management should be left free to select both their own arbitrators and their own arbitration procedures. In this section we wish to ask whether this freedom should extend to the parties' ability to select their own penalty structure to encourage one another to follow the prescribed procedures. That is, should it be the parties themselves, or should it be the government which establishes and levies the fines to be paid when one (or both) of the parties refuses to accept arbitration?

There are two reasons why we feel that the general assumption in favour of free market operations must be rejected in this case. First, assume that the imposition of compulsory arbitration would reduce the bargaining power of one of the parties relative to that of the other. That party would wish to minimise the penalties to be imposed for 'illegal' strikes or lockouts, as that would allow it to continue using the strike/lockout threat at little extra cost. If

140 Rethinking labour–management relations

that party's initial bargaining power was sufficiently strong it might be able to obtain agreement to a schedule of relatively low penalties. As a result, the goal of the compulsory arbitration provision would be denied.

More importantly, when selecting penalties for illegal work stoppages the firm and the union will be concerned only with the costs which those stoppages can be expected to impose upon *them*. No consideration will be given to the effect which stoppages will have upon third parties. Thus, from a social point of view, the penalties which would be chosen voluntarily by the two parties will be inadequate to deter all work stoppages for which the social costs of those stoppages exceed the social benefits (if any). For this reason, the government may have a legitimate role in the establishment of penalties.

However, if a system of compulsory arbitration is to operate effectively great care will have to be taken to ensure that both parties consider the penalties imposed to be fair. For this reason the use of statutory penalties will be inadvisable; for no statutory schedule will be able to anticipate all circumstances and devise the appropriate fine for each such circumstance. Instead, we would propose that the legislature simply outline the major criteria on which the calculation of penalties is to be based and then leave to the existing courts, or to a specially convened industrial tribunal, the task of tailoring the penalty to the specific circumstance. The reasoning of these courts on tribunals would then be made public in order that precedents could be established for the resolution of future disputes.

SUMMARY

In this chapter we have argued that the only roles which the government need take in the establishment of a system of binding arbitration are those of setting a legal requirement that certain groups settle their disputes through arbitration and of establishing a schedule of penalties to be imposed when this requirement is not met. We have also argued that all other aspects of binding arbitration can best be developed by the parties themselves. In the final two chapters of this book we will analyse a number of alternative institutional frameworks in order to determine which of them best meets these criteria.

Chapter 8

Wages councils

In the preceding three chapters we reviewed the most important characteristics of labour–management arbitration. In those chapters, we argued that arbitration could prove superior to the use of the strike as a method for resolving bargaining impasses. We also showed, however, that a wide diversity of techniques of arbitration is available. This leaves the question of whether any one of these techniques can be considered to be preferable to the others. It is this question which we take up now.

We begin our analysis of this issue by reviewing the operation of the system of Wages Councils which has been in place in Britain since the early years of this century. Our reason for initiating the analysis at this point is that the Wages Councils had many factors in common with a compulsory arbitration system. Therefore, an analysis of their operation may provide some insight into the manner in which a compulsory arbitration system might function and into the drawbacks which might be associated with such a system.[1] Because the Wages Act 1986 removed many of the arbitration-like powers which had characterised the Wages Councils over most of their history, we concentrate in this chapter on the operation of those Councils as they were constituted under the Wages Council Acts of 1945, 1959, and 1979. In the first section of the chapter, we provide a brief history of the operation of the Wages Council system. In the second, we apply to this system the four criteria which were developed in Chapter 2 – collective voice, efficiency, equity, and legal structuring – in order to identify its merits.

THE WAGES COUNCIL SYSTEM

Towards the end of the nineteenth century, the middle- and upper-classes of British society began to show increasing concern for the plight of the urban poor. One practice which drew particular attention was that of 'sweating', which a House of Lords committee defined as a combination of 'a rate of wages inadequate to the necessities of the workers or disproportionate to the work done, excessive hours of labour, and the insanitary state of the houses in which the work is carried on'.[2] Following a lengthy period of public debate, the Trade Boards Act 1909 was passed as an experiment to determine whether sweating could be controlled through the use of statutory instruments.

The 1909 Act established four separate Trade Boards to determine minimum time rates of wages and, if they wished, general minimum piece-work rates in each of: ready-made tailoring, paper box making, chain making, and machine-made lace and net finishing. These Boards consisted of equal numbers of employer and employee representatives together with three independent members appointed by the government. The wage minima which were to apply to each trade were selected by a vote of the members of the Board and were enforced by a government inspectorate.[3]

The initial experiment was sufficiently successful that a committee of Parliament (the Whitley Committee) recommended in 1917 not only that the Trade Boards system should be extended to all other sweated industries, but that this system should also encompass all low-wage trades or industries in which there was insufficient organisation to allow for the establishment of voluntary collective bargaining procedures. These recommendations were embodied in the Trade Boards Act 1918. Minor changes to this Act were then made in the Wages Councils Act 1945, which did little more than change the name of the Trade Boards to Wages Councils, and in the Wages Council Acts 1959 and 1979. Dramatic changes were made in the Wages Act 1986.[4] As it is the Wages Council system which existed prior to 1986 which is of greatest interest to us, we discuss the operation of this system first. A brief analysis of the 1986 changes is provided at the end of this section.

Pre-1986

The system which developed betwen 1909 and 1986 was one in which most low-wage workers had their wage floors established by one of the Wages Councils or Agricultural Wages Boards. Unlike their North American counterparts, these Boards did not restrict themselves to the establishment of only one or two wage minima. In 1980, for example, the Retail Bread and Flour Confectionery (England and Wales) Wages Council set separate wage minima for managers and manageresses, roundsworkers, assistant roundsworkers, transport workers, and 'all other workers'; workers in London, 'Provincial Area A', and 'Provincial Area B'; managers of shops doing a weekly trade of £160 to £740 (in £20 increments); and workers with 0–3 months' experience, 3–6 months' experience, and over 6 months' experience.[5] Other Councils differentiated on the bases of such factors as the size of motor vehicle which was driven[6] and the amount and type of education which had been received by operatives.[7]

Wages Councils were also empowered to set the duration of annual holidays, the number of 'customary' holidays (for example, Christmas Day, Boxing Day, and Easter), overtime rates, and severance pay. In addition, thc Councils could make recommendations to any government department with respect to industrial conditions affecting the workers and employers in its trade and the Department concerned was required to take such recommendations 'into consideration'.[8]

Typically, Wages Councils had ten to twenty members on each side plus three independent members, one of whom was designated as chairperson. As workers in the affected trades were generally not well organised, their representatives were usually selected by those trade unions which were most closely associated with the trade in question.[9] Turner and McCormick, for example, reported that restaurant workers were represented primarily by officials drawn from the Union of Shop, Distributive, and Allied Workers, the National Union of General and Municipal Workers, the Transport and General Workers' Union, and the National Union of Railwaymen.[10] As employers tended to be better organised, their representatives were generally chosen from trade associations such as, in the restaurant trade, the Caterers' Association, the Licensed Trade Defence Association, and the British Hotels and Restaurant Association.[11] The independent members, who were chosen by the Minister, were usually university professors or members of the legal profession.[12] In trades with a large percentage of women, one of the independent members was to be a woman.[13]

Although no regulations governed the times and places of meetings, most Councils established a pattern of meeting once a year. The majority of these meetings, except the Scottish ones, took place in London.[14] Partly as a result of the distance of these meetings from the average worker's place of employment, but also because of the lack of organisation among workers and employers, those who were affected by Wages Council orders had little opportunity to provide input into the initial round of negotiations. However, the Councils were required to make their decisions known to every employer and employee who could be expected to be affected by those decisions and to provide at least fourteen days for those parties to make written representations to the Council. Any such representations had to be considered by the Council and if, as a result of this consideration, the Council altered its initial decision, notice had to be given again to the affected parties.[15]

The only statutory regulations governing the method by which the Councils were to reach their decisions stated (i) that for a quorum there should be present at least one independent member and 'one third of the whole number of persons appointed by nominated employers' associations or trade unions';[16] and (ii) that the independent members would only cast their votes if the employer and employee representatives reached a deadlock.[17] Thus, dispute resolution procedures could, and did, vary among Councils. However, a close reading of the available literature indicates that most Councils adopted the following general procedures.[18]

First, in the early stages of discussion, the independents' role was primarily that of chairpersons. If no agreement was reached, they became actively involved as conciliators,[19] meeting with the two sides separately in an effort to obtain a voluntary agreement. If no agreement could be reached at the conciliation stage, the full Council reconvened and the independents cast the deciding vote. Because this left the ultimate decision to the independent members, their role in the last stage could be considered to have been that of an arbitration tribunal.

Wages councils 145

In this system, it was unusual for the independent members to put forward a compromise position of their own. Thus, the last stage of negotiations could not be likened to conventional arbitration; rather, it more closely reflected what, in Chapter 5, we called 'full-information, final-offer arbitration'. That is, if the independent members came to believe, in the conciliation stage, that no mutually satisfactory agreement was going to be reached, they announced whether it was the employers' or the employees' position (final offer) which they would support if the issue went to a vote – that is, the parties were kept 'fully informed' concerning the independents' preferences. Furthermore, the party whose final offer was not supported by the independents experienced considerable pressure to modify that offer. Indeed, the theory of bargaining under full-information, final-offer selection arbitration predicts that the pressures on the parties to modify their positions would be so great that most disputes would be settled without the independents (arbitrators) having to cast the deciding vote.[20] This hypothesis was supported in Bayliss's finding that in 1945 (the only year for which such data are available), 71 per cent (37 out of 52) of the settlements were achieved by agreement between the two sides.[21]

From this introduction it is apparent that, prior to 1986, British Wages Councils provided a rudimentary industrial relations system for those low-wage workers who would otherwise have had only limited access to a formal collective bargaining procedure. This system allowed for bargaining over a number of factors of interest to workers, including pay scales, vacations, piece rates, terms and conditions of employment, and overtime rates. It also provided a *de facto* form of binding arbitration for the resolution of impasses; and it provided for a limited amount of input from the affected workers.

Post-1986

The philosophy upon which the Wages Act of 1986 was founded was entirely different from that which had formed the basis of all of the preceding Wages Council statutes.[22] The premise which underlay the Trade Boards Act 1918 and the subsequent Wages Council Acts 1945, 1959, and 1979 was that all workers were to be provided with the benefits of collective bargaining. In those industries which were difficult to organise into formal trade unions, these benefits were to be provided through the institution of centralised regulatory committees – the Wages Councils. The Wages Act, on the other hand, is based upon the philosophy of the minimum wage – that the function of the Wages Councils is to combat poverty. Thus, whereas Wages Councils had previously set pay scales, vacation entitlements, and terms and conditions of employment for all workers within the covered industries; the Wages Act provides for the establishment of only a single minimum hourly rate of pay for all workers aged 21 or over within each industry (or a single minimum hourly rate for all hours worked in a week up to a maximum and a single minimum overtime rate for additional hours worked). No longer is the model one in which workers and employers meet on equal footing to settle the terms of employment of all workers within an industry. Instead, it has become one in which a paternalistic regulatory body imposes upon employers the requirement that they raise the wages of only those who would otherwise fall below the poverty line. It is for this reason that the provisions of the Wages Act cannot act as a prototype for the development of an arbitration-based system of collective bargaining and why, in the analysis which follows, we employ the provisions of the Wages Council Act 1979 for this purpose.

WAGES COUNCILS AS A SYSTEM OF COLLECTIVE BARGAINING

Collective voice

In Chapter 2 we argued that one of the most important functions of any system of industrial relations is to provide a means through which workers can collectively convey their views to their employers. This expression can achieve a number of objectives, including the reduction of alienation, the coordination of worker preferences, the gathering of information, and the enforcement of long-term 'implicit' contracts. Although Wages Councils were able to make a limited contribution to the achievement of these objectives, we submit that alterations could have been made to that system which would have improved its performance significantly.

Wages Councils were very poorly placed, for example, to provide any reduction in worker alienation. There was no provision in the Wages Council Acts for the establishment of grievance procedures; and workers were not permitted to bargain over many factors of importance to them, such as lay-off procedures, seniority provisions, and pension plans. Furthermore, with respect to those factors over which workers were allowed to bargain, no provision was made to identify worker preferences before the bargaining began. It was only after the first round of negotiations had taken place, and the Wages Councils had reached a tentative agreement, that any formal procedure was instituted to obtain worker input.

A further criticism of the Wages Council system was that no provision was made for workers to form their own organisations. Indeed, it could be argued that the presence of the Wages Councils acted to discourage the development of employee organisations, despite the introduction of Statutory Joint Industrial Councils (SJIC) which were intended to provide a 'half-way house' to full collective bargaining. By providing workers with some of the rudimentary elements of a collective bargaining system, the incremental benefits from organisation were lower than they would have been had there been no access to bargaining at all. The absence of labour organisations meant that there was virtually no means by which workers could coordinate their approaches to the bargaining process. It was up to the workers' 'representatives' to divine what the workers' preferences might be. Similarly, in the absence of formal organisations, it was extremely difficult for workers to coordinate the collection of information concerning the economy and their employers' bargaining positions.

Finally, it has been suggested that an important function of collective bargaining is to provide a means by which workers can enforce the terms of 'implicit contracts' with their employers. For example, they might wish to agree to accept relatively low wages during 'boom' periods in the economy in return for the implicit promise that they would not be laid off during recessionary periods. That the Wages Council system provided no means for enforcing implied contractual terms, therefore, represents a criticism of that system.

These criticisms suggest that it is not sufficient that a system of industrial relations provide workers with a means of obtaining

148 Rethinking labour–management relations

higher wages and improved working conditions. It must also provide some mechanism through which workers' preferences can be identified and, where those preferences are inconsistent with one another, through which compromises can be made in order to present a common front to the employer. In addition, workers must be able to submit grievances to their employers without concern for reprisals; and some control over non-pecuniary benefits, such as lay-off and promotion procedures, must be provided.

Efficiency

Like trade unions, Wages Councils may have influenced economic efficiency through their effects on labour productivity, profits, investment, unemployment, and inflation. With respect to productivity, it seems likely that these effects were not significant. Unlike trade unions, Wages Councils did not reduce worker productivity by setting direct constraints, such as 'featherbedding' rules, on the ability of employers to allocate their workers among tasks; but, equally, they provided no means by which worker productivity could be improved – such as by fostering worker–management collaboration.

The effects which both trade unions and Wages Councils have upon profits, investment, and inflation are felt through the influence which they have upon wages. As both act to increase wages, and costs, both can be expected to have the same effect upon each of these factors. Accordingly, following from the evidence which we reported in Chapters 2 and 3 with respect to trade unions, we conclude that Wages Councils reduced profits but had relatively little effect upon investment or inflation.

Finally, there is reason to believe that the British Wages Council system had a greater effect upon unemployment than a system of union–management bargaining would have. Whereas unions are able to bargain over both wages and employment, the Wages Councils could act only to increase wages. This implies that the empirical results with respect to trade union effects upon employment – which find that unions may have little effect upon either employment or unemployment – cannot be transferred to the analysis of Wages Councils. Rather, the effect of Wages Councils on employment can be expected to have been similar to that which arises in other countries when minimum wage laws are imposed. In all cases in which wages are increased, the costs to employers of hiring workers increase, and employers can be expected to reduce their demand for labour. When the wage has been increased by a union, this reduction in demand can be offset to some extent by the union's insistence that employment levels be maintained. But when the wage is increased by statutory (minimum wage legislation) or regulatory (Wages Council order) fiat, no counterbalancing force prevents employers from laying workers off. Thus, as the economics literature is virtually unanimous in finding that increases in wage minima lead to increases in unemployment,[23] it can be concluded with some confidence that Wages Council edicts also had the effect of increasing unemployment in Britain.

To summarise, we have concluded that Wages Councils and trade unions have similar effects on productivity, profits, investment, and inflation. Where they differ is with respect to their effects upon unemployment. Because Wages Councils had no control over employment, we conclude that the increases in wages which they imposed resulted in greater decreases in employment than would have resulted had similar increases been introduced through direct employer–employee bargaining. Hence, on this criterion, a Wages Council system can be considered to be inferior to a system based on true collective bargaining.

Equity

In Chapter 2 we argued that an industrial relations system can affect equity through four factors: improvement of workers' access to basic liberties, redistribution of income from capital to labour, and redistribution of income among workers according to considerations of both vertical and horizontal equity. In this section, we will suggest that with respect to access to basic liberties Wages Councils were inferior to collective bargaining based on either the strike or arbitration; that with respect both to the redistribution of income between workers and employers and to horizontal equity it is superior to collective bargaining based on the strike; and that with respect to vertical equity it has the same effect as most forms of collective bargaining.

Wages Councils were less successful in providing equal access

150 Rethinking labour–management relations

to basic liberties than are most forms of collective bargaining. They provided neither the means through which workers could complain to their employers without fear of reprisal nor the forums through which workers could raise social and political issues of common concern. Furthermore, Wages Councils were unable to overcome one of the primary criticisms of collective bargaining, that the views of the individual are subjugated to those of the majority. Indeed, because Wages Councils imposed conditions upon much larger groups of individuals than do collective agreements and because Wages Councils provided no means by which those affected could vote on wages and working conditions, it is to be expected that the views of the individual received less consideration under the Wages Council system than they would have in any system based upon collective bargaining.

Because strike-based bargaining requires greater cohesion of organisation than did representation to a Wages Council, the Wages Council system was able to extend bargaining rights to a larger number of workers than could a strike-based system. Accordingly, with respect to both the distribution of income between labour and capital and the horizontal distribution of income among workers, Wages Councils proved superior to strike-based bargaining. No similar conclusion can be reached with respect to the comparison between Wages Councils and arbitration-based bargaining, however. Because the degree of organisation required for arbitration is much less than that required for a strike, it is possible that an arbitration-based system of bargaining could provide coverage for as many workers as did the Wages Council system.

In the preceding chapters we argued that collective bargaining generally acts to reduce vertical equity. The reason for this is that in most bargaining units the wage structure is pyramidical, with a concentration of workers in the lower wage categories. Accordingly, in a democratic vote, the wishes of the low-wage workers predominate. To the extent, therefore, that these workers are motivated by self-interest, unions can be expected to prefer policies which compress wage differentials. It is possible that, as the worker representatives to Wages Councils were not democratically chosen, Wages Councils may have been less inclined to favour low-wage workers than are trade unions and, therefore, may have been better able to maintain horizontal equity. However, it should be noted that no empirical evidence to this effect is available.

What this analysis suggests is that the ability of an industrial relations system to influence equity is a function of two factors: (i) the percentage of workers to which it offers coverage; and (ii) the extent to which it is able to offer a forum in which workers can coordinate their views and organise their actions. On these bases, we conclude that the Wages Council system was inferior to an arbitration-based system of collective bargaining. Although these systems offer approximately the same capability of extending representation to most workers, the arbitration-based system clearly offers far greater facility for allowing workers to work in concert with one another and, hence, for allowing 'equal access to basic liberties'. It is less clear whether it can be concluded that the Wages Council system was superior to a strike-based system of collective bargaining. On the one hand, Wages Councils were able to extend representation to a far greater number of workers than could strike-based bargaining and, therefore, represented a superior means of redistributing income and obtaining horizontal equity. On the other hand, the Wages Councils provided no method by which workers' views could be collected and coordinated – indeed, it has been argued that the presence of Wages Councils discouraged the development of formal worker organisations – and, therefore, were less able than strike-based bargaining to provide workers with 'equal access to basic liberties'.

Legal structuring

Industrial relations systems may also provide an important benefit to workers by creating the circumstances in which workers can influence the development of both common and statutory labour law. Whereas individual workers will lack the knowledge and the finances to lobby for statutory changes or to mount appeals of common law decisions, trade unions can pool worker resources to undertake these tasks. Wages Councils, on the other hand, provided no means by which workers' views or finances could be mobilized. On this criterion, as with the criterion relating to the provision of equal access to basic liberties, therefore, the Wages Council system is seen to be inferior to both the arbitration- and the strike-based systems of collective bargaining.

SUMMARY

In Chapters 6 and 7 we suggested that an arbitration-based industrial relations system might be superior to other forms of worker-employer interaction – such as bargaining based on the strike threat or the operation of a free market in labour. What we did not consider in those chapters, however, were the specific details of how such an industrial relations system might function. One possible model for this functioning is the system of Wages Councils which was employed in Britain between 1918 and 1986. These Councils represented an advance on the strike-based system of collective bargaining in the senses (i) that they extended collective representation to a much larger group of workers than would have been possible under strike-based bargaining and (ii) that they introduced a method of dispute resolution which did not require the use of work stoppages. Relative to both the strike-based and arbitration-based systems of collective bargaining, however, the Wages Council system suffered from a number of drawbacks which, in our view, significantly weakened its attractiveness. Paramount among these drawbacks was the system's inability to encourage the establishment of worker organisations. In the absence of this development, workers had little input into the decisions which affected them and one of the major advantages of collective bargaining, the provision of a collective voice, was lost. Workers could not develop grievance procedures, they could not coordinate their approaches to their employers, and they could not enforce the terms of long-term implicit contracts with their employers. The lack of formal organisations also made it difficult for workers to fight for changes in laws and government policies – such as those concerning public education – which benefited both them and many less-advantaged groups in society. Finally, the restriction of Wages Councils' scope to wages and working conditions meant that they could not discourage employers from laying off workers when wages were raised.

For all of these reasons, we conclude that the Wages Council system cannot act as a model for arbitration-based systems of industrial organisation. It is not sufficient that arbitration be provided. Some method must also be devised by which workers can be encouraged to form groups for the purpose of collating information and lobbying for changes in social and legal policy. It is such a system which we will discuss in Chapter 9.

Chapter 9

The arbitration of industrial disputes: a proposal

The purpose of this study has been to argue that binding arbitration represents a viable alternative to the strike-threat system of industrial relations. In this concluding chapter we wish to outline the characteristics of the system of arbitration which we feel would best achieve the general goals of industrial relations.[1] Before doing this, however, we will first (i) suggest a number of criteria against which any system of industrial relations must be evaluated and (ii) identify the reasons why we believe that the arbitration schemes which have previously been introduced in Britain have failed.

THE GOALS OF INDUSTRIAL RELATIONS SYSTEMS

Throughout this book, we have argued that the goals of any industrial relations system must be to supply workers with the means to voice their concerns collectively, to encourage the efficient and equitable operation of the labour market, and to provide the conditions in which workers and employers have equal influence over the development of the legal system. It is our view that these goals will be achieved if the following criteria are met:[2]

(a) *Communication*: In Chapter 2, we argued that any industrial relations system must provide workers with a means through which their views can be represented collectively to their employers. This requires not only that workers be able to coordinate their approaches to their employer, but also that the two parties be encouraged to communicate with one another, to understand one another's problems, and, where possible, to resolve those problems

154 Rethinking labour–management relations

through mutual agreement.[3] Particularly in Chapter 7, we suggested that this can be achieved only if procedures for resolving disputes are left to be as informal as possible, as formality restricts the range of choices open to the parties and thereby closes options for communication.[4] (Where labour and management have historically had an unsatisfactory relationship, however, this goal may have to be compromised simply in order to bring them into contact with one another.) Furthermore, as tactics of confrontation and the use of force are anathema to an environment of communication and compromise, peaceful means of dispute resolution must be encouraged.[5]

(b) *Responsibility*: Parties which have voluntarily reached their own agreements can be expected to feel a greater responsibility for ensuring that those agreements are followed than those which have had settlements imposed upon them, either under threat of force or through third party intervention.[6] For, although force or the threat of penalties (from an external agency such as the government) can obtain compliance with the letter of agreements, conformity with the spirit of agreements lies beyond such regulation. Furthermore, where external agencies become involved, the parties can never be certain that decisions have been made on a completely impartial basis. When a suspicion of bias arises, the parties can be expected to refuse to participate in the negotiation process and the system will fail. Thus, the ideal industrial relations system should impose as few external constraints upon the parties' bargaining process as possible.

(c) *Flexibility*: Systems of dispute resolution should be flexible both *laterally* and *temporally*. Laterally, it is advantageous that each set of parties be allowed to devise its own procedures in order that those procedures can be matched to the parties' particular situations[7] and also in order that the experimentation which is essential for the evolution of new, efficient procedures can be carried out. Temporally, flexibility allows labour and management to alter their procedures as the industrial relations situation changes, as well as allowing them to adopt new techniques as they are developed elsewhere.[8]

(d) *Equity*: The improvement of equity is a fundamental goal of any industrial relations system. This goal has implications not only for the distribution of income *between* workers and employers, but also for the distribution *among* different groups of workers. For example, although the provision of bargaining rights to a particular set of workers may be considered to improve the distribution of income between workers and employers, at the same time it may reduce horizontal equity by increasing the incomes of some workers relative to those of others. Thus, equity requires both that bargaining power between workers and employers be equalised as much as possible *and* that all workers be able to share equally from the benefits of the industrial relations system.

(e) *Minimisation of external costs*: Those who are immediately involved in work go-slows, overtime bans, work stoppages, and other forms of industrial action are able to bring such actions to an end once they have decided that the incremental costs exceed the benefits. They do not need government protection against the consequences of their own decisions. However, third parties also experience the costs of industrial actions. Because they neither obtain significant benefits from such actions nor have any control over them, it becomes desirable that the government intervene on their behalf to keep the external costs of the industrial relations system at a minimum. As Donn has argued:

> The community has the right to insist that instances of industrial conflict which occur are necessary to make the system work and it should frown on conflict which does not help resolve problems.[9]

(f) *Lack of transitional friction*: Finally, if a new industrial relations system is to be introduced to replace one which has been in place for some time, resistance from labour and management can be expected – particularly from those parties which have obtained the greatest benefits from the existing system. Thus, it may be desirable to rank new systems according to their abilities to avoid transitional friction. In this respect, for example, it is our belief that a system which allowed the parties to build on, or at least to retain elements of, their traditional procedures would have a greater chance of success than one which attempted to introduce wholesale changes.

ARBITRATION PRACTICES IN BRITAIN

Although the arbitration of labour disputes is generally associated with Australia and the United States, this practice has an old and respected tradition in Britain as well. Before attempting to develop a model of arbitration to meet the criteria established on pp. 153–5 of this chapter, it will prove useful to reconsider very briefly a number of British systems of arbitration which either exist or have existed to determine whether any of them provides the basis on which that model could be constructed.

Employer conciliation – the York Agreement

From 1922, the engineering industry employed a dispute resolution procedure based upon the use of employer conciliation panels. In this procedure, which was originally established in the Agreement for Manual Workers, or the York Agreement, workers had the right to have their grievances heard by a succession of employers' representatives. That is, the employee initially took his case to his immediate supervisor. If he was not satisfied with the response at that level he was then empowered to refer successively to his head shop foreman, a Works Committee, a Works Conference, a Local Conference, and, ultimately, the Central Conference. At no stage in this procedure were the findings considered to be binding on either of the parties. However, both agreed that no strike or lockout would be initiated until the procedure had been exhausted.

Marsh and McCarthy[10] reported that this procedure was able to dispose of more than 95 per cent of the cases raised above the domestic level in the period 1955–1966. Furthermore, in a study of 125 cases referred to the York Central Conference in 1959, Marsh and Jones[11] found that only 19, or 15.2 per cent, had been subject to unconstitutional work stoppages. Thus, there is some evidence to indicate that the employer conciliation technique was able to reduce the incidence of strikes. However, two major criticisms of this technique remain. First, as the Conferences were composed exclusively of employers' representatives, considerable doubt must exist concerning their ability to reach decisions acceptable to both sides. Indeed, although the system as a whole was able to 'dispose of' 95 per cent of the cases considered by it, the Local and Central Conferences, which would have dealt with the most important cases, were able to dispose of fewer than 60 per cent of the cases brought to them. Furthermore, in a majority of these cases 'disposal' simply meant that the Conference referred the dispute back to the establishment from which it originated.[12] Second, that workers are unable to obtain an impartial hearing from a third party, or to impose sanctions directly, implies that the system will not be an effective method of reducing worker alienation. In the case of the engineering industry, this alienation would have been reinforced by the employers' consistent refusal to adopt a system of joint conciliation. To conclude, in our view the York Agreement of the engineering industry represents an inappropriate model on which to base industrial relations legislation. Because it placed workers in the position of supplicants before their employers, they would always question its impartiality and could be expected to mount concerted opposition to the introduction of any system based on that model.

Voluntary arbitration

A number of British industries have grievance procedures which resemble the York Agreement in the sense that workers are provided with a number of steps through which a dispute may be pursued and in the sense that both sides have agreed to forestall industrial action until all procedures have been exhausted. Agreements which include such clauses include those involving the Humberside Regional Joint Council for the Road Haulage (Hire or Reward) Industry,[13] British Home Stores and the USDAW,[14] The National Joint Council for Retail Pharmacy,[15] the Joint Industrial Council for the Wholesale Grocery and Provision Trade,[16] the Furniture Manufacturing Trade,[17] and the Retail Multiple Grocery and Provisions Trade.[18] However, these agreements differ from the York Agreement in that they provide for equal representation of workers and employers at the various stages of conciliation and also in that some provide for the possibility that unresolved disputes may be referred to an umpire or arbitrator.[19] In some industries the arbitrator is selected by the parties themselves, whereas in others the arbitrator is selected from a panel by the Advisory, Conciliation, and Arbitration Service (ACAS) or the Central Arbitration Committee (CAC).[20]

158 Rethinking labour–management relations

Thus, the procedures employed in these industries meet many of the criteria outlined on pp. 153–5. As these procedures have been developed by the parties themselves, some *responsibility* for the results is engendered and both lateral and temporal *flexibility* are maintained. Furthermore, the use of joint consultative committees encourages *communication* between the parties and reduces the degree of alienation felt by workers.

Voluntary arbitration, however, presents a number of problems which may prevent it from becoming generally applicable. The first, and most important, of these is that its continued success is dependent on the parties' perceptions that the use of arbitration does not significantly alter their relative bargaining powers. That is, as arbitration is voluntary, if one party feels that it consistently obtains less favourable decisions from an arbitrator than it would obtain from use of the strike threat it may choose simply to withdraw from the arbitration agreement. Thus, voluntary arbitration only *minimises external costs* in the unlikely event that the parties consider arbitration to offer them the same relative powers as does the strike threat. Second, because employers will normally enter voluntary agreements to arbitrate disputes only if unions are able to threaten work stoppages or other disruptions, weak unions and unorganised workers will be unable to obtain access to this form of dispute resolution. Thus, it is an ineffective method for obtaining *horizontal equity*.

Compulsory arbitration

In 1940 an Order in Council established a system of compulsory arbitration in Britain. Under this Order, strikes and lockouts were prohibited and parties were required to submit all unresolved disputes to the Minister of Labour. If the Minister was unable to obtain a voluntary agreement to a dispute he was required to submit it to a National Arbitration Tribunal (NAT). This Tribunal was composed of five members, of whom three were appointed members while the remaining two were chosen from panels established in cooperation with the Confederation of British Industry and the Trades Union Congress respectively. The decision of the Tribunal was binding on the parties in that it became incorporated into the individual contracts of employment between the firm and its employees.

Following the Second World War, the ban on strikes and lockouts became increasingly difficult to enforce, largely because the judiciary was unwilling to impose the available sanction, a prison sentence, on striking trade unionists. Accordingly, the ban was lifted in 1951 and a newly created Industrial Disputes Tribunal (IDT) was substituted to carry on a modified form of compulsory arbitration. With the exception of the removal of the ban on strikes, the IDT operated in a manner very similar to that of the NAT. That is, it was empowered to hear any case submitted by one of the parties to a dispute and it could make its decisions binding by incorporating them into the employment contracts of the workers concerned. The failure to ban strikes, however, led employers to oppose the IDT; for it was their contention that unions who had been unable to obtain the desired award from the Tribunal would simply call a strike in order to obtain that outcome through confrontation.[21] As a result, compulsory arbitration by the IDT was terminated in 1959.

In spite of its ultimate rejection, the compulsory arbitration system provided by the NAT and the IDT fulfilled two important functions. First, it provided a method whereby impasses could be resolved without the use of work stoppages. And, second, as this method of impasse resolution could be imposed by either party without resort to the strike or lockout threat, it provided bargaining power to previously weak employer and employee groups. For example, McCarthy[22] has argued that the NAT was used by NALGO (National and Local Government Officers' Association) to organise local government workers and that the IDT was used by weak employee groups more often than by strong groups.

However, the NAT and the IDT both failed because they did not deal in a satisfactory manner with the strike threat. Whereas the experience of the IDT indicates that retention of the strike is inconsistent with compulsory arbitration, the operation of the NAT indicates that if strikes are to be banned a socially acceptable method of penalising striking workers must be found. Furthermore, both the NAT and the IDT removed from the disputing parties the right to select their own arbitrators and their own system of arbitration. Thus, parties felt no *responsibility* for the awards which were produced and often reacted to unfavourable awards either by engaging in work stoppages or, more commonly, by calling for

160 Rethinking labour–management relations

a repeal of the compulsory arbitration system. Finally, although the IDT increased the power of previously weak groups, it accepted representations only from organisations which '"habitually" took part in the settlement of such terms and conditions, or which represented a "substantial proportion" of the workers or employers involved'.[23] Thus, as it was difficult to organise occupations composed of part-time and transient workers, these occupations were denied access to the arbitration process.

Wages councils

Unlike most other industrialised nations Britain has no minimum wage. Instead, the Secretary of State was empowered to establish Wages Councils in those industries or occupations in which the workers were considered to be too poorly organised to initiate collective bargaining themselves. Although these Councils were not normally thought of as arbitration panels, their operation shared many important characteristics with compulsory arbitration and, as such, merits attention here. (A more detailed analysis of Wages Councils was provided in Chapter 8, see pp. 141–52.)

Each of the Wages Councils was responsible for the establishment of *minimum* remuneration, standard hours of work, overtime provisions, customary and annual holiday provisions, and related matters within the industries and occupations covered by that Council.[24] Furthermore, Councils could establish different minima for men and women, for different districts and regions, and for different grades of workers. Each Council was composed of representatives of labour and management as well as containing three government-appointed 'independents'. In practice, the independents acted as conciliators unless the labour and management representatives could not reach agreement, in which case they acted as final-offer arbitrators on an issue-by-issue basis.[25]

Thus, Wages Councils provided employees in poorly organised occupations with at least some collective influence on their working conditions. Furthermore, they provided an improvement on the standardised wage minima of other countries in the sense that they were able to take into consideration differences in conditions across industries, occupations, regions, and age–sex groups. On the other hand, as an industrial relations system Wages Councils suffered from a number of defects. First, as they provided only minimum levels of remuneration they left a large number of workers unrepresented. Second, the number of issues which could be considered by Wages Councils was severely limited. For example, such important factors as safety conditions, promotions, pensions, and lay-off policies were left to the unilateral control of employers. Thus, Wages Councils were unable to deal satisfactorily with worker feelings of alienation. Third, as the structure of Wages Councils and the manner in which they operated was dictated by legislation there was no opportunity for those affected to influence the procedures by which they were governed. As a result, they felt no responsibility for the decisions of the Councils. Finally, the Wages Council system did not envisage that arbitration would be the final step in a progressively centralised process of mutual compromise between labour and management. Rather, the decisions of the Wages Councils were made in isolation, by a centralised committee[26] which may have had little contact with the workers it was supposed to represent.

COMPULSORY ARBITRATION

In Chapter 3 we outlined a number of drawbacks which are associated with the use of strike-based bargaining. These included disruption of the provision of essential services, reduction of worker and employer incomes, furtherance of inflationary pressures, failure to distribute income equitably *among* workers, and failure to provide assistance to the least-advantaged members of the labour force. In Chapters 6 and 7 we argued that most of these problems could be overcome if a system was introduced in which disputes were resolved through the use of arbitration. However, we also noted in those chapters that not all arbitration systems can be expected to perform equally well. For this reason it is proposed, in this final section, to outline a system which we believe offers the greatest chance for success. This proposal is presented in three parts. In the first we outline the government legislation which would be necessary. In the second, we identify a number of optional provisions which would contribute to the smooth functioning of the proposed system. And, finally, we measure our proposal against the six criteria identified on pp. 153–5 of this chapter.

The main proposal

The legislation which we envisage would contain five basic elements:

(a) *Selection of dispute-resolution procedure:* At the request of any employee group which meets the current definition of a bargaining unit, or at the request of any employer, firms would be required to enter into negotiations with their employees to establish: (i) a procedure for identifying, discussing, and resolving disputes over the construction ('interests') and interpretation ('rights') of the terms and conditions of employment; and (ii) a procedure for identifying, discussing, and resolving disputes concerning the modification of the procedures required in (i). In no case would these requirements preclude the possibility that the two sides might wish to cooperate with other workers and employers to create industrial, occupational, regional, or national procedures.

Requirement (i) is not intended to induce the parties to follow a course of action different from the one which most follow as a matter of course already. We include it primarily to emphasise our view that it is *imperative that the parties should be left to choose their own dispute-resolution procedures* and not have them imposed by the government. As we argued in Chapters 2 and 7, when the procedures or arbitrators are selected by an external agency over which one (or both) of the parties has no control, it is inevitable that suspicion will develop that the procedures are biased. When this occurs, that party can be expected to find it to its advantage to 'opt out' of the system, relying instead upon such extra-legal tactics as go-slows, wild-cat strikes, and punitive lay-offs.

Requirement (ii) has been introduced in order to meet a problem raised by Marsh and McCarthy,[27] namely that although many British industries have become saddled with dispute-resolution procedures which no longer suit their circumstances, unions and employers have been unable to reach agreement as to how those procedures should be modified.

(b) *Special dispute-resolution procedures:* The Secretary of State in Britain (or appropriate authority in other countries) should have the power to establish special dispute-resolution procedures in those industries or occupations in which workers are not sufficiently well organised to establish that machinery themselves.

The arbitration of industrial disputes: a proposal   163

These procedures will not necessarily follow a standard pattern but, wherever possible, will be modified to suit the circumstances of the industry involved. Furthermore, they will apply to all aspects of the employment relationship and will place special emphasis on the mutual resolution of disputes at the level at which they arise. Finally, the Secretary of State (or other authority) will be instructed to ensure that the employer and employee representatives to the dispute procedures are selected in a manner which is as democratic as is possible.

This recommendation calls, in the case of Britain, for the continuation of the Wages Council system in a modified form, rather than (at the time of writing) its proposed abolition. These modifications are intended to overcome what we perceive to be the four major failings of that system: that it does not cover all aspects of the employment relationship; that it provides no means of resolving disputes at the local level; that it does not allow for alteration of the dispute-resolution procedure to meet the requirements of different industries and occupations; and that it provides no assurance that the employer and employee members of the Councils are truly representative of their constituents.

(c) *Selection between strike and arbitration:* The procedures selected (see p. 162) must indicate that the ultimate method of resolving disputes is to be *either* a work stoppage *or* binding arbitration. No procedure may employ both and every procedure must include one of these provisions unless permission is first received from the Secretary of State (or appropriate authority).[28] Furthermore, in those cases in which the parties wish to use the strike or lockout option, permission for such a course must first be received from an independent commission – composed, in Britain, of representatives chosen by the Confederation of British Industry, the Trades Union Congress, and the Secretary of State and in other nations by the equivalent bodies – which would also be free to accept submissions from the government and the public.

Requirement (c) has a number of functions. First, it ensures that the parties to a dispute will possess the means to impose costs of disagreement upon one another, thereby encouraging the voluntary resolution of disputes. Second, it ensures that all disputes will reach *some* conclusion. Third, it avoids the problem encountered under the operation of the Industrial Dispute Tribunals that unions which were dissatisfied with arbitration awards were able to use the strike threat to overturn those awards. Finally, in recognition of both the fact that many sectors have developed harmonious relationships in the face of the strike threat and the fact that strikes can have important external effects, requirement (c) allows the parties to retain the strike threat only if they can convince an independent commission that retention of that threat would produce benefits which exceeded the costs.

(d) *Penalties:* Legislation would be introduced to provide financial penalties against those who had defied no-strike, no-lockout agreements. These penalties, payable to the government, would be equivalent (or greater) in value to the gains which the offending party had obtained through imposition of a work stoppage. For example, if a union had used a strike to obtain a wage increase which was 3 per cent greater than it had been awarded in arbitration, the government would tax those gains away from the individual workers who had benefited; and if an employer had used the threat of a lockout or layoffs to induce workers to work longer hours than had been provided by arbitration, the government would tax the firm an amount which was *at least* equal to the profits it had earned from those additional hours. Furthermore, in any situation in which the size of penalty was in dispute, the government would select the larger penalty in order to ensure that no benefit could be gained by circumventing the agreed procedures.

The purpose of this provision is not to penalise the act of striking (or locking out) *per se*, but to remove from the participants any gains which such an action might bring. Thus, whereas observance of the accepted procedure would hold out some possibility of gain at little cost, a work stoppage would offer no gains yet would impose the cost of lost wages and profits.

It might be argued that if parties are to be allowed to establish their own procedures for resolving disputes they should also be allowed to devise and enforce their own penalties. We have rejected this view because the party with the stronger bargaining power can often make the waiving of penalties a condition for the cessation of an illegal work stoppage. In our view, if labour contracts are to be enforced the penalties must be constructed and imposed by an impartial third party, such as the Secretary of State.

The arbitration of industrial disputes: a proposal   165

(e) *Roles of ACAS and CAC:* The Advisory, Conciliation, and Arbitration Service (ACAS) and the Central Arbitration Committee (CAC) in Britain are to be retained in their present forms.

Although we have stressed that labour and management should be free to choose their own arbitrators, there are a number of institutional reasons why a government-provided arbitration service might prove useful. First, until the requirements of condition (a) above have been met, labour and management will have no procedure for resolving disputes. The government may, therefore, wish to provide an arbitration service to assist them in developing those procedures. Indeed, as no group would have the right to strike at this stage, (as that right is dependent on condition (c)), it might be necessary to impose compulsory arbitration to ensure that condition (a) was met. Second, as there is not an extensive tradition of arbitration in Britain, disputants may initially find it difficult to identify an impartial set of arbitrators. To meet this need, the government may wish to offer the services of ACAS. Finally, even after the arbitration system has been operating for some time, some groups will have difficulty agreeing on the selection of the chairman of the arbitration panel. In these cases, they may wish to call upon an agency such as ACAS to recommend such an individual.

Finally, we wish to emphasise that our recommendation that certain parties be required to submit their disputes to arbitration does not imply that the arbitration procedures which they employ are to be dictated to them. That arbitration must be compulsory rather than voluntary (where it substitutes for the strike threat) results from the initial imbalances of power between different labour and management groups. Once the requirement to arbitrate has been imposed, however, there is no reason why the parties could not agree between themselves such issues as the method by which the arbitration process is to be initiated, the role of mediation, the number and selection of arbitrators to be used, the type of decision procedures to be employed by the arbitrator(s), and the role of precedent. Indeed, in Chapter 7, we argued at some length the advantages of self-selection of arbitration procedures. At the micro-economic level these included the ability of labour and management to tailor their procedures to the particular historical–institutional situation in which they found themselves, to adopt successful practices from

166 Rethinking labour–management relations

other sectors, and to alter their procedures in response to changes in their own industrial relations environment. In a broader sense, individualised choice of procedures allows for the experimentation which is necessary if new, efficient techniques are to evolve; it reduces opposition to the new system by removing a certain amount of compulsion; and it encourages the development of a class of independent, unbiased arbitrators by allowing arbitrators to offer their services in a competitive market.

Additional recommendation

One of the major drawbacks of a strike-based system is that the interruptions of services associated with work stoppages often harm the international competitive positions of firms and may also impose severe costs on the consumers of 'essential' goods and services. In spite of this, governments which are committed to the preservation of the strike-based system are unable to take steps to mitigate these costs, for the ability to impose 'costs of disagreement' is an integral element of that system. Under binding arbitration, however, there should be no need for work stoppages as the required costs of disagreement are internal to the arbitration process itself. Thus, if one of the parties to a binding arbitration procedure was to instigate a work stoppage in violation of that procedure, the government would be free to compensate the 'victims' of the stoppage without compromising the operation of the procedure. Indeed, the provision of such compensation might even strengthen the arbitration system in the sense that it would reduce the ability of the instigator of the work stoppage to impose (strike-based) costs of disagreement.

Furthermore, although we believe that there is no rationale for the standardisation of arbitration procedures across industries, some general principles do appear to apply and it may prove fruitful to summarise them here. First, for minor disputes, a single arbitrator is preferable to a panel because of the greater speed at which he can work. For major disputes, however, a tripartite board composed of two sidemen and a chairman is advantageous as each of the parties will be assured that at least one member of the panel will be fully apprised of its position. Second, the parties should inform themselves as fully as possible concerning the preferences of the arbitrator as this will enable them to reach their

The arbitration of industrial disputes: a proposal 167

own, efficient agreements. Third, in our view it is important that arbitrators publish the reasons for their findings as this provides a basis on which the parties can avoid or resolve future disputes and because it provides a means by which labour and management can select arbitrators. Finally, it is submitted that conventional arbitration is generally preferable to final-offer arbitration as the former avoids the possibility that the arbitrator will be forced to choose between two unacceptable offers.[29]

ARBITRATION AS AN INDUSTRIAL RELATIONS SYSTEM

In the opening section of this chapter six criteria were proposed against which all industrial relations systems could be measured. In this concluding section we wish to argue that the system outlined above meets all of these criteria.

(a) *Communication:* The industrial relations system outlined in this section encourages both communication between the parties and voluntary resolution of disputes by allowing the parties to tailor their dispute-resolution procedures to their own needs and by discouraging the use of confrontation tactics.

(b) *Responsibility:* It is our belief that most disputes which arise will be settled without resort to arbitration, thus placing responsibility for those settlements firmly with labour and management. But even when resort is made to the arbitration process, the fact that both the arbitration procedures and the arbitrator have been chosen by mutual agreement between the parties will provide a sense of responsibility for the outcome which is selected.

(c) *Flexibility:* Clearly, a system in which the parties are free to select their own dispute resolution procedures and in which explicit provision is made for the introduction of new procedures will allow for the tailoring of procedures to specific circumstances and for the evolution of new procedures to meet changing conditions.

(d) *Equity:* The current industrial relations system provides very little power to non-unionised workers or to groups who are unable to withstand lengthy strikes. Arbitration, on the other hand, can be extended to unorganised workers and, through the use of unbiased arbitrators, can be used to equalise the bargaining

168 Rethinking labour–management relations

powers of labour and management. Furthermore, whereas the strike-based system offers much greater bargaining power to some groups of organised workers than to others, arbitration offers all workers equal access to the industrial relations system.

(e) *Minimisation of external costs:* Although the imposition of compulsory arbitration cannot guarantee the cessation of industrial disruptions, through the provision of a framework in which the parties are encouraged to settle their disputes through cooperation rather than confrontation, it can be expected that hostility between labour and management will be reduced. Furthermore, in those cases in which the parties do agree to abide by the decision of an arbitrator rather than engage in strike activity, disruptions are by definition avoided.

(f) *Lack of transitional friction:* The system proposed in this chapter minimises transitional frictions by restricting its application to those sectors in which the benefits of arbitration are generally held to be the greatest and by allowing the parties to base their arbitration procedures on the dispute resolution procedures which they follow already.

CONCLUSION

Clearly no industrial relations system will be without its detractors. The system of binding arbitration proposed in this chapter is no exception. Any government which attempts to introduce this system can expect to encounter vigorous opposition. The transition period from the old system to the new will be a turbulent one. Nevertheless, we believe that the evidence presented in this work indicates that the long-term gains to be made from such a change would far outweigh the temporary costs. Furthermore, we also believe that an arbitration system in which the parties are encouraged to develop their own procedures will minimise short-term frictions while maximising the long-term benefits which arbitration can provide.

Notes

Preface

1 For an important exception, see Philip Bassett, *Strike Free* (London: Macmillan, 1986).

2 Examples of this may be seen in the British Employment Act 1980, s.17, the Trade Union Act 1984, ss. 10 and 11 as amended by the Employment Act 1988 and the Employment Act 1990.

3 For example, the teachers' bargaining machinery in England has been suspended, albeit on a temporary basis, and the government has taken over its role.

1 The origins of the strike-based system

1 See, in particular, Paul Rubin, 'Why is the Common Law Efficient?', *Journal of Legal Studies*, VI(1), January 1977, pp. 51–63; and Richard Posner and William Landes, 'Adjudication as a Private Good', *Journal of Legal Studies*, VIII(2), (March 1979), 281–98.

2 Sidney and Beatrice Webb, *The History of Trade Unionism* (London: Longmans, Green, & Co., 1894).

3 *Ibid.*, pp. 41 *et seq.*

4 The British wages council system is discussed in Chapter 8.

5 E.J. Hobsbawm, *Labouring Men*, 2nd edition (London: Weidenfeld and Nicolson, 1968), p. 7.

6 See Louis Adamic, *Dynamite*, Revised edition (New York: Viking Press, 1934), Chapter 2.

7 Robert Owen, a philanthropic cotton manufacturer, was an influential leader of the socialist/utopian union movements in Great Britain of the 1820s and 1830s.

8 See Pauline Gregg, *A Social and Economic History of Britain, 1760–1965*, 5th edition (London: George Hangs & Co., 1965), pp. 25–6.

170 Rethinking labour–management relations

2 'Perfect' collective bargaining

1 This definition implies that the parties have 'equal bargaining power', *if* it is presumed that equality of bargaining power will lead to maximisation of *joint* utility.

2 The concept of 'collective voice' was first developed by Hirschman and later expanded by Freeman and Medoff. See Albert O. Hirschman, *Exit, Voice, and Loyalty* (Cambridge, MA: Harvard University Press, 1970); and Richard Freeman and James Medoff, 'The Two Faces of Unionism', *The Public Interest*, 57 (Fall 1979), 69–93.

3 Lloyd Ulman and Elaine Sorensen, 'Exit, Voice, and Muscle: A Note', *Industrial Relations*, 23 (Fall 1984), 424–8.

4 See Paul Blumberg, *Industrial Democracy* (London: Constable 1968).

5 See F. Herzberg, *Work and the Nature of Man* (London: Staples), 1968.

6 See Ontario Quality of Working Life Centre, *QWL Focus* (various issues), Ontario Ministry of Labour.

7 See A.A. Thompson and I. Weinstock, 'Facing the Crisis in Collective Bargaining', *MSU Business Topics* (Summer 1968).

8 Research carried out by one of us (Carby-Hall) in a sample of four European Community countries, found that employees in both the public and private sectors wished to have a say in the management of the firms for which they worked. The percentages of employees expressing this desire were: in France, 94; in the United Kingdom, 93; in Belgium, 93; and in Luxembourg, 85. Furthermore, employees expressed a wish to experience a sense of belonging within the establishment – 89 per cent in Luxembourg; 83 in Belgium; 81 in France; and 73 in the United Kingdom. See J. Carby-Hall, *Worker Participation in Europe* (London: Croom Helm, 1977), pp. 15 *et seq.* and 26.

9 Cyril Grunfeld, 'Discussion', in Institute of Economic Affairs, *Trade Unions: Public Goods or Public 'Bads'?* (London: Institute of Economic Affairs, 1978), p. 109.

10 Philip Bassett (in *Strike Free*, London: Macmillan, 1986, p. 169) reports that there is some reluctance among employees at IBM (UK) to use the employer-established grievance procedure.

11 See Peter Doeringer and Michael Piore, *Internal Labor Markets and Manpower Analysis*, 2nd edition (Armonk, NY: M.E. Sharpe, 1985).

12 This suggests that it might be desirable to have multiple unions within an establishment, to provide a better representation of the views of the various types of workers employed there.

13 See, for example, Robert Hall, 'The Importance of Lifetime Jobs in the U.S. Economy', *American Economic Review*, 72 (September 1982), 716–24; and Doeringer and Piore, *supra* note 11.

14 See especially Gary Becker, 'Investment in Human Capital: A Theoretical Analysis', *Journal of Political Economy: Supplement*, 70 (October 1962), 9–49; and Walter Oi, 'Labor as a Quasi-Fixed Factor', *Journal of Political Economy*, 70 (December 1962), 538–55.

15 See Edward Lazear, 'Why is there Mandatory Retirement?', *Journal of Political Economy*, 87 (December 1979), 1261–84.

Notes 171

16 See, for example, Andrew Oswald, 'Unemployment Insurance and Labor Contracts under Asymmetric Information: Theory and Facts', *American Economic Review*, 76 (June 1986), 365–77.
17 Greg Duncan and Frank Stafford, 'Do Union Members Receive Compensating Differentials?', *American Economic Review*, 70 (June 1980), 355–7.
18 Greg Hundley, 'Things Unions Do, Job Attributes, and Union Membership', *Industrial Relations*, 28 (Fall 1989), 335–55.
19 Henry Farber, 'The Extent of Unionization in the United States', in Thomas Kochan, ed., *Challenges and Choices Facing American Labor* (Cambridge, Mass.: MIT Press, 1985) pp. 15–44.
20 A. Flanders, *Management and Unions* (London: Faber & Faber, 1970), p. 42. See also Albert Rees, *The Economics of Trade Unions* (Cambridge, England: Cambridge University Press, 1962), p. 195.
21 See Annette Davies, *Industrial Relations and New Technology* (London: Croom Helm, 1986), Chapter 3.
22 *Ibid.* p. 59.
23 *Ibid.* p. 47.
24 *Ibid.* p. 64.
25 Richard Caves, 'Productivity Differences Among Industries', in Richard Caves and Lawrence Krause, eds, *Britain's Economic Performance* (Washington, DC: Brookings Institution, 1980) pp. 135–98.
26 D. Gallie, *In Search of the New Working Class* (Cambridge, England: Cambridge University Press, 1978).
27 William Cooke, 'Improving Productivity and Quality Through Collaboration', *Industrial Relations*, 28 (Spring 1989), 299–319.
28 For a survey of this literature see John Addison and Barry Hirsch, 'Union Effects on Productivity, Profits, and Growth: Has the Long-Run Arrived?', *Journal of Labor Economics*, 7 (January 1989), 72–105.
29 *Ibid.*
30 Richard Freeman and James Medoff, *What Do Unions Do?* (New York: Basic Books, 1984), p. 183.
31 Kim Clark, 'Unionization and Firm Performance: the Impact of Profits, Growth, and Productivity', *American Economic Review*, 74 (December 1984), 893–919.
32 Barry Hirsch and Robert Connolly, 'Do Unions Capture Monopoly Profits?', *Industrial and Labor Relations Review*, 41 (October 1987), 118–36.
33 See Addison and Hirsch, *supra.* note 28.
34 See Clark, *supra.* note 31.
35 Alan Carruth, Andrew Oswald, and Lewis Findlay, 'A Test of a Model of Trade Union Behaviour: The Coal and Steel Industries in Britain', *Oxford Bulletin of Economics and Statistics*, 48 (February 1986), 1–18.
36 See T.E. MacCurdy and John Pencavel, 'Testing Between Competing Models of Wage and Employment Determination in Unionized Markets', *Journal of Political Economy*, 94 (June 1986), S3–S39; and James Brown and Orley Ashenfelter, 'Testing the Efficiency of

172 Rethinking labour–management relations

Employment Contracts', *Journal of Political Economy*, 94 (June 1986), S40–S87.

37 John Pencavel and Catherine Hartsog, 'A Reconsideration of the Effects of Unions on Relative Wages and Employment in the United States, 1920–1980', *Journal of Labor Economics*, 2 (April 1984) 193–232.

38 Steven Allen, 'Union Work Rules and Efficiency in the Building Trades', *Journal of Labor Economics*, 4 (April 1986), 212–42.

39 Edward Montgomery, 'Employment and Unemployment Effects of Unions', *Journal of Labor Economics*, 7 (April 1989), 170–90.

40 Montgomery, *ibid.*, also found that unions reduced the length of the workweek.

41 This hypothesis is often referred to as the cost-push hypothesis.

42 In the United Kingdom, the most common form of the inflationary initiation hypothesis is that a small number of relatively powerful unions initiate inflationary pressures and that other unions follow. This form of the hypothesis also leads to the prediction that in periods of union-induced inflation, union wages will rise relative to non-union.

43 See Derek Carline, 'Trade Unions and Wages', in Derek Carline, *et al. Labor Economics* (New York: Longman, 1985), pp. 198–200.

44 See H. Gregg Lewis, *Union Relative Wage Effects: A Survey* (Chicago: University of Chicago Press, 1986).

45 Orley Ashenfelter, 'Union Relative Wage Effects: New Evidence and a Survey of their Implications for Wage Inflation', in Richard Stone and William Peterson, eds, *Econometric Contributions to Public Policy* (New York: St Martin's Press, 1978), pp. 31–60.

46 Charles Mulvey and Mary Gregory, 'Trade Unions and Inflation in the UK – an Exercise' (Discussion Paper in Economics No. 22, University of Glasgow, 1977).

47 See Barry Hirsch and John Addison, *The Economic Analysis of Unions* (Boston: Allen & Unwin, 1986), p. 149; Carline, *supra* note 43, p. 197; and William Moore and John Raisian, 'Cyclical Sensitivity of Union/Nonunion Relative Wage Effects', *Journal of Labor Research*, 1 (Spring 1980), 115–32.

48 See R. Layard, D. Metcalf, and S. Nickell, 'The Effect of Collective Bargaining on Relative and Absolute Wages', *British Journal of Industrial Relations*, 16 (1978), 287–308.

49 Layard *et al.*, *ibid.*, presented two sets of estimates; one showed that the primary increase occurred over the period 1970–1972, the other over 1970–1975.

50 Many of the following arguments were made by Carline, *supra* note 43, pp. 213–15.

51 John Rawls, *A Theory of Justice* (Cambridge, Mass.: Belknap, 1971).

52 John Rawls, 'Some Reasons for the Maximin Criterion', *American Economic Review*, 64 (May 1974), 141–6, at p. 141.

53 *Ibid.* p. 142.

54 See, for example, R.T. Gill, *Great Debates in Economics, Vol. II* (Pacific Palisades, CA: Goodyear, 1976), pp. 55–112; and 'Symposium', *Quarterly Journal of Economics*, 88 (November 1974), 597–655.

55 We assume, in setting out this criterion, that any redistribution of income which has left the non-employed no worse off must not have been associated with such a large reduction in national income that those in the original position would reject that redistribution.

56 For a more detailed analysis of vertical and horizontal equity, as applied to collective bargaining, see David M. Winch, *Collective Bargaining and the Public Interest* (Montreal: McGill-Queen's University Press, 1989) 20–9.

57 See Richard Freeman, 'The Effect of Unionism on Fringe Benefits', *Industrial and Labor Relations Review*, 34 (July 1981), 489–509.

58 Beth Rubin, 'Inequality in the Working Class: The Unanticipated Consequences of Union Organization and Strikes', *Industrial and Labor Relations Review*, 41 (July 1988), 553–66.

59 Alan Caniglia and Sean Flaherty, 'Unionism and Income Inequality: A Comment on Rubin', *Industrial and Labor Relations Review*, 43 (October 1989), 131–7.

60 We know of no studies which have attempted to identify the effects of unions on horizontal equity.

61 In Britain there is a great deal of both common law and statutory law which govern their relationship. For example, the contract of employment and the status of the employee is primarily governed by the common law. The reciprocal implied duties of the employer and the employee are also common law based, as is the law of wrongful dismissal. Statute law also plays an important role in the relationship. The employee's right to maternity leave, redundancy payments, medical suspension, fair dismissal, and time off for certain activities are all governed by statute.

62 Marc Galanter, 'Why the "Haves" Come Out Ahead: Speculations on the Limits of Legal Change', *Law and Society*, 9 (Fall 1974) 95–160 .

63 This is readily seen in the British unfair dismissal legislation where a large proportion of cases are settled out of the tribunals.

64 Since the introduction in February 1972 (originally under the Industrial Relations Act 1971) of the law of unfair dismissal, some British employers are developing an expertise in unfair dismissal cases.

65 An example was the International Management Centre, Buckingham, having drafted on its behalf a Parliamentary bill.

66 Galanter's views are shared by many economists studying the legal system. See particularly Paul Rubin, 'Common Law and Statute Law', *Journal of Legal Studies*, 11 (June 1982), 205–23.

67 *Supra* note 62, p. 141.

3 The strike-based system

1 N.W. Chamberlain, *A General Theory of Economic Process* (New York: Harper & Row, 1955) esp. Ch. 6, 'Bargaining Power'.

2 Although we will deal explicitly with Chamberlain's model only, reference to Harsanyi's paper on Nash and Zeuthen bargaining

174 Rethinking labour–management relations

models indicates a close affinity among all three models. See J.C. Harsanyi, 'Approaches to the Bargaining Problem Before and After the Theory of Games', *Econometrica* (April 1956), 144–57; and F. Zethuen, *Problems of Monopoly and Economic Warfare* (London: Routledge & Sons, 1930) pp. 104–50.

3 Note: To this point we have not mentioned unions, employers, or strikes. The Chamberlain model is very flexible and can be used to analyse virtually any situation in which two parties bargain with one another – from situations of marital discord to those of international war. It will be seen in Chapter 6, for example, that Chamberlain's model provides a useful tool for the analysis of bargaining in the face of arbitration.

4 Utility is the term used by economists to measure 'happiness' or 'satisfaction'.

5 Price elasticity of demand is the percentage change in quantity demanded which results when the price of the product is changed, divided by the percentage change in price. If the percentage change in quantity is greater (lesser) than the percentage change in price, demand is said to be price elastic (inelastic).

6 To our knowledge, only anecdotal evidence is available concerning the argument that unions will be more successful in 'essential' industries than in 'non-essential'. The evidence concerning the hypothesis that the union/non-union differential will be higher in concentrated than non-concentrated industries is, at best, mixed – reflecting the theoretical weakness of the hypothesis. See H. Gregg Lewis, *Union Relative Wage Effects: A Survey* (Chicago: University of Chicago Press, 1986), pp. 154–5; and Barry Hirsch and John Addison, *The Economic Analysis of Unions* (Boston: Allen & Unwin, 1986), pp. 136–7.

7 Empirical studies find that unionism is significantly higher in industries which are dominated by large firms. See for example, George Bain and Farouk Elsheikh, 'An Inter-industry Analysis of Unionisation in Britain', *British Journal of Industrial Relations*, 17 (July 1979), 137–57; Colin Crouch, *Trade Unions: The Logic of Collective Action* (Glasgow: Fontana, 1982), p. 70; and Hirsch and Addison, *supra* note 6, pp. 61–2.

8 It has consistently been found that women and part-time workers are less likely to belong to unions than are males and full-time workers. Most commentators attribute these differentials to differences in labour force attachment among these groups. See for example, Crouch, *supra* note 7, p. 71; and Hirsch and Addison, *supra* note 6, p. 59.

9 The issue of the substitutability of replacement workers for striking workers is considered in some detail by Crouch, *supra* note 7, pp. 93–101.

10 Hundley has recently presented evidence to suggest that workers whose skills are specific to the firms and industries in which they work – that is, those with a considerable amount of 'on-the-job' training –

Notes 175

are more likely to belong to unions and have more bargaining power than are workers whose skills are easily transferred from firm to firm. See Greg Hundley, 'Things Unions Do, Job Attributes, and Union Membership', *Industrial Relations*, 28 (Fall 1989), 335–55.

11 Pradeep Kumar, Mary Lou Coates, and David Arrowsmith, eds, *The Current Industrial Relations Scene in Canada, 1988* (Kingston, Ontario: Queen's University, Industrial Relations Centre, 1988), p. 449.

12 See the references cited in *supra* note 8.

13 See the references cited in *supra* note 8.

14 See the references cited in *supra* note 7.

15 See Hundley, *supra* note 10.

16 'Industrial Stoppages in 1988', *Employment Gazette* (July 1989), 349–59.

17 If firms stockpile inventories in *anticipation* of strikes, the costs of storage and any excess of costs of production over normal costs must also be attributed to the strike threat system, *even if no strike is called.*

18 A considerable amount of evidence has been presented to suggest that production lost due to strikes in manufacturing industries can be recouped either through sale of inventories or through increased production following the strike. See Crouch, *supra* note 7, p. 89 (re: 1980 British steel strike); George Neumann and Melvin Reder, 'Output and Strike Activity in US Manufacturing: How Large are the Losses?', *Industrial and Labor Relations Review*, 37 (January 1984) 197–211 (re: US manufacturing); and Morley Gunderson and Angelo Melino, 'Estimating Strike Effects in a General Model of Prices and Quantities', *Journal of Labor Economics*, 5 (January 1987) 1–19 (re: US automobile manufacturing).

19 If it is assumed that the average worker works 240 days per year, of which he loses one half-day to strikes, strikes reduce his annual production by 0.208 per cent. (A similar conclusion was reached twenty years ago by T.G. Whittingham and B. Towers, 'The Strike Record of the United Kingdom: An Analysis', *Industrial Relations Journal*, 2(3), (Autumn 1971) 2–8.)

20 'Industrial Stoppages in 1988', *supra* note 16, p. 356.

21 *Ibid.* p. 354.

22 A.I. Marsh, E.O. Evans, and P. Garcia, *Industrial Relations in Engineering* (Oxford: Oxford University Press, 1971), p. 24.

23 Richard Caves, 'Productivity Differences Among Industries', in Richard Caves and Lawrence B. Krause, eds, *Britain's Economic Performance* (Washington, DC: Brookings Institution, 1980) pp. 135–98, see pp. 173–4.

24 *Supra* note 19, p. 6.

25 For eloquent arguments that trade unions in the United States are at least as democratic as the governments of most 'western' democracies, see Richard Freeman and James Medoff, 'The Two Faces of Unionism', *The Public Interest*, 57 (Fall 1979), 69–93, especially 88–90; and Richard Freeman and James Medoff, *What Do Unions Do?* (New York: Basic Books, 1984), pp. 210–13. A number of authors have also suggested that trade unions in the United Kingdom are fundamentally democratic. See Michael P. Jackson, 'Internal

176 Rethinking labour–management relations

Democracy', in *Trade Unions* (London: Longman, 1982) pp. 53–85; H.A. Clegg, *The System of Industrial Relations in Great Britain*, 3rd edition (Oxford: Blackwell, 1976), p. 112; and, on the Trade Union Act 1984, see J.R. Carby-Hall, *Recent and Future Developments in Labour Law* (Bradford: MCB University Press, 1989) and *Trade Union Democracy* (MCB University Press, 1984), pp. 2–5. See also Bryn Perrins, *Trade Union Law* (London: Butterworth, 1985), p. 14.

26 J.R. Carby-Hall (*The Juridical Nature of the Collective Agreement* (Unpublished Ph.D. thesis, University of Hull, 1986), pp. 122 *et seq.*) argues that the views of workers are not always adequately represented by their unions in collective bargaining. He suggests, however, a number of solutions in 'The Trade Union as Representative of its Members when Concluding Collective Agreements' in *Studies in Law*, University of Hull Law School Publication, 1991.

27 In the United Kingdom in 1986 the twenty-four unions which had over 100,000 members each accounted for approximately 80.8 per cent of the total union membership in the country.

28 See also Carby-Hall, *supra* note 26, pp. 118 *et seq.*

29 Many of the following arguments have been made by David M. Winch in *Collective Bargaining and the Public Interest* (Kingston, Ontario: McGill-Queen's University Press, 1989), pp. 77–80 and 94–7. See also Colin Crouch, *supra* note 7, pp. 68–71; and Greg Hundley, *supra* note 10.

30 *Supra* note 6, p. 156.

31 *Supra* note 6, pp. 149–51.

32 *Supra* note 6, pp. 139–46 and 156.

33 Orley Ashenfelter, 'Union Relative Wage Effects: New Evidence and a Survey of their Implications for Wage Inflation', in Richard Stone and William Peterson, eds, *Econometric Contributions to Public Policy* (New York: St Martin's Press, 1978) pp. 31–60.

34 See the provisions relating to the 'political objects' of the trade union and the expenditure of money for those and related purposes in the Trade Union Act 1913 s.3(3) as amended by the Trade Union Act 1984 and Employment Act 1990, s.5.

35 In Britain there is generally held to be no 'right' to strike, but rather only a 'freedom' to strike. This freedom emanates from various statutes which protect workers who act 'in contemplation and furtherance of a trade dispute' from liability in tort. The right to strike is seen as only a 'right to withdraw labour in combination without being subject to legal consequences' (Donovan Report, Cmnd 3623 (London: HMSO, 1968), para. 935). Bryn Perrins (*supra* note 25, p. 265), argues that 'if the worker cannot participate without breaking his contract, then he has no *right* to participate and to that extent the right to strike is abrogated'.

36 Ronald Dworkin, 'Liberalism', in Stuart Hampshire, ed., *Public and Private Morality* (Cambridge, England: Cambridge University Press, 1979), pp. 116–17.

37 Otto Kahn-Freund and Bob Hepple, *Laws Against Strikes* (London: Fabian Society (n.d.)), Fabian Research Series 305, p. 7.

Notes 177

38 A flamboyant example in Britain was the attitude of the Court of Appeal in a series of cases in the 'winter of discontent' and the late 1970s which limited the immunities available to striking workers. See J.R. Carby-Hall, *The Employment Act 1980 – A Means of Redressing the Balance* (Hull: Barmarick Publications, 1981), pp. 15–18 for a brief discussion of some of the more important cases. There also exist statutory limitations to the legal immunities. See J.R. Carby-Hall, *Industrial Conflict – the Civil Liability and Statutory Immunities of Trade Unions and their Officials* (Bradford: MCB University Press, 1987), particularly p. 20 *et seq.*

4 Possible modifications to the strike-based system

1 See J.R. Carby-Hall, *Industrial Conflict – the Civil Liability and Statutory Immunities of Trade Unions and their Officials* (Bradford: MCB University Press, 1987), where the civil and criminal liabilities and immunities of trade unions are discussed in some detail.

2 See *Simmons* v. *Hoover Ltd.* [1977] ICR 61 (EAT); *Wilkins* v. *Cantrell and Cochrane (GB) Ltd.* [1978] IRLR 483; *Haddow* v. *ILEA* [1979] ICR 202; and *Morgan* v. *Fry* [1968] 2 QB 710 (CA). In the latter, Lord Denning argued that where strike notice of adequate length is given, the strike is not unlawful and has the effect of *suspending* the contract of employment, a view which had been rejected by the Donovan Report, Cmnd 3623 (London: HMSO, 1968), para. 943 and which was also rejected in a series of subsequent cases, including the *Simmons* case (above). For a fuller discussion, see J.R. Carby-Hall, *The Law of Wrongful Dismissal* (Bradford: MCB University Press, 1986), pp. 4 and 5.

3 See, for example, *National Coal Board* v. *Galley* [1958] 1 All ER 91 and *Strathclyde Regional Council* v. *Neil* [1984] IRLR 14.

4 The employee on strike will also be affected by employment legislation so that if dismissed, he *may* not be able to sue for unfair dismissal (Employment Protection (Consolidation) Act 1978, s.62). See J.R. Carby-Hall, *Unfair Dismissal – Statutory Qualifications and Excluded Employment* (Bradford: MCB University Press, 1988), pp. 8 and 9. See also the Employment Act 1990, s.9(1) relating to unofficial industrial action.

5 See *Heath* v. *Longman Ltd.* [1973] ICR 402 and particularly Sir Hugh Griffiths who said (p. 410) that the 'overall purpose' of the 1978 legislation 'is to give a measure of protection to the employer if his business is faced with ruin by a strike. It enables him . . . if he cannot carry on business without a labour force, to dismiss the labour force on strike; to take on another labour force without the stigma of it being an unfair dismissal.' See also J.R. Carby-Hall, *Industrial Tribunal Procedure in Unfair Dismissal Claims* (Bradford: MCB University Press, 1986), p. 9.

6 See Roger Rideout with Jacqueline Dyson, *Rideout's Principles of Labour Law*, 4th edition (London: Sweet & Maxwell, 1983), Chapter 10.

7 See Alvin Goodman, *Labor Law and Industrial Relations in the United States of America* (Antwerp: Kluwer, 1984), Chapter V.

178 Rethinking labour–management relations

8 *Quebec Labour Code*, R.S.Q. 1977 C-27 as amended, s.109.1(a).

9 See, in Britain, the cases which came before the courts in the latter part of the 1970s, e.g. *Express Newspapers Ltd.*, v. *McShane* [1979] ICR 210 (CA); *Associated Newspapers Group Ltd.* v. *Wade* [1979] ICR 664; *United Biscuits Ltd.* v. *Fall* [1979] IRLR 110; *NWL Ltd.* v. *Woods* [1979] ICR 867; and *Beaverbrook Newspapers Ltd.* v. *Keys* [1978] ICR 582 (CA).

10 [1980] ICR 490 (H.L.)

11 Trade unions as democratic bodies are discussed by Bryn Perrins, *Trade Union Law* (London: Butterworth, 1985), pp. 14 *et seq.* and 99 *et seq.*

12 Statement by Mr Tom King, then Secretary of State for Employment, when introducing the Trade Union Act 1984.

13 Trade Union Act 1984, s.1(1)(a).

14 *Ibid.* s.1(1)(b) as amended by the Employment Act 1988, s.12.

15 *Ibid.* s.1(4).

16 *Ibid.* s.2(4)(a)(b).

17 *Ibid.* s.2(1)(5)(7)(8). See the discussion in J.R. Carby-Hall, *Recent and Future Developments in Labour Law* (Bradford: MCB University Press, 1989).

18 Trade Union Act 1984, s.3(1).

19 Employment Act 1988, s.14.

20 Trade Union Act 1984, s.10.

21 *Ibid.* s.11.

22 For a fuller discussion of trade union democracy, see J.R. Carby-Hall, *Trade Union Democracy* (Bradford: MCB University Press, 1984).

23 The miners' strike in 1985 in Britain, which led to the formation of a breakaway union (the Democratic Mine Workers' Union), is a recent example of this.

24 See LeRoy Marceau and Richard Musgrave, 'Strikes in Essential Industries: A Way Out', *Harvard Business Review*, 27 (May 1949), 286–92; N.W. Chamberlain, *Social Responsibility and Strikes* (New York: Harper & Row, 1953), pp. 279–86; and David B. McCalmont, 'The Semi-Strike', *Industrial and Labor Relations Review*, 15 (January 1962) 191–208.

25 Assume, for example, that firefighters agreed to continue working without pay. It is not clear what the employer-tax against their employer, the government, would be, nor to whom that tax would be paid.

5 Arbitration systems: a taxonomy

1 Much of the argument in this paragraph has been made by K.W. Wedderburn and P.L. Davies, *Employment Grievances and Disputes Procedures in Britain* (Berkeley: University of California Press, 1969). It should be noted, however, that there has recently been a move away from national and company-wide agreements in Britain, particularly in 'multiple food retailing, textiles, roadstone quarrying, cement, commercial broadcasting, . . . airports . . . merchant shipping . . . and the water industry'. (See ACAS *Annual Report*, 1988, p. 9.)

Notes 179

2 See, especially, Philip Bassett, *Strike Free* (London: Macmillan, 1986).

3 Leonard Rico, 'The New Industrial Relations: British Electricians' New-Style Agreements', *Industrial and Labor Relations Review*, 41 (October 1987), 63–78.

4 William M. Timmins, 'Arbitration in Political Campaigns', *Arbitration Journal*, 31(2), (June 1976), 77–89.

5 Duane H. Heintz, 'Medical Malpractice Arbitration: A Viable Alternative', *Arbitration Journal*, 34(4) (December 1979), 12–18.

6 Janet M. Spencer and Joseph P. Zammit, 'Reflections on Arbitration Under the Family Dispute Services', *Arbitration Journal*, 32(2) (June 1977), 111–22.

7 John Schlicher, 'The Patent Arbitration Law: A New Procedure for Resolving Patent Infringement Disputes', *Arbitration Journal*, 40 (December 1985), 7–18.

8 Dwight Golann, 'Taking ADR to the Bank: Arbitration and Mediation in Financial Services Disputes', *Arbitration Journal*, 44 (December 1989), 3–14.

9 See, however, the references in notes 2 and 3, *supra*.

10 In Britain, ACAS has reported that the percentages of disputes heard before a single arbitrator were: in 1983, 86% (151/176), 1984, 89% (158/178), 1985, 91% (135/148), 1986, 95% (164/172), 1987, 92% (123/133), and 1988, 97% (122/126). See ACAS *Annual Report*, 1983 to 1988.

11 For a detailed analysis of the advantages and disadvantages of tripartite arbitration, see Thomas Kochan, *et al.*, *Dispute Resolution Under Fact-Finding and Arbitration: An Empirical Evaluation* (New York: American Arbitration Association, 1979), pp. 97–100.

12 John Lockyer, *Industrial Arbitration in Great Britain* (London: Institute of Personnel Management, 1980), p. 47.

13 The state of New Jersey maintains a hybrid system in which the state-funded Public Employment Relations Commission (PERC) provides each party with a list of seven potential arbitrators. Each party is asked to strike up to three names from this list and to rank the remaining arbitrators in order of preference. The PERC assigns the arbitrator with the highest preference ranking from the combined lists. See Richard Lester, 'Analysis of Experience Under New Jersey's Flexible Arbitration System', *Arbitration Journal*, 44 (June 1989), 14–21.

14 The question of who should pay the arbitrator's fees is discussed in Chapter 7, *infra*.

15 Employment Protection Act 1975, sch. 1 Part III, para. 29(a), (b).

16 In Britain, the Employment Protection Act 1975 s.3(1) provides that where a trade dispute exists, or is apprehended, ACAS may, at the request of one or more of the parties to the dispute, and with each of the parties' consent, refer the matter to the CAC for settlement by arbitration. Section 3(2) provides, however, that in 'exercising its functions under subsection (1), the Service shall consider the likelihood of the dispute being settled by conciliation and where there

180 Rethinking labour–management relations

exist appropriate agreed procedures for negotiation or the settlement of disputes shall not refer a matter for settlement to arbitration . . . unless those procedures have been used and have failed to result in a settlement or unless . . . there is special reason which justifies arbitration'. (Similar requirements are in place with respect to mediation.)

17 Mediation provides a 'half-way' house between conciliation and arbitration. Whereas a conciliator helps the parties to the dispute to reach their own negotiated agreement by making suggestions where appropriate, the mediator also conciliates but, in addition, he is expected to make his own recommendations. These may be accepted by the parties, or may provide a springboard for further negotiations and an eventual settlement. The arbitrator's award, on the other hand, is final and binding upon the parties.

18 ACAS has commented that 'mediation/arbitration is particularly well-suited to complex, multi-faceted disputes in which the parties request arbitration-type assistance but want to retain the discretion to be able to resolve voluntarily some or all of the constituent parts of a wider problem.' See ACAS, *Annual Report*, 1987, p. 31. See also, ACAS, *Annual Report*, 1988, p. 23.

19 See Richard Lester, *supra* note 13, p. 18.

20 Mediation and arbitration were combined for the first time in Britain in 1987, in the BBC and the Broadcasting and Entertainment Trades Alliance (BETA) dispute concerning a proposed reduction in shift work and the method to be used to recruit additional supervisors. The mediator/arbitrator was able to secure some agreement between the parties on almost half of the issues in dispute. The remaining issues were resolved through an arbitration award. See ACAS, *Annual Report*, 1987, pp. 30–1.

21 The analysis in this section is taken from C.J. Bruce, 'The Role of Information Concerning the Arbitrator's Preferences', *Relations Industrielles*, 36(2) (1981), 386–402.

22 One such agency is the Pay Research Bureau of the Federal Government of Canada.

23 Kenneth F. Walker, 'Compulsory Arbitration in Australia', in J. Joseph Loewenberg *et al. Compulsory Arbitration* (Lexington, Mass.: D.C. Heath & Co., 1976), p. 21.

24 C.H. Rehmus, 'Is a "Final Offer" Ever Final?', *Monthly Labor Review*, 97(9) (September 1974), 44.

25 Sir John Wood, 'The Central Arbitration Committee – A Consideration of Its Role and Approach', *Department of Employment Gazette*, 87(1) (January 1978); cited in John Lockyer, *supra* note 12, pp. 109–10.

26 Typical of the general nature of the arbitration guidelines set by statute are the following from the Essential Services Dispute Act of British Columbia, Canada:

> 7.(1) . . . the single arbitrator or the arbitration board shall *have regard to*
>
> (a) the *interests of the public*
> (b) the terms and conditions of employment in *similar* occupations

Notes 181

(c) the need to maintain *appropriate* relationships . . . between different classification levels

(d) *any other factor* that the . . . arbitrator . . . considers relevant.

(Statutes of British Columbia 1977, c.83, emphasis added) In Britain, the CAC determines 'its own procedure' (Employment Protection Act 1975, sch. 1. para. 20).

27 We do not wish to imply that arbitrators are *able* to identify society's welfare function with any precision; only that that is the *goal* which conventional arbitration procedures implicitly set them.

28 In Britain, the Central Arbitration Committee found that a 'careful examination of cases shows that arbitrators do not in fact crudely split the difference . . . where awards do fall between offer and claim this is likely to be the result of an evaluation of a complex of different arguments: ability to pay, cash limits, labour market factors on the one hand versus comparability, cost of living, going rate arguments on the other' (Central Arbitration Committee, *Annual Report*, 1984, p. 18).

29 See M.H. Bazerman and H.S. Farber, 'Arbitrator Decision-Making: When are Final Offers Important?', *Industrial and Labor Relations Review*, 39 (October 1985), 76–89.

30 *Ibid.*

31 ACAS, *Annual Report*, 1984, p. 39.

32 *Ibid.*

33 See CAC *Annual Report*, 1984, pp. 18–19.

34 Gary Long and Peter Feuille, 'Final-Offer Arbitration: "Sudden Death" in Eugene', *Industrial and Labor Relations Review*, 28 (January 1975), 186–203.

35 Clifford Donn, 'Games Final-Offer Arbitrators Might Play', *Industrial Relations*, 16 (October 1977), 306–14.

36 V.P. Crawford, 'On Compulsory Arbitration Schemes', *Journal of Political Economy*, 87 (February 1979), 131–60.

37 Charles M. Rehmus, 'Varieties of Final Offer Arbitration', *Arbitration Journal*, 37 (December 1982), 4–6.

38 This procedure has been employed in Iowa. (See Daniel Gallagher and Richard Pegnetter, 'Impasse Resolution Under the Iowa Multistep Procedure', *Industrial and Labor Relations Review*, 32(3) (April 1979), 327–38.) It has also been employed in the British printing industry, where it is known as the Birkett method, after Lord Birkett. (See Seyfarth, Shaw, Fairweather, and Geraldson, *Labor Relations and the Law* (Ann Arbor: Graduate School of Business Administration, University of Michigan, 1968) pp. 117–18.)

39 John Magenau, 'The Impact of Alternative Impasse Procedures on Bargaining: A Laboratory Experiment', *Industrial and Labor Relations Review*, 36 (April 1983), 361–77.

40 *Ibid.*, p. 375.

41 For example, in Britain, the Employment Protection Act 1975, sch. 1, para. 19 provides that if 'in any case the Committee cannot reach a unanimous decision on its award the chairman shall decide the matter with the full powers of an umpire, or, in Scotland, an oversman'.

182 Rethinking labour–management relations

42 For example, in Britain, the CAC procedure in their arbitration awards is to identify the parties; state the terms of reference; give the background to the dispute; identify the main submissions on behalf of the union and the employer; give the general considerations; and make a declaration. See, for example, Award No. 88/1 (*Smith Meters Ltd. and MATSA*); Award No. 88/3 (*Mersey Probation Committee and National Association of Probation Officers*); and Award No. 87/4 (*Christian Salvesen (Ford Services) Ltd. and TGWU*).

6 The role of arbitration

1 Numerous studies have found that 'voluntary' agreements reached in the face of arbitration do not differ significantly from those which would have been imposed by an arbitrator. See especially, James L. Stern, Charles M. Rehmus, J. Joseph Loewenberg, Hirschel Kasper, and Barbara D. Dennis, *Final Offer Arbitration – The Effects on Public Safety Employee Bargaining* (Lexington, Mass.: D.C. Heath & Co., 1975), pp. 77–115; and John T. Delaney, 'Strikes, Arbitration, and Teacher Salaries: A Behavioral Analysis', *Industrial and Labor Relations Review*, 36 (April 1983), 431–46.

2 M. and M.L. Handsaker ('Arbitration in Great Britain', *Industrial Relations*, 1(1) (October 1961), 117–36), for example, find that the British use of joint industrial councils allows the unions and employers' associations to develop what Allan Flanders has described as 'a close relationship and interdependence' removed from the militancy of the rank-and-file workers (p. 129).

3 Hoyt N. Wheeler, 'An Analysis of Fire Fighter Strikes', *Labor Law Journal*, 26(1) (January 1975), 17–20; J. Joseph Loewenberg, Walter J. Gershenfeld, H.J. Glasbeek, B.A. Hepple, and Kenneth F. Walker, *Compulsory Arbitration* (Lexington, Mass.: D.C. Heath & Co., 1976), p. 165; James L. Stern, *et al., supra.* note 1, p. 189; Peter Feuille, *Final Offer Arbitration*, Public Employee Relations Library Series No. 50 (Chicago: International Personnel Management Association, 1975), pp. 10–11; and Peter Feuille, 'Selected Benefits and Costs of Compulsory Arbitration', *Industrial and Labor Relations Review*, 33(1) (October 1979), 64–76.

4 In a survey of the literature, Downie found that wage increases were approximately the same in jurisdictions which employed arbitration as in those which employed the strike. See Bryan M. Downie, *The Behavioural, Economic, and Institutional Effects of Compulsory Interest Arbitration* (Ottawa: Economic Council of Canada, Discussion Paper No. 147, 1979), pp. 47–50. A similar result was subsequently obtained by Delaney, *supra* note 1. Saunders, however, found that interest arbitration had had a slight depressing effect upon wage increases in the Canadian federal public service. See George Saunders, *Interest Arbitration and Wage Inflation in the Federal Public Service* (Ottawa: Economic Council of Canada, Discussion Paper No. 162, 1980).

5 In the *Iveco Ford Truck Ltd. and TGWU Award* (ACAS *Annual Report*,

Notes   183

1987, p. 32), the arbitrator had to choose between two positions in pendulum arbitration. He found in the company's favour, but commented that a compromise award was suitable in this case but that he was not empowered to order one. Although the parties implemented the pendulum award, a new agreement was subsequently reached which brought about the compromise suggested by the arbitrator. Although this was not strictly arb–med, its results were very similar. In *Hebridean Spinners Advisory Committte and TGWU* (ACAS *Annual Report*, 1986) the arbitrator adjourned the hearing to give both parties the opportunity to consider the compromise offer made by the employer. In this case, the parties did not agree and arbitration was resumed.

6 In Britain it often happens that the parties request an arbitrator who has experience in the field or the industry concerned. In *Rolls Royce Ltd. and AUEW (TASS)* (ACAS *Annual Report*, 1985), an arbitrator was appointed who had experience as an engineering apprentice, had shop floor experience, and had worked in the design department of an AEW-engine manufacturer, since the case required a person who had engineering knowledge and was familiar with technical authors' work and the use of manuals in operations. This may not only command confidence in the parties to the dispute, but also the arbitrator's experience in the field enabled the award to be disposed of quickly and efficiently. In this case, written statements weighing 15 pounds were considered by the arbitrator and this only took him a two-day hearing. Similarly, an arbitrator experienced in the textile industry was appointed in *Hebridean Spinners Advisory Committee and TGWU (ACAS Annual Report*, 1986). The parties specifically requested such an arbitratror because of the technical nature of the case.

7 Frederick Wheeler, 'Industrial Relations – A Public Service Point of View', *Journal of Industrial Relations*, 12(2) (July 1970), 145–65.

8 A.J. Geare, 'Final Offer Arbitration: A Critical Examination of the Theory', *Journal of Industrial Relations*, 20(4) (December 1978), 373–85.

9 See Peter Feuille, 'Final Offer Arbitration and the Chilling Effect', *Industrial Relations*, 14(3) (October 1975), 302–10.

10 J. Lockyer, *Industrial Arbitration in Great Britain* (London: Institute of Personnel Management, 1980), p. 106.

11 V.P. Crawford, 'On Compulsory Arbitration Schemes', *Journal of Political Economy*, 87 (February 1979), 131–60.

12 The following analysis is developed in greater detail in C.J. Bruce, 'The Role of Information Concerning the Arbitrator's Preferences', *Relations Industrielles*, 36(2), 1981, 386–402.

13 Recently, the CAC has commented that 'even where bargaining arrangements are well developed, there appears to be a possibility that a small group of workers can genuinely feel ignored. There is no guarantee that their trade union will insist on remedial action . . . and the employer himself may be reluctant to make changes. It appears convenient to put these matters to a third party' (CAC *Annual Report*, 1984, p. 14).

184 Rethinking labour–management relations

14 See, for example, A.V. Subbarao, 'The Impact of the Two Dispute Resolution Process in Negotiations', *Relations Industrielles*, 32(2) (1977), 216–33; and George Saunders, 'Impact of Interest Arbitration on Canadian Federal Employees' Wages', *Industrial Relations*, 25 (Fall 1986), 320–7.

15 W.E.J. McCarthy, 'Compulsory Arbitration in Britain: The Work of the Industrial Disputes Tribunal', in Royal Commission on Trade Unions and Employers' Associations, *Three Studies in Collective Bargaining*, Research Paper 8 (London, 1968), p. 37.

16 *Ibid.*

17 John T. Delaney, *supra* note 1, pp. 443–4. (Delaney does suggest that arbitration *may* have reduced dispersion slightly. The evidence is too weak to provide conclusive evidence, however.)

18 John Delaney, Peter Feuille, and Wallace Hendricks, 'Police Salaries, Interest Arbitration, and the Leveling Effect', *Industrial Relations*, 23 (Fall, 1984), 417–23.

19 A. Ponak and H. Wheeler, 'Choice of Procedures in Canada and the United States', *Industrial Relations*, 19 (Fall 1980), 292–308.

20 Richard Lester, 'Analysis of Experience Under New Jersey's Flexible Arbitration System', *Arbitration Journal*, 44 (June 1989), 14–21.

21 H.J. Glasbeek, 'Compulsory Arbitration in Canada', in J. Joseph Loewenberg *et al. supra* note 3, p. 60.

22 See, for example, Donald P. Crane and John B. Miner, 'Labor Arbitrators' Performance: Views from Union and Management Representatives', *Journal of Labor Research*, 9 (Winter 1988), 43–54 .

23 *Supra* note 20, p. 21.

24 K.G.J.C. Knowles, *Strikes – A Study in Industrial Conflict* (Oxford: Blackwell, 1952), pp. 5–6.

25 For evidence concerning the North American experience, see Orley Ashenfelter and David Bloom, 'Models of Arbitrator Behavior: Theory and Evidence', *American Economic Review*, 74 (March 1984), 111–24; Max Bazerman, 'Norms of Distributive Justice in Interest Arbitration', *Industrial and Labor Relations Review*, 38 (July 1985), 558–70; Max Bazerman and Henry Farber, 'Arbitrator Decision Making: When are Final Offers Important?', *Industrial and Labor Relations Review*, 39 (October 1985), 76–89; Henry Farber and Max Bazerman, 'The General Basis of Arbitrator Behavior: An Empirical Analysis of Conventional and Final-Offer Arbitration', *Econometrica*, 54 (November 1986), 1503–28; and Susan Schwochau and Henry Farber, 'Interest Arbitrators and their Decision Behavior', *Industrial Relations*, 27 (Winter 1988), 37–55.

In Britain, the CAC *Annual Report*, 1984, concludes that '[a] careful examination of cases shows that arbitrators do not in fact crudely split the difference. Where awards do fall between offer and claim this is likely to be the result of an evaluation of a complex of different arguments: ability to pay, cash limits, labour market factors on the one hand versus comparability, cost of living, going rate arguments on the other' (p. 18).

Notes   185

26 See Bazerman, *ibid*.; Bazerman and Farber, *ibid*.; and Schwochau and Farber, *ibid*.

27 See Bazerman and Farber, *supra* note 25, p. 86.

28 These penalties have been discussed by James E. Meade, in *The Fixing of Money Rates of Pay*, unpublished manuscript (Cambridge: Department of Applied Economics, Cambridge University, June 1979).

29 On the other hand, the use of fines has been partly responsible for the low strike incidence in New Zealand. See John M. Howells, 'New Zealand', in *International Encyclopedia for Labour Law and Industrial Relations* (Antwerp: Kluwer, January 1980).

30 In the United Kingdom, it is a breach of contract to go on strike. Further, legal immunities against a common law action for inducing breaches of contract, etc., are removed if the provisions of the statutes giving these immunities are not slavishly observed. See J.R. Carby-Hall, *Principles of Industrial Law* (London: Charles Knight & Co., 1969).

31 Of course, a particularly strong employer may be able to resist this pressure. The American government, for example, responded to the illegal strike of federal air traffic controllers in 1981 by firing all strikers. This policy may not be open to most private sector employers, however.

32 There is also the danger that pickets and strikers put in jail will become 'martyrs', as happened in the United Kingdom with the 'Shrewsbury six' in the early 1970s.

33 There are numerous references concerning the reduction in the incidence of strikes under arbitration. See in particular, Bryan Downie, *supra* note 4; Thomas Kochan *et al. Dispute Resolution Under Fact-Finding and Arbitration: An Empirical Evaluation* (New York: American Arbitration Association, 1979), p. 164; and Jeffrey Tener, 'Interest Arbitration in New Jersey', *Arbitration Journal*, 37 (December, 1982), 9–12.

34 Canadian examples include the strike of Ontario prison guards in the late 1970s and the strike of Alberta nurses in the late 1980s.

35 John Howells, *supra* note 29, p. 38.

36 The benefits which could be removed from registered unions need not be restricted to the ones mentioned above. It might also be possible, for example, to remove union immunity from common law actions.

37 In most circumstances, economists argue that the fine for undertaking an undesirable activity should equal the cost which that activity imposes on society. The rationale for this prescription is that a fine which exceeded the cost imposed by an activity might discourage firms or individuals from partaking in activities whose benefits exceeded their costs. For example, it would be inefficient to fine a polluter £1 million for pollution which produced costs of £500,000 and benefits of £800,000. However, this prescription does not apply in cases in which we are certain that we wish to prevent the activity in

186 Rethinking labour–management relations

question. To take an extreme case, as there are no social benefits from murder, economic theory would suggest only a lower, and not an upper, bound on the punishment of murderers. Similarly, as all of the socially desirable objectives which devolve from the use of the strike can also be obtained from the use of arbitration, there is no economic rationale for setting an upper limit on the penalties for the use of the strike.

38 The state of New York has had some success in the levying of penalties such as those suggested here. See L. Zimmer and J. Jacobs, 'Challenging the Taylor Law: Prison Guards on Strike', *Industrial and Labor Relations Review*, 34 (July 1981), 531–44; A. Peterson, 'Deterring Strikes by Public Employees: New York's Two-For-One Salary Penalty and the 1979 Prison Guard Strike', *Industrial and Labor Relations Review*, 34 (July 1981), 545–62; and Craig Olson, 'Strikes, Penalties, and Arbitration in Six States', *Industrial and Labor Relations Review*, 39 (July 1986), 539–51.

39 For example, the administrative costs of taxing each member of a large union may outweigh the benefits.

7 The market for arbitration

1 This prediction is strongly supported by the virtual absence of voluntary agreements to send interest disputes to arbitration. For one important British exception, see the discussion of the York Agreement in Chapter 9, pp. 157–8.

2 This problem is becoming more significant in Britain where the closed shop concept has been virtually destroyed by the Employment Acts 1988 and 1990. See J.R. Carby-Hall, *Trade Union Law* (Bradford: MCB University Press, 1990).

3 For example, the dockers' strike of July and August 1989 had a significant effect on the United Kingdom's international trade position.

4 As we noted in Chapter 5, there is a wide array of arbitration systems from which to select. Not all of these systems will prove equally effective in providing workers with collective bargaining rights. We contrast alternative arbitration systems in the remaining sections of this chapter and in Chapter 9.

5 This section draws heavily from Christopher Bruce, 'The Adjudication of Labor Disputes as a Private Good', *International Review of Law and Economics*, 8 (June 1988), 3–19.

6 We define an 'inefficient' decision to be one which *both* parties consider to be inferior to some alternative outcome. For example, rather than a 5 per cent wage increase coupled with a 10 per cent increase in employer contributions to a pension plan, both parties might prefer a 6 per cent wage increase coupled with no change in pension plan contributions. Thus, it is tautologically true that the parties would prefer an efficient outcome to an inefficient one, regardless of their views concerning distributional gains.

Notes 187

7 Lon Fuller, 'The Forms and Limits of Adjudication', in Kenneth Winston, *The Principles of Social Order* (Duke, N.C.: Duke University Press, 1981), pp. 87–124.

8 Melvin Eisenberg, 'Private Ordering Through Negotiation: Dispute Resolution and Rulemaking', *Harvard Law Review*, 89 (1976), 637–81.

9 William Landes and Richard Posner, 'Adjudication as a Public Good', *Journal of Legal Studies*, 8 (March 1979), 235–84.

10 J. Lockyer, *Industrial Arbitration in Great Britain* (London: Institute of Personnel Management, 1980), p. 86.

11 It has been suggested to us that there is a tension between the parties' desire for innovative arbitral decisions and their desire for consistent, precedent-following decisions. We believe that this tension is more apparent than real. On the one hand, there is no doubt that if a decision has been announced which negotiators agree is superior to all other known decisions, they will wish to ensure that arbitrators employ that decision. On the other hand, negotiators can be expected to be willing to experiment somewhat if they feel that there is some chance that arbitrators will be able to produce decisions which are superior to those which have been employed in the past.

12 Of course, many alternative forms of public involvement in arbitration are possible. We discuss a number of these, including Britain's system of wages councils and its Advisory, Conciliation, and Arbitration Service (ACAS) in Chapters 8 and 9. A number of other alternatives are also discussed in Bruce, *supra* note 5.

13 In developing the following model we have relied primarily upon: Thomas Borcherding, *Toward a Positive Theory of Public Sector Supply Arrangements* (Simon Fraser University, Toronto, Dept. of Economics, Discussion Paper 79–15–3, 1979); Borcherding, 'Toward a Positive Theory of Public Sector Supply Arrangements', in J. Robert Prichard, ed., *Crown Corporations in Canada* (Toronto: Butterworths, 1983) pp. 99–184; Louis de Alessi, 'The Economics of Property Rights: A Review of the Evidence', *Research in Law and Economics*, 2 (1980) pp. 1–48; P.M. Jackson, *The Political Economy of Bureaucracy* (Deddington: Philip Allan, 1983); and W.A. Niskanen, *Bureaucracy and Representative Government* (Chicago: Aldine, 1971).

14 Phillippe Nonet (*Administrative Justice*, New York: Russell Sage Foundation, 1969) chronicles the growth of the referees' office in the California Industrial Accident Commission (responsible for administration of workers' compensation) from that of an informal administrative position to that of a full-blown court of record with the associated salaries and trappings of office – including 'elevated benches for referees', 'dignified furnishings', 'proper acoustics', and 'private chambers located adjacent to the referees' personal hearing rooms' (p. 217).

15 Richard Posner, in a letter of 1 November 1985 to one of the authors (Bruce), and in his book *The Federal Courts* (Cambridge, Mass.: Harvard University Press, 1985, pp. 147–60), argues that it is desirable that judges do not specialise. He notes that specialist judges might

188 Rethinking labour–management relations

become bored; that it would be easier for a specialised court, consisting of only a few judges, to become 'captured' by one sociolegal school of thought than it would be for a more broadly based court; and that specialist courts might become centralised in a single city, such as Washington, DC, thereby reducing regional representation. These are all valid and important points. But they do not answer the central concern of this section. That concern is that if these benefits were to be outweighed by the benefits derived from specialisation, the government might yet prevent the courts from specialising – because, whereas the government can easily measure the benefits of non-specialisation outlined by Posner, it will encounter difficulty measuring the increased quality of arbitral decisions which specialisation would bring.

16 There is ample evidence from the literature on commercial arbitration to indicate that the parties to contract disputes will prefer arbitrators who have a long association with their industry to those who have less specialised knowledge. See for example, Soia Mentschikoff, 'Commercial Arbitration', *Columbia Law Review*, 60, (1961) 846–69 and Robert Bonn, 'The Predicatability of Nonlegalistic Adjudication', *Law & Society Review*, 6, (1971–2) 563–78.

17 This argument was suggested by a comment made by Armen Alchian in Victor Goldberg, 'Discussion by Seminar Participants', *Journal of Legal Studies*, 8, (1979), pp. 323–98.

18 *Supra* note 9.

19 See Christopher Bruce, 'The Role of Information Concerning the Arbitrator's Preferences', *Relations Industrielles*, 36, (1981), 386–402; and Henry Farber and Harry Katz, 'Interest Arbitration, Outcomes, and the Incentive to Bargain', *Industrial and Labor Relations Review*, 33 (1979), 55–63.

20 See Robert Cooter, 'The Objectives of Private and Public Judges', *Public Choice*, 41 (1983), 107–32.

21 *Supra* note 9.

22 These are: *B.C. Labour Relations Board Decisions* (Western Legal Publications), *Canadian Labour Relations Board Reports* (Butterworths), *Labour Arbitration Cases* (Canada Law Book), *Western Labour Arbitration Cases* (Continuing Legal Education Society of B.C.), and *Labour Arbitration News* (Lancaster House).

23 See Frank Elkouri and Edna Asper Elkouri, *How Arbitration Works*, 4th edition (Washington, DC: Bureau of National Affairs, 1985).

24 See Earl Palmer, *Collective Agreement Arbitration in Canada* (Toronto, Butterworths, 1978).

25 The citation index to Palmer, *ibid.*, lists approximately 1,700 arbitration decisions.

26 Paul Weiler, 'The Code, the Collective Agreement, and the Arbitration Process: As Seen from the Arbitration Board', in M.A. Hickling, ed., *Grievance Arbitration: A Review of Current Issues* (Vancouver, BC: Institute of Industrial Relations, University of British Columbia, 1977), p. 9.

Notes 189

27 Killingsworth, 'Twenty-five Years of Labor Arbitration – and the Future', in Barbara Dennis and Gerald Somers, eds, *Labor Arbitration at the Quarter-Century Mark* (Washington, DC: BNA Inc., 1973) 11, p. 18.

28 *Supra* note 23, p. 18.

29 See Herbert Heneman and Marcus Sandver, 'Arbitrators' Backgrounds and Behavior', in Barbara Dennis, ed., *Proceedings of the 35th Annual Meetings of the Industrial Relations Research Association* (Madison, Wisc.: Industrial Relations Research Association, 1983), pp. 216–26; Joseph Cain and Michael Stahl, *Academy of Management Journal*, 26(1) (1983), 140–7; K. Dow Scott and Stephen Taylor, 'An Analysis of Absentee- ism Cases Taken to Arbitration', *Arbitration Journal*, 38 (1983), 61–70; and Robert Rodgers and I.B. Helburn, 'The Arbitrariness of Arbitrators' Decisions', in Barbara Dennis, ed., *Proceedings of the 37th Annual Meetings of the Industrial Relations Research Association* (Madison, Wisc.: Industrial Relations Research Association, 1985) pp. 234–41.

30 *Supra* note 9, p. 241.

31 See D. Plowman, S. Deery, and C. Fisher, *Australian Industrial Relations* (Sydney: McGraw Hill, 1980), p. 146.

32 Note: Arthur Stark ('The Presidential Address', in Barbara Dennis, ed., *Truth, Lie Detectors, and Other Problems in Labor Arbitration* (Washington, D.C.: BNA Inc., 1979), pp. 1–29), cites a small number of situations in which trade union contracts have provided for the appeal of arbitral decisions. That the parties are *able* to construct such provisions, but generally have not done so, provides further evidence that they find appeal procedures unnecessary.

33 H. Arthurs, *Without the Law* (Toronto: University of Toronto Press, 1985), p. 85.

34 *Supra* note 16, p. 571.

35 The New York State Board of Mediation, the Federal Services Impasse Panel, the Federal Mediation and Conciliation Service, and the British Columbia Labour Relations Board all offer public arbitration services. But spokesmen at each of these organisations indicated to one of us (Bruce) that they do not encourage use of these services.

36 Stephen Hayford and Richard Peguetter, 'Grievance Arbitration for Public Employees', *Arbitration Journal*, 35, (1980), 22–9.

37 Michael Brookshire and Michael Rogers, *Collective Bargaining in Public Employment* (Lexington, Mass.: Lexington, 1977).

38 Betty Binns Fletcher, 'Arbitration of Title VII Claims: Some Judicial Perceptions' in James Stern and Barbara Dennis, eds, *Arbitration Issues for the 1980's* (Washington, DC: BNA Inc., 1982) pp. 218–29.

39 *Ibid.*, p. 220. On the other hand, the presence of these delays suggest that the public court system is less responsive to demand than is the private arbitration system.

40 See Plowman *et al. supra* note 31, p. 51.

41 Whereas Australia loses approximately 500 days per 1,000 worker years to strikes (Plowman, *et al. ibid.*, p. 60; and International Labour Office, *Yearbook of Labour Statistics*, various issues); the United States

190 Rethinking labour–management relations

loses approximately 250 (W.D. Wood and P. Kumar, *The Current Industrial Relations Scene in Canada* (Kingston, Ont.: Industrial Relations Centre, Queen's University, 1985), p. 386).

42 See, especially, Edward Sykes, 'Labour Arbitration in Australia', in J.E. Isaac and G.W. Ford, eds, *Australian Labour Relations: Readings*, 2nd edition (Melbourne: Sun Books, 1971), pp. 352–87.

43 E.P. Kelsall, 'Industrial Conflict in Australia', *Economic Record*, 35, (1959), 255–63.

44 Plowman, *et al.* (*supra* note 31, p. 155) reported that there were approximately 200 wages boards in Victoria. They also reported that in 1979 there were ten 'panels' of arbitrators in the federal Australian system. But each of these panels 'must deal with so many industries that adequate specialisation is difficult' (p. 124). For example, Panel 6 dealt with industries as disparate as cement manufacture, chemists, felt hatting, health inspectors, meat, municipal employees, and woolclassing, among many others.

45 Plowman, *et al.*, *ibid.*; and Kenneth Walker, *Australian Industrial Relations Systems* (Cambridge, Mass.: Harvard University Press, 1970).

46 John Herrick, 'Profile of a Labor Arbitrator', *Arbitration Journal*, 37, (June 1982), 18–21.

47 Plowman, *et al. supra* note 31, p. 127.

48 R.W. Fleming, 'The Labor Arbitration Process: 1943–1963', in Mark Kahn, ed., *Labor Arbitration* (Washington, DC.: BNA Inc., 1964), p. 40.

49 Plowman, *et al.*, *supra* note 31.

50 *Supra* note 46, p. 19.

51 Plowman, *et al.*, *supra* note 31.

52 Source: letter from Earl Baderschneider, Vice President – Publications, American Arbitration Association, 17 January 1986.

53 Source: telephone conversation with James McCabe, Mediator, New York State Board of Mediation, 13 March 1986.

54 Source: telephone conversation with Patrick Halter, Staff Associate, Federal Labor Relations Authority, 13 March 1986.

55 Robert Garrett, 'One Management Point of View', in James Stern and Barbara Dennis, eds, *Arbitration – Promise and Performance* (Washington, DC.: BNA Inc., 1984), pp. 29–36.

56 Thomas Kochan, Mordehai Mironi, Ronald Ehrenberg, Jean Baderschneider and Todd Jick *Dispute Resolution Under Fact-Finding and Arbitration* (New York: American Arbitration Association, 1979).

57 Chief Justice Warren E. Burger, 'Using Arbitration to Achieve Justice', *Arbitration Journal*, 40, (December 1985), 3–6.

58 Byron Abernethy, 'The Presidential Address: The Promise and the Performance of Arbitration: A Personal Perspective', in Stern and Dennis, eds, *supra* note 55, p. 1.

59 Source: US Department of Commerce, Bureau of the Census, *Statistical Abstract of the United States* (various years).

60 Fleming (*supra* note 48) reports that the average fee was $129.00 in 1962; while Garrett (*supra* note 55) reports that it had risen to $299.62 by 1981.

Notes   191

61 Paul Prasow and Edward Peters, *Arbitration and Collective Bargaining*, 2nd edition (New York: McGraw-Hill, 1983).

62 Thomas Kochan, *Collective Bargaining and Industrial Relations* (Homewood, Ill.: Irwin, 1980).

63 *Ibid.*, p. 400.

64 This argument applies only to those situations in which the government exerts direct control over the selection of the arbitrators and of the arbitration procedures. It would not apply, for example, to the Advisory, Conciliation, and Arbitration Service (ACAS) of Britain. In that system, arbitrators are selected, by ACAS, from a panel of private citizens and the arbitrators thus-chosen are free to select their own criteria for resolving disputes (Employment Protection Act 1975, s.3). Nor does it apply to the Central Arbitration Committee (Employment Protection Act 1975, sch. 1, Part II, para. 1412).

65 That differing conditions may produce the need to develop different procedures for resolving disputes is exemplified by the wide variations in such procedures across British industries. See, for example, A.J. Marsh and W.E.J. McCarthy, *Disputes Procedures in Britain*, Research Paper 2 (Part 2), U.K. Royal Commission on Trade Unions and Employers' Associations (London: HMSO, 1966); and K.W. Wedderburn and P.L. Davies, *Employment Grievances and Disputes Procedures in Great Britain* (Berkeley: University of California Press, 1969), Chapter 5.

66 If the parties have a poor record of industrial relations, they may find it difficult to reach agreement voluntarily. Yet agreements reached voluntarily are generally held to be preferable to those which are imposed by a third party, if only because a third party will not be as well-informed concerning the facts of the case as will the parties themselves. Thus, the parties may find it advantageous to employ an arbitration system such as final-offer selection (see pp. 85–8 of Chapter 5), which penalises them for failing to reach their own settlement.

67 A.J. Marsh, *Disputes Procedures in British Industry*, Research Paper 2 (Part 1), UK Royal Commission on Trade Unions and Employers' Associations (London: HMSO, 1966), p. 15.

68 Clifford P. Donn, 'Australian Compulsory Arbitration – Some Proposed Modifications', *Journal of Industrial Relations*, 18(4), (December 1976), 330.

69 See Allen Ponak and Hoyt Wheeler, 'Choice of Procedures in Canada and the United States', *Industrial Relations*, 19(3), (Fall 1980), 292–307; and David Bloom, 'Customized "Final-Offer": New Jersey's Arbitration Law', *Monthly Labor Review*, 103(9) (September 1980), 30–3.

It is also interesting to note, in this context, that one of the main reasons the majority of Canadian federal civil servants have chosen the conciliation-strike route in preference to binding arbitration is that the rules and procedures which the government requires arbitrators to follow are seen to be too constricting and inflexible. (See George Saunders, *Interest Arbitration and Wage Inflation in the Federal Public Service*, Discussion Paper No. 162, The Centre for the Study of

192 Rethinking labour–management relations

Inflation and Productivity, Economic Council of Canada, Ottawa, February 1980).

70 For example, assume that arbitrators are known to be reluctant to accept union 'packages' which include a demand for a 4 day week. The union may wish to avoid making such a demand in order to improve the probability that its other demands will be accepted.

71 For example, ACAS, in virtually all its Annual Reports, has consistently expressed this opinion.

72 Such privately published digests already exist in Canada and the United States. For Canadian references, see *supra* note 22. In the United Kingdom arbitration awards are reported sometimes in privately published journals (e.g., *Industrial Relations Law Reports* and *Industrial Relations Review and Report*). It should also be noted that some CAC awards are published and hold a Crown copyright.

73 An exception to this conclusion occurs when arbitration is voluntary; that is, when the parties are free to choose between the use of arbitration and the use of the strike. In this case one of the external benefits of arbitration will be that consumers of the firm's product (and suppliers of its inputs) will not be inconvenienced by a work stoppage. As these parties will have no means of 'bribing' disputants to take their case to arbitration, the government may wish to act on their behalf by offering to subsidise the costs of arbitration.

74 See the various CAC award structures which treat (i) the parties; (ii) the terms of reference; (iii) the background; (iv) main submissions on behalf of employers; (v) union submissions; (vi) general considerations; and (vii) the award.

75 The first four of the following objections are taken from a statement of the British industrial court, reported in K.W. Wedderburn and P.L. Davies, *supra* note 65 pp. 172–3; the remaining two are taken from J. Lockyer, *supra* note 10, p. 47. Points (ii) and (iv) were also raised by Sir George Honeyman in his submission to the Royal Commission on Trade Unions and Employers' Associations. (See Sir George Honeyman, 'Written Memorandum of Evidence', *Minutes of Evidence – 50* (London: HMSO, 1963), pp. 2166–7).

76 Even then, few arbitrators will find it worthwhile to refer to precedent. In a study of 250 American cases, Philip Harris found that arbitrators referred to previous decisions in only 76 instances. (Philip Harris, 'The Use of Precedent in Labor Arbitration', *Arbitration Journal*, 23(2), (June 1977), 26–34).

77 Marsh, for example, argues that the absence of formal dismissal procedures in British industry has resulted in a situation in which 'problems of dismissals ... are normally decided ... after a demonstration of strength by workers in the form of unconstitutional action'. (A.J. Marsh, *Disputes Procedures in British Industry*, Research Paper 2 (Part 1), UK Royal Commission on Trade Unions and Employers' Associations (London: HMSO, 1966, p. 18.)

78 Lord Amulree, *Industrial Arbitration in Great Britain* (Oxford: Oxford University Press, 1929); cited in John Lockyer, *supra* note 10, p. 52.

Notes 193

79 *Ibid.*, p. 82.
80 See also Employment Act 1975, sch. 1, para. 19.
81 This argument is developed, with respect to use of the common law courts, by Paul Rubin, 'Why Is the Common Law Efficient?', *Journal of Legal Studies*, 6(1), (January 1977), 51–63.
82 John Lockyer, *supra* note 10, p. 86.
83 This argument is due to Philip Harris, *supra* note 76.
84 See Employment Act 1975, sch. 1, para. 24.

8 Wages Councils

1 For discussions of the Wages Council system under the Wages Council Acts 1959 and 1979, see J.R. Carby-Hall, *Principles of Industrial Law* (London: Charles Knight & Co., 1969), pp. 159–75; and J.R. Carby-Hall, *Modern Employment Protection Law – Managerial Implications* (Bradford: MCB Publications, 1979), pp. 124–8.
2 Fifth Report of the House of Lords Select Committee on the Sweating System, H.L. No. 62, 1890, p. xliii; cited in F.J. Bayliss, *British Wages Councils* (Oxford: Blackwell, 1962), p. 2.
3 An uneven number of independents was appointed in order to ensure that there were no tied votes.
4 Subsequent to the consultative document published by the government in 1988, there appears to be a strong possibility that the complete abolition of the Wages Council system is imminent.
5 Retail Food and Allied Trades Wages Council (Great Britain), *The Wages (Retail Food and Allied Trades) (Amendment) Order 1980* – Schedule 1, London, 3 March 1980, pp. 2–5.
6 Transport workers in retail bookselling and stationery received different wage minima depending upon whether they drove a truck with a carrying capacity of 1 ton or less, 1–2 tons, 2–5 tons, or over 5 tons. See Retail Trades (Non-Food) Wages Council (Great Britain), *The Wages (Retail Non-Food Trades) (Amendment) Order 1980* – Schedule 1, London, March 7, 1980, p. 3.
7 Hairdressers, for example, had different minima for first- and second-year apprentices, college-trained students, shampooists, manicurists, managers, and non-apprentice hairdressers with less than one, two, and more than two years of experience. See Hairdressing Undertakings Wages Council (Great Britain), *The Wages (Hairdressing Undertakings) Order 1979*, London, 26 November 1979, p. 3.
8 Wages Council Act 1979, s.9(2).
9 Not all workers covered by Wages Council orders were non-unionised. Although most industries covered by these orders had very few unionised establishments, the orders applied to unionised and non-unionised workers equally.
10 H.A. Turner and B. McCormick, 'The Legal Minimum Wage, Employers, and Trade Unions: An Experiment', *The Manchester School of Economic and Social Studies*, 25 (September 1957), pp. 284–316, p. 309.

194 Rethinking labour–management relations

11 *Ibid.*, p. 308.

12 In 1961, of 180 independent seats on Wages Councils, 87 (48 per cent) were held by university professors, 41 (23 per cent) by members of the legal profession, 19 (11 per cent) by individuals classified as 'social welfare, settlement, and educational' workers, 15 (8 per cent) by ex-civil servants, and 18 (10 per cent) by 'others'. See F.J. Bayliss, *supra* note 2, p. 160.

13 C.W. Guillebaud, *The Wages Council System in Great Britain*, 2nd edition (Welwyn, Herts: James Nisbet & Co., 1962), p. 6.

14 Personal correspondence with T. Campbell of the Department of Employment, London, 23 September 1980.

15 Statutory Instrument 1975 No. 2138 (*The Wages Councils and Statutory Joint Industrial Councils (Notices) Regulations 1975*), Regulations 2, 3, and 5; and C.W. Guillebaud, *supra* note 13, p. 11.

16 Statutory Instrument 1975 No. 2136 (*The Wages Councils (Meetings and Procedure) Regulations 1975*), Regulation 2.

17 *Ibid.*, Regulation 3.

18 Information for the discussion which follows has been obtained from: C.W. Guillebaud, *supra* note 13, pp. 13–18; F.J. Bayliss, *supra* note 2, pp. 102–37; H.A. Turner and B. McCormick, *supra* note 10, pp. 304–7; D.J. Robertson, *Minutes of Evidence*, 44, Royal Commission on Trade Unions and Employers' Associations, Cmnd 3623 (London: HMSO, 1967), pp. 1903–5; and D.J. Robertson, 'Additional Memorandum of Wages Councils', *Selected Evidence Submitted to the Royal Commission*, The Royal Commission on Trade Unions and Employers' Associations (London: HMSO, 1968), pp. 654–5.

19 The independent members can be referred to as conciliators, rather than as mediators, in the sense that if no agreement was reached, they would not put forward a recommendation of their own.

20 See also C.J. Bruce, 'The Role of Information Concerning the Arbitrator's Preferences', *Relations Industrielles*, 36 (1981) 386–402; and H.S. Farber and H.C. Katz, 'Interest Arbitration, Outcomes, and the Incentive to Bargain', *Industrial and Labor Relations Review*, 33 (October 1979), 55–63.

21 See F.J. Bayliss, *supra* note 2. That 29 per cent of the decisions required a vote of the independent members may be due to the fact that many Councils settled their disputes on an issue-by-issue basis. Thus, even though most issues may have been decided without a vote, even if one issue was decided that way, Bayliss's figures would have shown that a vote was taken. (For evidence that an issue-by-issue approach was often used, see H.A. Turner and B. McCormick, *supra* note 10, pp. 305–6.)

22 See I. Smith and J.C. Wood, *Industrial Law*, 4th edition (London: Butterworths, 1989), pp. 418–21; and J.R. Carby-Hall, *Proposed Changes in Wages Legislation* (Bradford: MCB University Press, 1986), pp. 3–5.

23 For a recent review of this literature see Charles Brown, 'Minimum Wage Laws: Are They Overrated?', *Journal of Economic Perspectives*, 2 (Summer 1988), 133–45. See also Robert Meyer and David Wise, 'The

Notes 195

Effects of the Minimum Wage on the Employment and Earnings of Youth', *Journal of Labor Economics*, 1 (January 1983), 66–100.

9 The arbitration of industrial disputes

1 It should be noted that these characteristics are of a general nature and are not intended to apply to a particular country.

2 This list is adapted and extended from Clifford Donn, 'Australian Compulsory Arbitration – Some Proposed Modifications', *Journal of Industrial Relations*, 18 (December 1976), 326–36.

3 In Britain this has been the view expressed by both the CAC and ACAS in their various Annual Reports. See also the advice given in the ACAS Industrial Relations Code of Practice (1972), particularly paragraphs 51 to 70, where communicaton and consultation are treated in detail.

4 For example, see what the Industrial Relations Code of Practice has to say on this issue, particularly paragraph 121, which suggests that 'there should be a formal procedure, except in very small establishments where there is close personal contact between the employer and his employees'. See also paragraphs 126–9, which talk of arbitration being 'particularly suitable for settling disputes of right'.

5 See the Industrial Relations Code of Practice, paragraph 127 (iii).

6 Similar views have been expressed in Britain by ACAS in virtually all of its Annual Reports.

7 Indeed, in Britain, there is a statutory requirement under the Employment Protection (Consolidation) Act 1978, s.1, for the particulars of employment to be given to the employee within the first thirteen weeks of his employment, to contain, *inter alia*, the disputes procedures available in the establishment.

8 For a more detailed analysis of the advantages of flexibility see Chapter 7, pp. 131–3 of this study.

9 Clifford Donn, *supra* note 2, p. 331.

10 A.I. Marsh and W.E.J. McCarthy, *Dispute Procedures in Great Britain*, Research Paper 2 (Part 2) (Royal Commission on Trade Unions and Employers' Associations) (London: HMSO, 1968), p. 20.

11 A. Marsh and R.S. Jones, 'Engineering Procedure and Central Conference at York in 1959: A Factual Analysis', *British Journal of Industrial Relations*, 2 (June 1964), pp. 243–4.

12 Marsh and McCarthy, *supra* note 10, pp. 20–1.

13 Commenced 9 November 1979, as amended 15 December 1980.

14 In 1976.

15 Fifth Agreement relating to Pharmacists, 1980.

16 Signed by five employers and three trade unions .

17 January 1973, Clause 24(ii).

18 April 1980, Clause 6(b).

19 Details concerning these procedures may be found in K.W. Wedderburn and P.L. Davies, *Employment Grievances and Dispute*

196 Rethinking labour–management relations

Procedures in Britain (Berkeley: University of California Press, 1969) Chapter 5; and in Marsh and McCarthy, *supra* note 10.

20 Whereas ACAS selects its arbitrators from panels of external experts, the CAC selects its arbitrators from its own permanent employees. See Advisory, Conciliation, and Arbitration Service, *The ACAS Role in Conciliation, Arbitration and Mediation* (London: ACAS, 1989).

21 W.E.J. McCarthy was able to find only three cases in which it might be argued that unions had behaved in this manner. However, that it was possible that unions would be able to manipulate the IDT to their advantage was sufficient reason for the employers to question the IDT's impartiality and, therefore, to lose confidence in its ability to resolve disputes equitably. See W.E.J. McCarthy, 'Compulsory Arbitration in Britain: The Work of the Industrial Disputes Tribunal', in Royal Commission on Trade Unions and Employers' Associations, *Three Studies in Collective Bargaining*, Research Paper 8 (London: HMSO, 1968), pp. 40–1.

22 *Ibid.*, p. 37.

23 *Ibid.*, pp. 32–3.

24 Department of Employment, *Statutory Minimum Wages and Holidays with Pay: The Wages Councils Act Briefly Explained* (London: HMSO, June 1979).

25 See D.J. Robertson, 'Additional Memorandum on Wages Councils', in Royal Commission on Trade Unions and Employers' Associations, *Selected Written Evidence Submitted to the Royal Commission* (London: HMSO, 1968), p. 654.

26 Most Councils hold their meetings in London.

27 *Supra* note 10, esp. Chapter 7.

28 A similar recommendation has been made by John Niland, *Collective Bargaining and Compulsory Arbitration in Australia* (Kensington: New South Wales University Press, 1978).

29 Note also that if final-offer arbitration is to be avoided, the chairman of a tripartite arbitration panel must be allowed to impose a settlement without obtaining the agreement of either of the sidemen. (See Chapter 5, pp. 84–8.)

Cases and statutes

LIST OF CASES

	Page
Associated Newspapers Group Ltd v. *Wade* (1979)	178
Beaverbrook Newspapers Ltd v. *Keys* (1978)	178
Express Newspapers Ltd v. *McShane* (1979)	178
Haddow v. *ILEA* (1979)	177
Merkur Island Shipping Corporation v. *Laughton* (1980)	70
Morgan v. *Fry* (1968)	177
National Coal Board v. *Galley* (1958)	177
NWL Ltd v. *Woods* (1979)	178
Simmons v. *Hoover Ltd* (1977)	177
Strathclyde Regional Council v. *Neil* (1984)	177
United Biscuits v. *Fall* (1979)	178
Wilkins v. *Cantrell and Cochrane (GB) Ltd* (1978)	177

CHRONOLOGICAL TABLE OF STATUTES AND STATUTORY INSTRUMENTS

Trade Boards Act 1909	142
Trade Boards Act 1918	142, 145
Wages Council Act 1945	141, 142, 145, 147
Wages Council Act 1959	141, 142, 145, 147
The Wages Councils (Meetings and Procedure) Regulations (1975)	194
The Wages Councils and Statutory Joint Industrial Councils (Notices) Regulations (1975)	194
Wages Council Act 1979	141, 142, 145, 146, 147, 194
Wages Act 1986	141, 142, 145

Arbitration awards

CAC ARBITRATION AWARDS

	Page
Christian Salvesen (Ford Services) Ltd and TGWU	182
Mersey Probation Committee and National Association of Probation Officers	182
Smith Meters Ltd and MATSA	182

ACAS ARBITRATION AWARDS

Hebridean Spinners Advisory Committee and TGWU	183
Iveco Ford Truck Ltd and TGWU	183
Rolls Royce Ltd and AUEW (TASS)	183

Index

Abernethy, Byron 129
ACAS, 96, 103, 157: on final-offer arbitration 86; lists of arbitrators 79; payment of fees 80; proposals for a future role 165
actions in tort 67
Addison, John 23
Advisory, Conciliation and Arbitration Service, *see* ACAS
Agreement for Manual Workers, *see* York Agreement
Agricultural Wages Boards, *see* Wages Councils
Alberta, Canada, University of Lethbridge 83
alienation 15–18, 93, 161
Allen, Steven 24
Amalgamated Society of Engineers 10
Ambulance Service, industrial action (1988–89) 45
American Arbitration Association (AAA) 103; fees 128, 129; selection procedure 79–80
American Federation of Labor (AFL) 10
Amulree, Lord 137
anti-combination laws 42
anti-management bias 94
appeal courts in public arbitration systems 124
apprenticeship, in arbitration 121
arbitration: in 19th century 7; as an industrial relations system 167–8; conventional, *see* conventional arbitration; final-offer, *see* final-offer arbitration; general principles 166–7; goals of 112–14; levels of information 82–4; market for 109–40; (threats to competitiveness 121); practices in UK 156–61; proposals 153–68; (for selection of option 163–4); quality of decisions 118–21, 124–8; role of 90–108; selection of outcome 88; self-imposed regulation 132–3; *see also* compulsory, private, public, voluntary
arbitration law textbooks 123–4
arbitration panels, selection 88; size of 78
arbitration procedures, selection of 131–3, 165; types 112–31
arbitration systems: costs 128–9; equity criteria 97–102; goals 112–14; information in 81–4; legal structure 76–8; operational difficulties 102–7; selection procedure 84–8; taxonomy 75–89
arbitration–mediation (arb–med) 82, 95
arbitrators 78–80: number of 78; payment of fees 80; preferences 81–4; selection of

200 Index

79–80; specialist 118, 127; supply of 121, 129–30; *see also* impartiality
Arthurs, H. 124
Ashenfelter, Orley 26, 62
Association of University Teachers 16
Australia, arbitration system 77, 82, 95, 115, 124, 126–7
automation 2

ballots, secret postal 72
bargaining: comparison of relative strengths of unions 47–50; in good faith 104–5
bargaining process, model 43–50, 90–2, 110
Bayliss, F.J. 145
benefits, non-pecuniary 148
Bentham, Jeremy 64
blacking 69
blue-collar workers 61
Bonn, Robert 124
breach of contract 67–8
Britain: arbitration practices 156–61; Wages Councils 141–52
British Coal 46
British Columbia 104
British Home Stores 157
British Hotels and Restaurants Association 143
Brookshire, Michael 125
'business unionism' 10

CAC, *see* Central Arbitration Committee
Canada 68, 99, 104, 120, 123
Caniglia, Alan 35
capitalism 6, 10
Carruth, Alan 24
Caterers' Association 143
Caves, Richard 21, 53
Central Arbitration Committee (CAC) 103, 157; problem-solving approach 82; proposals for future role 165
chairman of arbitration panel 79, 88

Chamberlain, N.W. 43–7
Chartered Institute of Arbitrators 103; list of arbitrators 80
Clark, Kim 23
coercion 5
collective action, and industrialisation 2–3, 8, 9
collective bargaining: goals of 153–5; governments and 11; history of 2–7; and Industrial Revolution 2–3; and the least advantaged 29–31, 34–5, 100; 'perfect' 12–40; (definition 13); Wages Councils 146–51
collective voice 14–20, 39, 50–2; in arbitration 92–3; and Wages Councils 146–8
Combination Acts (1799, 1800) 5
common law 37–8, 68, 151
communication 153–4, 158, 167
compensation for victims of stoppages, proposed 166
compulsory arbitration 110–31, 158–60, 161–7; bargaining process in 90–2; in Britain 158–60; coverage 111–12; enforcement problems 106–7; proposals 161–7; recommendations 166–7
conciliation 80
Confederation of British Industry (CBI) 158, 163
consistency in arbitration 120–1, 122–4
conspiracy 67
construction industry 62
contract, breach of 67–8
contract of employment, as contract of adhesion 2
contracts: implicit 19–20, 147; long-term 19–20, 93
control, workers' 15
conventional arbitration 80, 84–5: split-the-difference method 105
Cooke, William 22
coordination of worker preferences 18, 20, 93

costs, of arbitration systems 128–9, 133–5
craft-based unions 10
Crawford, V.P. 87, 96
criminal law 67

Davies, Annette 21
demand, time-specificity of 46, 55
democracy 57, 63, 71–3, 97–9
disputes: resolution procedures 106, 162–3; types of 75–6
Donn, Clifford 87, 132, 155
Duncan, Greg 20
Dworkin, Ronald 63

economic rights 64
efficiency 20–8, 39; in arbitration system 93–6, 124–8; and strike-based system 52–6; and Wages Councils 148–9
Eisenberg, Melvin 114
elections, of principal executive committee 71–2
Electrical, Electronic, Telecommunications and Plumbing Union (EETPU) 76
Electricity Generating Board 46
Elkouri, Edna Asper 123
Elkouri, Frank 123
employer conciliation panels 156–7
employers, ability to influence price 48, 91–2
Employment Acts: (1980) 69; (1988) 71–2; (1990) 69, 71
employment levels: and unionisation 23–5; and Wages Councils 148–9
Employment Protection (Consolidation) Act (1978) 17
enforcement problems, in compulsory arbitration 106
engineering industry 55, 156–7
equity 28–37, 40; and arbitration 97–102, 167–8; criteria 28–32; horizontal, *see* horizontal equity; in industrial relations systems 154–5; *maximin*

criterion 29–31; and strike-based system 56–62; vertical, *see* vertical equity; and Wages Councils 149–51
essential goods and services 55, 57, 77, 111, 166
Eugene, Oregon 86–7
export industries, effect of strikes on key 56
external costs: and arbitration 168; minimisation 155, 158; of strikes 55, 73

'fact-finders' 87
factory system 2
Farber, Henry 20
'featherbedding' 21, 148
Federal Mediation and Conciliation Service (FMCS), US 127, 128, 129
Federal Services Impasse Panel 128
fees, arbitrators' 128–9; payment of 80, 133–5; subsidisation of 133–4
final-offer arbitration 80, 85–8, 105; multiple issue 87; multiple offer 86–7; revised offers 88; single package 85–6
fines 64, 107
Flaherty, Sean 35
Fleming, R.W. 127
Fletcher, Betty Binns 125–6
flexibility in dispute resolution 154, 158, 167
foreign subsidiaries, extra production in 47
free market 13–14
Freeman, Richard 23
Fuller, Leon 114
funds, strike 46, 106
Furniture Manufacturing Trade 157

Galanter, Marc 37–8
Gallie, D. 22
GNP (gross national product), effect of strikes on 52–6

202 Index

Gompers, Samuel 10
governments: and arbitration 92, 130–1; and collective bargaining 11; and compulsory imposition of arbitration 110–11; enforcement of arbitration decisions 106–7; intervention in strikes 73–4; selection of arbitrators 79; support for strikers 50
government agencies 74; and public arbitration 114–18
Grand National Consolidated Trades Union 5
Gregory, Mary 26
grievance procedures 17, 126, 148
Grunfeld, Cyril 16
guild system 2, 3

Harsanyi, J.C. 43
Hayford, Stephen 125
Hepple, Bob 64
Herrick, John 127
Hirsch, Barry 23
Hobsbawm, E.J. 5
horizontal equity 35–6, 59–62, 100, 150, 158; definition 32
Humberside Regional Joint Council for the Road Haulage (Hire or Reward) Industry 157
Hundley, Greg 20

impartiality 79, 92, 103–4, 117
imprisonment, threat of 106
income, redistribution of 28, 34–5; in arbitration system 99–100; and strike-based system 59
individual representation 42, 51, 58, 98
industrial democracy 14, 15
Industrial Disputes Tribunal (IDT) 101, 159–60
industrial relations system: arbitration as an 167–8; goals of 153–5; principles 9–10

Industrial Revolution, and collective bargaining 2–3, 8
Industrial Workers of the World ('wobblies') 6
inflation: in arbitration system 94; and unionisation 25–7
inflationary continuation hypothesis 25–6
inflationary initiation hypothesis 25
information, in arbitration systems 81–4
information gathering, and unionisation 18–19
interest disputes 75–6, 80
international trade, effect of strikes on 55–6, 166
International Transport Workers' Federation (ITWF) 70
International Typographical Union 24
investment, and unionisation 22–3
Iowa 87

job enrichment 15
Joint Industrial Council for the Wholesale Grocery and Provision Trade 157
Jones, R.S. 156

Kahn-Freund, Otto 64
Kelsall, E.P. 126–7
Killingsworth, Charles 123
Knights of Labor 5, 10
Knowles, K.G.J.C. 104
Kochan, Thomas 129

Labor Arbitration Awards 123
Labor Arbitration Reports 123
labour: freedom to dispose of one's 64; involvement in arbitration process 132; percentage of costs accounted for by 47–8, 91
laissez-faire 4–5, 8
Landes, William 114, 120, 122, 124
lawyers, as arbitrators 127

Index 203

least advantaged, and collective
 bargaining 29–31, 34–5, 100
legal evolution, theory of 1
legal structuring 37–8, 40, 62–3;
 and arbitration systems 76–8,
 102; (coverage 77–8);
 foundations 76–7; and
 strike-based system 62–3; and
 Wages Councils 142, 151
legislation: employment 17; on
 secondary industrial action
 69–71; on strikes 67–8
Lester, Richard 104
Lewis, H.Gregg 61
liberties, equal access to basic 29,
 31, 32–4; in arbitration system
 97–9; and strike-based system
 57–9; and Wages Councils
 149–50
Licensed Trade Defence
 Association 143
loans, to be used as strike pay 47
lockouts, banned (1940) 158

McCarthy, W.E.J. 101, 156, 159,
 162
McCormick, B. 143
Magenau, John 88
majority views 57, 61, 72–3, 150
manufacturing industries 55, 62
Marsh, A.J. 132, 156, 162
mass production 3
Massachusetts 87
mediation: fusion with
 arbitration 81; role of 80–1
Medoff, James 23
Merkur Island Shipping Corporation
 v. *Laughton* 70
Michigan 82
'middle ground' 112
militancy, union 26–7, 104
miners' strike (1973) 46
minimum wage 11, 146, 148–9
mining 24
'Molly Maguires' of Pennsylvania
 coalfields 5
Montgomery, Edward 24
Mulvey, Charles 26

NALGO 101, 159
National Academy of Arbitrators
 129
National Arbitration Tribunal
 (NAT) 101, 158–9
National Joint Council for Retail
 Pharmacy 157
National Union of General and
 Municipal Workers 143
National Union of Railwaymen 143
National Union of the Working
 Classes 5
Nevada 78
New Jersey 104
'New Model Unions' 10
New South Wales 126–7
New York State Board of
 Mediation 128, 129
New Zealand, compulsory
 arbitration 95–6, 107
North America 96, 106, 126

oil industry 22
oil prices 27
One Big Union, Canada 5
Ontario 104
Order in Council (1940), banning
 strikes and lockouts 158
overtime rates 143
Owen, Robert 5

Palmer, Earl 123
Pareto efficiency in exchange 94,
 95–6
part-time workers 51, 57, 60, 98,
 100
paternalism 14, 146
Peguetter, Richard 125
penalties 106–7, 139–40, 154, 164
pendulum arbitration, *see*
 final-offer arbitration
Peters, Edward 129
picketing 43
political factors, and union costs
 of agreeing 45
Ponak, A. 104
Posner, Richard 114, 120, 122,
 124

Index

Post Office strike, Britain (1988) 55

Prasow, Paul 129

precedents in arbitration 82, 120–1, 122–4; case against 135–8

private arbitration 118–22; compared with public 122–30; voluntary 77

private law model of arbitration 76–7, 112–31

productivity: in arbitration system 94; effect of strikes on 53, 70–1; and unionisation 20–2

profits, and unionisation 22–3

property rights 64

public arbitration 114–18; appeal courts in 124; compared with private 122–30; court system model 115–18

public law model of arbitration 76–7, 112–31

publication of arbitration awards 89, 119–20, 123, 135–9; case for 138; copyrighting 135; payment for 139

quality of working life 15

Quebec, prohibition of use of replacement workers 68–9

radical unions 6–7

Rawls, John, *A Theory of Justice* 28–9, 36, 56

redundancy payments 17–18

'registered' unions 107

Rehmus, Charles H. 87

replacement workers 49–50, 67–9, 100

resistance to change 21, 155, 168

responsibility 154, 158, 167

Retail Bread and Flour Confectionery (England and Wales) Wages Council 143

Retail Multiple Grocery and Provisions Trade 157

Rico, Leonard 76

right to strike 63–5

rights, constitutive and derivative 63–5; 'fundamental' 63

rights dispute, definition 75–6

Rogers, Michael 125

Rubin, Beth 35

sanctions 64, 93

'satisficing' 117

'scabs', *see* replacement workers

secondary industrial action 69–71

settlement, arbitration 88–9

severance pay 143

side members 79

sidemen 79, 88

small firms' employees, underrepresentation in unions 51

small unions 73, 98, 99; and strike-based system 58

Smith, Adam, *The Wealth of Nations* 4

socialism 5–6, 7, 8–9

solidarity 6, 43

Sorensen, Elaine 14

Stafford, Frank 20

statistics, official 81

Statute of Apprentices 4

statutes 4–5

statutory law 37–8, 151

statutory strikes 73–4

steel industry 24

stockpiling inventories 47, 53

storage, ease of product 48–9

strike, right to 63–5

strike threat 9, 51–2, 159–60

strike-based system 41–66; bargaining process 43–50; characteristics 41–50; deficiencies 65–6; definition 41–3; efficiency and 52–6; equity and 56–62; evolution of 8–10; legal structuring 62–3; modifications to 67–74

strikes 42; ban on 65; banned (1940) 158; days lost to, Australia compared with USA 126; effect on GNP 52–6;

illegal 106–7; law on 67–8; proposal for selection of option 163; statutory 73–4; sympathy 69; 'wildcat' 126
sub-contracting work in dispute 70
'sweating' 142

technological progress, and worker resistance to change 21–2
Tennessee Valley Authority 125
third party effects: in arbitration system 94; of strikes 140
Towers, B. 55–6
Trade Boards Acts: (1909) 142; (1918) 145
Trade Union Act (1984) 71–2
Trades Union Congress (TUC) 158, 163; goal 21
transitional friction, in industrial relations system 155, 168
Transport and General Workers' Union 143
Turner, H.A. 143

Ulman, Lloyd 14
unemployment: and unionisation 23–5; and Wages Councils 148, 149
union democracy, see democracy
union membership, concentration of 49, 60, 100
Union of Shop, Distributive and Allied Workers (USDAW) 143
union voice, see collective voice
unionisation: and arbitration legislation 77–8; efficiency and 20–8; proportion in Britain, Canada and USA 51
unions: based on common experience 9; control over available workers 49–50; economies of scale in large 58–9, 73, 93; radical 6–7; 'shock effect' on management 22; within capitalist system 10
university professors 50
USA: arbitration panels 78;

arbitration systems 120, 123, 125–6, 127; interest arbitration 104; reinstatement entitlement 68
USDAW 157
utopianism 5–6, 8–9

vertical equity 35–6, 61–2, 101, 150; definition 32
Victoria 126–7
voluntary agreements 80, 96
voluntary arbitration 77, 110–12, 157–8
voting, entitlement 72; method 72

wage differential: skilled/unskilled 36; union/non-union 25–6, 61, 62; (sector by sector 61)
wage elasticity of demand, and unionisation 24
wage laws, minimum 11, 146, 148–9
Wages Act (1986) 141, 142, 145
Wages Councils 5, 11, 141–52, 160–1, 163; composition 143–4; history of system 142–6; independents in 143–5, 160; meetings 144; statutory regulations 144; as a system of collective bargaining 146–51
Wages Councils Acts (1945, 1959, 1979) 141, 142, 145–6
Webb, Sidney and Beatrice 2
Weiler, Paul 123
Wheeler, H. 104
Whitley Committee 142
Whittingham, T.G. 55–6
wingmen 79
Wisconsin 78, 104
'wobblies', see Industrial Workers of the World
women, underrepresentation in unions 51
work stoppages: incidence Britain 52–3; ((1987–88) 54); incidence reduced by arbitration 94

206 Index

workers: attachment to labour force, and bargaining strength 49; preferences 147–8; skilled 3
workforce, dispersed 57, 60, 111
working classes 9, 35
workplaces, depersonalised 2, 15, 32

X and Y theories 15

York Agreement 156–7
young workers 62

Zeuthen, F. 43